The Smallest Color

Books by Bill Roorbach

Summers With Juliet

Writing Life Stories

The Art of Truth

Big Bend

The Smallest Color

~~~~~~~~~~~ A NOVEL

Bill Roorbach ~~~~~~~~~~~

COUNTERPOINT
WASHINGTON, D.C.

LIBRARY OF CONGRESS CATALOGING-IN-PUBLICATION DATA
Roorbach, Bill.
    The smallest color / Bill Roorbach.
      p. cm.
    ISBN 1-58243-252-X
    1. Brothers—Fiction. 2. Missing persons—Fiction.
    I. Title.
    PS3568.O6345 S6 2001
    813'.54—dc 21   2001028898

Printed in the United States of America on acid-free
paper that meets the American National Standards Institute
Z39–48 Standard.

Book design by Amy Evans McClure

COUNTERPOINT
387 Park Avenue South
New York, NY 10016-8810

Counterpoint is a member of the Perseus Books Group

10 9 8 7 6 5 4 3 2 1

For Elysia

What am I now that I was then?

May memory restore again and again

The smallest color of the smallest day:

Time is the school in which we learn

Time is the fire in which we burn

DELMORE SCHWARTZ

The Smallest Color

Chapter One

1

I am Coop Henry. Anthony Cooper Henry. A man who talks to his dead brother. Talk, talk, talk, a continuous loop for thirty years, not all of it in the middle of the night anymore, not all of it even safely in my *head* anymore. I can't hold the cracks closed; I'm losing my strength; I'm leaking lava.

Though probably no one much notices. Face to face I'm just a regular nice guy: calm, gentle, sweet, caring, rational, maybe a little emotional, good listener, good talker, funny sometimes, reasonably nice looking, decent shape for someone mid-forties, not too tall, not too short, true to my one and only wife. Everyone knows this. I'm trustworthy, brave, loyal, obedient, all that good Boy Scout stuff without the homophobia. Cheerful, kind, reverent, too.

Maybe a little dishonest. And about that, Mom is back on my case. She's in search of the truth, that's all, simple truth, and she has every reason to come to me. She writes and leaves messages, faxes Madeline at work, and now we've even moved on to e-mail: she's going to get to the bottom of things, and things, Hodge, is you.

Big brother, listen: you are dead, quite dead, thirty years dead. Tell her for me, okay? Tell her the whole appalling thing, please? Because the phone is about to ring again, and I don't know if I can perpetuate the lies: that you are in hiding, that you send your love.

When the phone rings, I pick it up fast, murmur a friendly "Hello," looking out the porch windows and across the river over there and up into the boulders. I gentle that phone. It's Mom all right. And brother, ask not for whom Mom calls, she calls for thee.

"Greetings," she says, sounding almost cheerful—she knows I know just why she's calling.

"He says he won't," I tell her, my kind and sweet and guilty self, lying without preamble.

"Did you even talk to him?" she says. "Sometimes I think you *protect* him."

"Protect Hodge?" I say. And I look around the living room at all the belongings Madeline and I have collected in almost twenty years, good chairs and that deep red rug from our perfect six weeks in Mexico those many years ago, a thousand books on drooping shelves, a hundred rocks and shells and bowls and photographs. I note the suddenly lovely and golden cone of light from the heavy floor lamp, light that falls inside the greater sunlight of the many morning windows. I see as if for the first time the old hand-built ranch cabinets hanging in the open kitchen. I see the big chairs Madeline and I read in, the counter we cook on, the table we eat on. I say, "It wasn't Hodge I protected."

Another silence, and I picture Mom in their house, hers and Dad's, she on her kitchen phone, cradling the receiver in her two spotted hands, something fragrant cooking on her stainless-steel restaurant-grade range. I picture her tennis sneakers, her unstooped height, her perfect halo of coifed white hair. "You!" she says. "You cryptic little . . . *turd!*" And she hangs up in my face.

Hodge, I'm called *turd* by Leslie Adams Keepnews Henry, our own sweet Ma, Daughter of the American Revolution, who has never said *turd* aloud in her life. And okay, I'll accept the charge. I'm a turd and cryptic as hell, a liar and a traitor. I'm going to have to tell her the truth and soon: you are dead. And it's worse than that. You and I, bro, we both know it's worse than that.

I stand in the living room seeing everything in it with great clarity, stand there for five long minutes to let her calm down a little and call back, truth at my tongue. But I get Dad, who just sighs and fumes and says, "Your mother will not talk to you, Cooper, and for goddamn good reason." He's fumbling with something as he speaks, probably sitting at his desk, maybe searching through his piles of papers for pliers or an old check or the slide rule he still maintains is faster than any (goddamn) computer. "She's at the end of her rope." Puffs of breath. "She's not going to talk to you or me or anybody till you tell her where your goddamn brother is. Your goddamn brother, Coop!" Papers rustling, the crash of something falling off his desk. "And it goddamn-well better be before this fiftieth-anniversary thing of hers." A snort as he finds whatever it is he's been searching for. "December tenth, Coop!"

I start to bridle, almost speak, but tell myself no.

The old man whispers then, his tone more vicious with each phrase: "You tell Hodge he best goddamn-well call, boy. If Mommy dies of a broken heart it's your ass I'm coming after. And your brother, well, for all I care that scamming scum can stay where he is till the gates of Hades *swing!*"

You'll stay, all right.

Clippings in the mail from our poor Mom, dressed up with yellow sticky notes, her bright, famous handwriting (*has Hodge seen this?!?*). A light sentence for Tonya Boudreau. Amnesty for Jackson DeBeers. Former Black Panthers starting fried chicken chains. Forgiveness. Compassion. Sixties radicals a dime a dozen. Implied: time for Hodge to come out, too. Unspoken: what's the worst that could happen?

Mom on the warpath, bro. Our own gentle mother. And if you

thought the campaign for your forty-fifth birthday was big, just wait. "This fiftieth-anniversary thing," it's coming, and Mom has *demanded* that you appear. Listen to this: she (by God) has resolved to hire a detective—and not just any detective—she's put away *thirty thousand* dollars to hire *the* number-one missing-persons man in New York City. *The same investigator that found Jimmy Hoffa,* she says. And she's determined, Hodge, she's going to find your *selfish soul* even if it means spending every cent she's got, and she's got plenty. She doesn't even pause when I explain that Jimmy Hoffa's still missing.

Why can't I just tell her? Hodge Henry is dead. You, brother, you know this. Thirty years dead! Madeline knows it. I certainly know it. Why the mortal secret? What was the point? What were we *thinking?* Maybe that we'd keep you alive by telling no one, that blame would disappear? Did I really think I could bury the unspeakable secret by laying it on your chest? That Mom would just accept your disappearance? Just like that? Forever? I threw dirt on you brother, one shovelful, then the next. The damage is done. You're dead, man. You're gone.

2

Anthony Cooper Henry liked what he saw. Mountains and dry gulches and cattle in spare pasture. Derelict barns and fields of wheat. Dust devils, tumbleweed, fireflowers, boulders. Machinery for watering, machinery for harvesting, machinery for baling up hay. It all rushed by click click click behind bare telephone poles, the grasses at roadside a blur, the mountains trundling along more stately, as if the world were turning beneath the car and Dad, that fuckhead, only steered to keep up.

Coop opened his window and held his harmonica out so the wind played every note. His little sister, Cindy, already eleven, shrieked and jumped across baby Jeremy to get at Cooper's arm. Mom reached back to spank her, but Cindy leapt out of the way and over the seat and into the way-back with Cherry, the huffing mutt, and with gentle Morton, who at seven years old was already tubby, cheerful for life, a boy-Buddha facing backwards across America. Cindy crouched behind Cooper, cackled in his ear. Cherry barked. The harmonica droned. "Get her back up here, Cooper," Mom barked, reaching. "And stop playing the harmonica."

"No way," Coop said. This mission was as bad as he had imagined. He didn't want to see his grandmother. He didn't care about Seattle. He wanted to be free like Hodge, his draft-dodging big brother. 1969, late June, and Coop almost sixteen. He wanted to be *underground* like Hodge, loud music and liberated girls and happening dope and the talk all pigs and protest and politics.

"Then he'll spank *you*."

"Jesus, Mom."

"Did you hear that Bob?"

"Cut out the language, Cooper, for the last time."

Mom said it again: "I'm frightened Bob! Every day more like his brother!"

The air in the car grew dense in a way Coop knew well and hated. He breathed, said, "This trip *sucks*." He liked the new word and the power of using it. "I'm just trying to look out the window a little, minding my own business, and now there's a *crisis*."

"*You* suck," Cindy said.

"Suck," Jeremy said, soulfully.

Mom spun in her seat to face him, blew up: "Anthony Cooper Henry, damnit all anyway, I'll snatch you bald."

"He'll shut up at the barbershop."

"Jesus *fucking* Christ," Coop said. He hauled the harmonica in and looked out the window, pretending not to notice his mother's awkward slap on his leg. Now the *haircut* again. He'd worked his ass off to get all A's for his whole high school career and skied his ass off for gold medals at every meet just so he wouldn't have to get a haircut and now he had to anyway because of Grandma Vanderhoop, supposedly, although he knew *she* didn't care. He'd put on his worst dirtiest ripped-up jeans and his giant flannel shirt at the motel that morning as a protest, but he was doomed: the haircut was going to happen.

"Well that's the limit," Mom said. She faced front sternly,

crossed her arms in front of her. From a peaceful car ride to disaster in two minutes flat. "Never you mind the haircut. We'll take you to a *psychiatrist.*"

This scene had been played with Hodge, and more than once, the last time two years past. What would Hodge have fired back? Something nasty: Mom was a *cunt.* Coop hadn't the heart.

Cindy pulled Morton's game book straight out of his hands and scrambled back over the seat. Morton said "Mahm," quietly. Jeremy crawled up on Cooper's lap. Coop picked him up, shook him, and put him on Cindy. Cindy shrieked again, her idea of grand fun. Jeremy wailed.

Dad roared: "I'm going to stop the car and thrash you all!"

Thrash who? Coop thought. He'd been there the day Hodge turned one of Dad's thrashings into a prizefight. And Hodge had almost won, eight hard shots to Dad's face before it was over, Hodge laid out on the floor and Dad all mopey and apologetic and man-to-man and fat lip and handshakes next morning. Thrash who? At sixteen you became an opponent and not a kid. Keep your *psycho* temper under control, thought Coop, but didn't speak—now that Hodge was gone, Coop was first in line.

"If you stop the car, we'll spank *you,*" Cindy said brightly. Somehow she got away with remarks like that.

Coop opened and closed the chrome ashtray lid snap snap snap and watched out the window. Mom had stiffened further yet, and the thunderheads were inside the car now, black, and the wind was blowing, fierce. Next, Coop knew—within minutes—she'd pretend to be calm and reasonably trot out her canned lecture on *choices* and *responsibility* and what Hodge had *done* to all of them with his *bad picks* for friends and his refusal to just *fit in.* Would Coop like to go away to school? Maybe a rehabilitative home? Because that's where he was headed, if he thought being a *psychopath* was *"cool."*

Coop thought of Hodge, whom he'd last seen almost exactly two years past. Hodge's graduation, whoa, how could Coop outdo *that?* The maniac told their parents—these same miserable parents—told them he'd peacefully go graduate and make them proud. But wait . . . there was an anti-war demonstration going on in Greenwich Village that same day.

And while Mom and Dad and two thousand other parents and every teacher in the high school and half the kids in town filed into the fenced confines of the football field, Hodge was driving very slowly through the high school parking lot in the giant new Athletics van—the keys straight off Coach Riley's pegboard. Coop was one of the innocents who'd climbed in—just a kid at thirteen! Just out of junior high! He'd climbed in the van for the joke of it along with Hodge's three girls—Missy Kirkbridge and Virginia Chance and Brittany Seusy (Missy in favor at the moment, all of them resigned to Hodge's ways). And they picked up whoever would get in, just a slow, bold ride around the parking lot, Dexter Blodgett still in his gown, Billy DiCresenzo in his gas station uniform, ten or eleven other kids till the van was full. Then Hodge turned up the heat in the sudden way he could. He pulled out onto South Avenue, drove right past the full football stands, drove right behind Mom and Dad and the other kids, drove right under the nose of every teacher he'd ever had, right past the coaches, zero to sixty in the Athletics van straight to the Merritt Parkway, New York City bound. On the fly he passed out joints, strong pot, enough for all to have their own, sent his special Zippo back. Seventy miles per hour, squeal and zoom, tight curves into the city; eighty miles an hour, Cross Bronx Expressway, West Side Highway; finally slower, poking through funny streets in the Village to Washington Square Park. Right there, Hodge heroically turned the smoke-filled van broadside in the middle of Thompson Street, stalled it to a chorus of honking, leapt out, flung the keys atop a trapped city bus with a whoop, and ran into the crowded park, his hair flowing golden behind him in bright sun, a warrior in worn blue jeans. Coop followed, loving him, Dexter hard at hand in flowing graduation gown, holding a mortarboard absurdly on his head, tassel flying. The others—Hodge didn't care or notice—the others were left behind. In the park the freaks had gathered, the hippies, the beatniks, the eggheads, the kids whose fathers meant to send them to war. Megaphones, pot smoke, beer cans slugged from paper bags. A hotdog vendor, too. Love, a poster said. Peace, all the symbols said. Coop felt big and gentle and floating. This was freedom. This was war. He better not puke. He better not get lost. He chased Hodge closely, Hodge raging through the crowd pushing at the hapless with his mighty arms, Hodge's back a rippling of muscles under black T-shirt, huge dude, faster than someone so big had any right to be. *Kill the pigs!* That's what Hodge shouted. Which was different from *Peace now!*, the chant coming from up ahead. Hodge yelled and pushed people out of his way, leaving Coop to take the glares and shoves, Dexter to take actual punches. Hodge shouted: *Kill the pigs! Kill the pigs!* He shouted it and bellowed it, like someone not kidding, made his way to the shade under the famous arch, pushed a bespectacled intellectual off the makeshift podium there, which was a park bench. *The means of production* . . . this man was saying mildly, but as Hodge would say: *Fuck that shit!* He jumped on the bench and knocked the old prof sideways. The crowd swelled forward, as if to get Hodge, but Hodge won them instantly: *Kill the pigs! Stop the war! Kill the pigs! Stop the war!* Fist raised over his head, pumping, the huge crowd with him all at once, fists raised, pumping. Coop too, *Kill the pigs!* He was beautifully high and thirteen back then and in the vast but dangerous protection of his big brother.

But he was fifteen now, almost sixteen, and what was he doing? Riding with his parents across the country to visit Grandma—

where was the life in that? What could be less cool? He clicked the ashtray lid at his elbow and watched the ranches go by and pictured the rally in very cool Greenwich Village those two years past perfectly.

The displaced little professor stood up tall then with his glasses askew and mouth open, not entirely displeased with the turn of events, the turn of the crowd. The others from the van were lost now, except Dexter in his gown, mortarboard missing, right beside Coop. The crowd surged and shouted and turned and pushed and began to move as one, marching up Fifth Avenue. With a thousand others Coop chanted Hodge's chant: *Kill the pigs! Stop the war! Kill the pigs! Stop the war!* He lost Hodge himself, though, and quickly lost Dexter, too. And then, suddenly, he was a boy thirteen and way too high and scared shitless and thoroughly abandoned by his fearsome brother. Whatever happened to Peace and Love? That was the part of the park Coop liked best—Peace and Love. The others from the van ride? Nowhere in sight, despite long searching. The van? Towed and gone. The train ride home alone after a bad collect call was terrifying. Dad would pick him up at the station.

And that was the last time any of them had seen Hodge, though polite FBI agents called regularly asking about him. Hodge was "associating" with some bad elements, they said. Hodge was on their "git-list." Hodge the wanted, Hodge the hero, Hodge the scourge—Hodge free of the draft, free of Al the barber, free of Dad's fists and buckle, free and fast as a bullet accelerating through air to the thing it would hit.

The happy family came to Tyco, Wyoming, a town from a Western movie, long main street, the sudden geometry of thirty or forty buildings. Cowboys steered huge pickup trucks. Banners proclaimed the coming of the rodeo. Coop saw four horses tied to a real rail in front of a real saloon. He liked Tyco big time, saw himself hired at a ranch and so good with the wild horses that the ranchers went ahead and gave the whole place to him, and Connie Kirkbridge heard about it and forgot about Ted DeMartino and came out west and finally let him touch her as much as he wanted, which was a lot and always.

Evenly, Mom said, "We've got to talk about *choices.*"

But Dad jerked the wheel, screeched the wagon into a gas station across Highway 87 from a perfect stainless-steel diner.

"*Choices,* Coop," Mom said, trimming the lecture to basics.

Thank God for gas. A lanky guy older than Dad gave a thumbs up to Dad's nod and shuffled to start the gas pumping. Mom, silenced, snagged Jeremy brusquely, pinched Cindy's ear, dragged them off to the ladies' room.

Dad just sat a second, rubbing his neck, saying nothing. Then he flung his door open, climbed out fast, yanked open Coop's door, wrenched him into the dry air, spun him, caught him by both biceps, hard. Coop wriggled in that furious grasp. The gas attendant watched with his eyebrows raised, hand on the nozzle grip, definitely cheering Dad, Coop thought, just the look on his face.

Dad breathed one of his dragon breaths, squeezed Coop's arms harder, pushed him against the car. He said, "I'll cut that wig of yours with a rusty axe, need be, you little shit."

Coop writhed in Dad's strong grip, pushed against Dad's hard belly with both fists, brought a knee up hard, caught Dad's thigh, spat in his reddened face, twisted free. Coop knew better than to run anywhere, stood ready for a blow, but Dad just glared and breathed hard, several puffing breaths, and abruptly marched right past Coop, cranked the back window open like he'd tear the handle off, tugged Morton out bodily, stormed off across the cement to the men's room with the little boy bouncing stoically sideways in his arms.

So Coop was alone, the gas guy lost under the massive hood of the spanking new station wagon. Sun hot, mountains all around, across the street a stainless-steel diner. Fast as the ski racer he was, Coop leapt back to the car, hawked two quarters from Dad's toll money and sprinted across the busy main drag, dodging cars.

The diner was long, ran narrowly back from the sidewalk, busy in there even though it was early for dinner. A waitress served the tables. Coop slunk along the length of the place to the bathroom at the back. People stared at him (of course people stared—his hair was a foot long and dirty, his demeanor 100% delinquent, his insides churning). Someone was in the bathroom so Coop gazed out the screened rear door at the mountains. Imagine the skiing around here come winter, the mountains of snow!

Far away and high on a grassy slope he saw a ranch, lots of cattle and twin silos, all of it baking in the sun. At the very ridge top, miles away, he made out a standing horse, silhouette before the hard blue sky, wavy and dreamish in the rising heat. He pictured cowboys jazzing him, the suburban greenhorn, heard the ridicule stop and turn to awe as he broke the one horse no one could break, the giant stallion called Wreckin' Ball.

After a leak he sauntered bowlegged up to the counter, mounted a spinning stool between a lady in a dress and a big man in overalls. But the fantasy didn't hold; he was just a kid without a driver's license, had never been in a restaurant alone before. The routine was familiar to him, though—frown a lot and don't look around. He picked up the menu, thinking he'd have a Coke, thinking Dad and Mom could pretty much come and get him. Through the big window and across the street he could see his father paying the gas guy.

The old man behind the counter bustled to Coop's spot, said, "What'll it be, kiddo?"

"I don't know. Maybe a Coke or something."

"Just a Coke? Maybe you better get yourself a bite. Hungry?"

"Sure."

"Take your time."

Coop looked out the window again. His mother was dragging Cindy to the car. Jeremy was in a world-class tantrum, face red, mouth open screaming, stubby hands hitting Mom around the face and neck. Mom, she looked about to explode.

Dad turned his head quick this way and that like a big chicken, looking for Coop, ha ha, looking every wrong direction there was, making tight fists. The gas guy just shrugged. Good. Coop had gone unseen.

The only thing on the menu for fifty cents was an egg sandwich. Even french fries were fifty-five. Coop Henry had never had an egg sandwich, but it sounded like something a cowpoke might eat. "Egg sandwich," he said.

"And the Coke."

"No, because I only have fifty cents."

"I see."

The man hobbled down the length of the counter and talked to a lady who was back behind a stainless-steel slot cooking. The lady peered at Coop like she felt sorry for him. She reminded him of his grandmother and that reminded him that he would have to get his hair chopped and that brought Dad's lava face to the front of his mind fast and caved him in on himself right there on his stool.

The old man behind the counter hobbled back. "You all right?"

"Yeah."

"Listen, special today, a Coke comes with the egg sandwich."

"Aw, thanks." Saying this, Coop saw himself in the mirrored wall across the counter, hair filthy and long past his shoulders, good, good. He sat up, squared himself. He was no Hodge, not in size, not in nerve. But, good, his shirt was big and ripped and really fuckingly dirty. He even had a brown streak across his forehead where Jeremy had swiped him after the chocolate bars they'd hawked from Mom's purse that morning.

The lady next to him made him nervous staring. These people

thought he was some kid bum, maybe a runaway from the rodeo or an orphan just escaped from the cruel orphanage, and they were trying to help. He straightened his spine to look tougher, maybe a little mean, and poor, sure. But the lady next to him kept staring.

"Here," she said, finally. "Take my rolls. I'm not going to eat them."

Coop deflated, gave her a baleful look, wrapped the rolls in a napkin, put them in his shirt pocket. The lady got a look of angelic pity on her face, clearly pleased to be of service. So in a way he was the one helping. He really did feel poor.

The counterman brought the sandwich. It had about five eggs in it, and lots of melted cheese, and they'd put it on a huge plate along with heaps of vegetables and french fries. The man wrote the bill out, right there, so Coop would know it was all right: fifty cents.

"Wow," Coop said.

"Don't say a thing," the counterman said. "We know what it's like. A kid needs a meal."

Now the big man next to Coop looked over. "Jeez. I can't finish this-here. Maybe you want it for later on, or somethin'?"

A pork chop. Coop wrapped it dolefully in another napkin to give a good effect of poverty and starvation, then stuck the package behind his rolls in his big shirt pocket. He bit his sandwich as if he were starving, bit it again, no match for Hodge, looked out the window. His father paced wrathfully back and forth between the station wagon and the gas pumps. Mom and Cindy tussled in the car, Cindy trying to get back out. Morton just stood there on the gas-drenched asphalt, peaceably detached, waiting to be told to climb back in.

Coop ate. *Let 'em linger*, as Hodge would say. The old counterman and the lady cooking watched him with love. What was he supposed to do? Leave and join his family, right there across

Highway 87? Everyone here could see he had a vicious brother and that he was a desperado himself. The two new suits and the wholesome snacks and the schoolbooks all a single slalom gate away were the falsity. The station wagon—brand new, fake wood paneling, the works—belied his true nature. He was a rebel, dangerous as Hodge, a man.

Now his father was practically strangling the gas guy, getting ready for the real thing on Coop. Mom was out of the car touching Dad, probably saying something soothing, as usual saving her fury for Coop at the same time she tried to protect him from Dad's. *Choices.*

Cooper gobbled his egg sandwich and fries. No time left: Dad was eyeing the diner. Coop thanked the lady in the dress and the big man in the overalls, stood tall as he could, square shoulders, well fed. At the cash register he quickly handed his guest check to the counterman, who looked at it just like Coop was a normal customer, took the fifty cents.

"And here's your change," the man said, handing the quarters back.

"Gosh, I can't."

"Not another word."

Through the window Coop saw Dad coming, saw Dad looking both ways to cross the road. But luck: a huge old truck came lumbering by, and many cars were stuck behind it. So the old man had to wait, bursting. Mom leaned on the car holding Jeremy, tapping her foot. *Responsibility.* Cindy practiced her bugaloo just this side of the pumps. Morton calmly waited.

"Well, thanks," Coop said, breathless. He looked at Cindy a moment, looked at the station wagon, saw Dad make a false start in front of a new row of cars, saw him raise his big fist and shout, saw him trying to use his mighty rage to stop traffic. And traffic did stop, *both ways,* and Dad came plunging across the highway, arms parting the air in front of him, face set hard and gory red with fury. This was going to be *bad.*

Coop leapt back through the diner. He ducked out the rear door and raced through grasses and tumbleweeds tall enough to hide him, jogged up and up the rocky slope, through pasture, past cattle, his father's roar in the diner behind propelling him upward. Coop climbed a barbed-wire fence, kept hiking in the dry wind, pasture after pasture, ascending the long hill to the mountains. He clambered through deep gullies, crunched through dry grasses collecting burrs and seeds in the laces of his work boots. He drank from a galvanized cattle tub, kept walking, always moving, moving through the afternoon, never resting, marching into the mountains. By dark he made the horse's high ridge and stopped to eat his pork chop and rolls.

3

Hey, Hodge, hi. I've told you how I love these parties at Frank Kobil's. At fifty-three he's suddenly become the perfect host. He shuttles back and forth to the kitchen, rattles the ice, runs the blender, makes strong margaritas with top-end tequila, and you forget he's head coach of the U.S. Ski Team, that except for Madeline, he's our *boss*. He fills two lovely old Mexican bowls from his collection of Mexican bowls with chips he's made from scratch somehow, watches with holy pleasure every bite and every sip his guests take, laughs hard at every crack we make, nods seriously when the talk gets sober. The five of us make a family for him, and he loves us without judgement. Roddy Manor, still his top woman downhiller, side by side with Julie Tinker, still his top woman freestyle star, the two of them growing riotous like college jocks, though they're not kids anymore, not really. I'm just a trainer now, an old skier with rackety knees, long past my racing days, Frank my old mentor, Frank my best friend. That's the right kind of boss to have.

Madeline's there, too, my other best friend—my wife—steady

and erect tonight, her head full of politics as always, sharp
Madeline, lawyer and full-time friend to the friendless, but a little
bored with my drunken buddies. I sit there holding her hand, joining the pleasant rip and roar of the after-dinner wit and gossip
and repartee, such as it is, and never want it to end. I don't even
mind that Rick Baldwin is present, just permit myself a little inter-
nal scoffing at Rick's tie and jacket—the guy thinks he's still a
Boston lawyer. But be nice, Coop! He's on-team now! Let kindness
prevail!

"Clever," Roddy says slyly, making fun of Julie, a bathing-suit
incident we all know lots about. "*Victoria's Secret* must have loved
that!"

I slurp at my drink, catch Madeline's disapproving eye, squeeze
her hand. But she drops mine, pushes away her glass of expensive
wine, unsipped. I know what's coming from her, see the tide going
out, laugh uneasily with Roddy and Julie.

Who are in each other's faces, mock catfight, choking with
laughter, Roddy tugging at Julie's shirt like she's going to pull it
off. And Jesus we're good friends and Jesus these young women
are funny. Their bodies don't embarrass them—they laugh, they
scream—Julie keeps her shirt on, goes after the straps of Roddy's
overalls, and though it's Julie whose great figure got her the
bathing-suit deal (thirty grand to wear a three-hundred-dollar
bikini top in competition, once!) it's Roddy I'm noticing. She's not
a kid anymore. Suddenly I'm thinking how *appealing* Roddy is—
Roddy whom I've known ten years with not a buzz. She's grown
into herself, she's comfortable as she's never been. No one safer to
have a crush on, either, if that's what's to call this glimmer.

Madeline sighs heavily, gives me the Madeline look: *Time to go.*
She drops my hand, rises slowly, takes a couple of long strides to
stand in Frank's grand living-room window.

"It wasn't *Victoria's Secret,* it was Jantzen," shrieks Julie.

"Speedo," Kobil shouts into the fray, but that's wrong too, which is the joke, something complicated and way inside about a business failure he once went through.

Lately—whoa—lately I've been seeing Roddy in a new light. And lately—whoa again—I've been thinking about Roddy at odd moments. Every train of thought seems to lead to her, some phrase she said in passing, some gesture she made saying it, some tilt of her head in listening. Tonight this new light upon her is warm, and seems to come from me, from my heart somehow, this old, cold heart suddenly warmed. By Roddy. She's no ski-slope bombshell like Julie, not an obvious beauty like Julie, nor Madeline (for that matter), not as tall as either of them. What Roddy looks like bouncing on the couch tonight, laughing and teasing, is what Roddy is: an athlete, strong and a little overwound. She's filled out lately—downtime due to injury (that bad broken ankle in the World Cups). The added mass—muscle from increased workouts and physical therapy—has cranked up her open-lane speed but slowed her overall times. That decrease is in addition to a new lag in reaction time (to the gates primarily, but to the buzzer, too, and to the icy tick of a coming fall), but that's age, and age slows reaction time first, even if like Roddy a skier's only thirty-two. Still, Roddy's got this subtle physical confidence: she walks like a boxer, up on her toes, swings her arms sweetly. She's cut her hair, too, straight line around her neck, and seems to have had it bleached; it's blonder than I recall, blond to the point of whiteness, darker underneath. She's laughing and I find I'm looking at her mouth.

It's just her mouth, Roddy's mouth, but to me, lately, and increasingly tonight, it's, I don't know, *darling*. What's this? Her appeal fills the great stone room, and it doesn't matter at all that the Euro swimwear gang ignores her, the makeup people, the fashion folks (instead, she gets equipment endorsements; you see her in trade magazines smiling and holding up her K2 Comps or making attractive muscles in front of high-end gym equipment, or the Leukemia Foundation for free, happy sick kids all around her): suddenly she's *charming*. Lucky I'm married! At Kobil's tonight she's wearing one of those thermal long-underwear tops half hidden by brand-new overalls, worn-out work boots like a farmer. She styles herself a country girl, even if she did have all the advantages—to the big city for college—and even if she has seen the world, skiing, even if her boyfriend's an Italian prince (or whatever old Claudio is). She's got a master's degree in art history, it's easy to forget. She's got her Ph.D. in progress. She's done all this learning while skiing *full blast*. She can talk art all night. She can talk art in such an abstruse way that I have no idea what she's saying, but the folks behind the desks in galleries and museums around the world light up when she says it. This, I've seen. Wherever she goes—whatever bleak motel room or skier's dorm—she sets herself up a desk and within a day her laptop is surrounded by books and computer disks and manuscripts and slides and gallery notices. Wherever she goes the phone is ringing—curators and professors, artists and dealers. This, I've seen, too. All of the paintings around Frank's big house have something to do with Roddy. She's got Frank collecting. The one true painting in our house I bought at her urging in Grenoble, and have come to love it dearly, stylized young girl, snow in the background, small canvas, plain frame. Her own collection has been growing since college, and it's nothing to sneeze at, apparently, though I can't make heads nor tails of half of it, strips of tar paper on glass beakers, I don't know. At Claudio's place there's an extraordinary marble sculpture though, something he bought for her in their flush of romance, something very, very old, her favorite possession, she has told me, two languid figures pointing upwards, life-size.

But here at Frank's she's the brazen athlete, once again. She's pushing Julie off the couch and the room is all laughter (except

Madeline, poor Madeline like a collapsed star over there, sitting now in the window seat, watching, gamely trying to take part, small forced smile—she's tired, is all), shouting with laughter. Roddy barks, "What concerns me here is how hard you had to be skiing to break the clasp like that. Topless for money! How long did you practice that move?"

"Acme Clasp Company's suing," Frank says laconically.

Rick Baldwin has stiffened nearly as much as Madeline: Julie and he are a brand-new item. He's proprietary in the extreme, thinks these are *his* breasts we're laughing about.

Frank says, "Jesus. Coop and me, in our generation, you didn't ski naked, all there is to it."

And all but one of us laugh absurdly. No wait, two. Baldwin's not laughing now, either.

Okay, brother, I know, absolutely: you had to be there. There's a two-woman pillow fight, Roddy and Julie, and Frank's off to the kitchen to make more drinks.

Madeline's staring out the window. At forty-eight she's much older than Roddy and Julie. Next to her, they're girls. Early thirties, you know, they don't yet know about middle age, don't quite believe they're going to die. Understandably, Mad gets stiff around their youth and their noisy good spirits, any sign of a party, really. Hodge, you remember Madeline. Remember her all too well, I imagine. But no reason to feel sorry for her. No, no. Her prodigious powers are intact, her beauty, too. Other women still turn to look at her in the street (ignoring me pointedly). She's smart to the point of brilliance, and you see this in her eyes, in the way she walks. So what if her teeth are big? So what if she's pushing fifty? She enters bike races and foot races and wins the goddamn things; she clumps around the house practicing some exotic brand of karate. She can read a thick legal tome in an hour and answer any question you might have about it, including case numbers and dates. She's got clout and gravity, though little tenderness (this she never had); she is magnificent, almost monumental. She's hard to love, I'm finding, hard to gentle. She's wearing the same type of long hippie dress she has always worn, the same stack of hard-won bracelets, the same sandals. And this is the same way she dresses for court or for a wedding (even her own, to me, all those years ago). She's consistently and assuredly her mighty self. She looks like an attorney, all right. The cowboy lawyers in the district still call her Lady Moonbeam and Ms. Flower Power here in 1998, but she beats them up all day. Me, I am her husband and admire her. But admiration is different from love and always was, I'm beginning to see.

Roddy, Jesus, still-immortal Roddy is sitting up, huffing and giggling on the back of the couch, her hair flagged across her face.

Julie sobers, sitting rumpled on the floor, says mildly, "What was I supposed to do? Quit the race?"

"You just *kept* going," Frank grants. He's got to be my best friend, though I don't have many competing for the honor. He's much quieter than when I was on the team those many years ago. Much quieter. It's he who got me every race I ever won, Hodge. I know that. He worked me and carried me and studied me and taught me. And I know it's he who brought me along into the coaching staff against a lot of pressure from the committee. And tonight before dinner while we were waiting for Rick and Julie to turn up, Frank got me aside, put his hand on my arm and said, "Things look pretty good, Coopsie. There's a bit of competition, granted. But what it's coming down to is this: the job's yours." The job in question is a big one: Alpine Director, U.S. Ski Team. "Rick Baldwin?" he says generously. "No way."

Here in his own house full of rioting guests Frank is calm and courtly, a man who will never look at the young women as anything but colleagues, a guy who has never (but never) put the moves on any woman I know about. I don't think he's so much as had a *date* since Billie died (her awful car wreck, Hodge, I've told you). He gives a party or two every week—skiers and bartenders and coaches and lift mechanics and board members and bums—and there's never been even a hint of a scandal. He's a drinker, but he's never drunk. He can down whiskey by the gallon like an old senator. Tonight at dinner he ate maybe one bite, nice tuna steaks burned perfectly on his gas grill (fish instead of the usual slabs of beefsteak in genuine and kind deference to Maddy). He's losing weight, he's withering, he's going to disappear.

He says, "Roddy, where's the videotape!"

"Not this again," I say.

Baldwin suddenly puffs himself up and says importantly, "What do you mean *your* generation, Frank? You and *Coop?* What, are you kidding?" He's smiling, but his mustache twitches so you know something's got under his skin. He looks like the new kid at the New York Stock Exchange, all stiff and earnest, anxious to manage, get control of the beast.

"Well," says Frank, "we're older than you."

"Maybe *you* are," says Rick. "But Coop?"

"Forty-five," I say.

"Thirty-eight," says Rick.

"Say, Richard," says Frank. "You'll be forty in 2000. That's got a nice ring to it. And it makes you a different generation. Coop had to deal with the draft. You didn't."

"I was in the first lottery," I say. I feel my foolish pride in this, and worry that maybe indeed it was the second lottery I was stuck in. But no matter, I keep on: "We watched it on TV in the beer hall at Colgate." And I tell the story I've told too many times to young skiers with hawkish views and no draft cards: how we watched this woman turn a crank to roll a drum full of every date in the year, then watched a little man in a suit reach in and pull out birthdays one by one, calling them out. And I mean, at each date, some kid in the room screamed. The student deferment was gone—a kid's birthday came up and that was it, off to boot camp. Kids in my classes would disappear and by the end of the semester they'd be dead or legs and fingers blown off. One of my profoundest memories of my abortive Colgate career was Professor Eiger announcing that our former classmate Carl Milton was dead, and asking for a prayer of *peace* right there in Astronomy 201! *Peace!* How about that, Rick! Not just a scientist but a well-known hawk, suddenly converted! *Peace!* Three kids I knew *intimately* were killed in futile action. A hundred kids I knew more or less well went off to live elsewhere. Canada, Scotland, Greece. Others went underground, as we so romantically called it, living depressive shadow lives in big cities or off on farms.

For Rick's benefit, I'm giving it all the drama I can and still stay relatively calm. I say: "It was traumatic coming up through high school in the midst of this! Nixon had 500,000 troops over there in 1971! And that's the year I'm *eighteen!*"

"Coop's already a senior in college when Nixon goes," says Frank seriously. He means I should have been a senior.

"I watched Watergate on TV," says Rick, fixing his tie. "That shaped us all, you can't claim that."

"Coop and me, we *feared* that war," says Frank. The good humor is drifting from the room.

"But Frank, *you* were *in* it," says Rick. "Coop was too young for that."

"I was in the lottery," I say.

"You were smoking dope and wearing bell-bottoms," says Rick dismissively.

"We were fighting on the home front," I say.

Rick spits, "The *hippie* thing."

That's it: my hackles rise.

"The sixties," says Roddy warmly.

"Rock and roll," says Julie.

"Oh, I was just an artilleryman," Frank says. "Just lobbing shells."

"Sex and drugs," says Roddy.

"Burnt-out idealism," says Richard P. Baldwin haughtily.

"Burned out?" I say. "Burned out? We changed the culture completely and forever. And for the *better*."

"And you'll claim credit," says Baldwin. "You were in, like, *fifth grade* when the Beatles came out."

"You were in *diapers*."

Baldwin twitches his mustache again. Belligerently, he says, "*Get real.*"

"But here's the point," says Frank. "Let's get back to the point here. It's a different generation."

"Nonsense," Baldwin says. He hates this discussion, disdains any whiff of idealism or activism. He's a backlash baby, one of the kids who went for the money as the eighties dawned and Reagan doddered forth.

"Coop never even saw *The Brady Bunch*," says Roddy. She's trying to lighten the mood. Bless her heart, her safe, enchanting heart under overalls.

"Never?" says Julie.

Frank says, "Richard? Confess."

"Sure," Rick says, seeing the humor here, seeing the need for humor. "I loved *Mar*-sha. Is that what I'm supposed to say? Marsha, Marsha, *Mar*-sha."

"Me and Coop, we're the Vietnam Generation," says Frank. Then, so seriously that it's clear he's kidding, he says, "You kids, you're the Brady-Bunch Generation."

"Not fair!" says Roddy.

"*Sesame Street*," says Julie soberly.

"We were afraid," chants Madeline from the shadows. This discussion, she likes. "Rick, you have to realize: we were genuinely afraid. They were killing us, actually shooting kids walking to class, actually sending boys to kill or die."

"Ah, crap," says Baldwin, but he's been instantly conquered—he knows better than to argue with Lady Moonbeam.

"Can we talk about my tits again?" says Julie, and we all roar with laughter, all of us but Madeline, who does despite herself manage a tolerant smile.

Julie Tinker, half naked in the snow. She lost the Jantzen bikini top at the end of a huge helicopter off the first mogul on the freestyle course—caught the clasp on a frayed slalom gate and *poing*, her boobs are bare. She just continued the event, ABC Sports and all: screw it. And you know, come on, In Europe they still show the clip on TV before every ski meet; they use it for TV commercials; it's great fun. Not here. As if a pair of human breasts, even a particularly splendid example thereof, were anything but hilarious in that situation. ABC Sports, they didn't show one inch of the run and didn't so much as explain why not. And Julie took the gold, nipples first. So Dapper Dan Drakesly, the ABC guy, is standing there interviewing her afterwards and congratulating her and nobody watching TV in the United States has seen her race or has the faintest idea what's happened or why the guys in the broadcast booth are audibly sniggering while she talks about fresh air and sunshine and Drakesly vamps and shivers. Sweetened her endorsement deals in Europe, half killed them here.

And now Frank's got his super high-tech VCR fired up so we can see the gate take the bra in stop motion—evidence—and everyone's laughing and he's rewinding miles of race tapes.

Which is exactly when Madeline rises up, flushed as a pastor's wife. She glares at Frank and strides over to him, puts her face straight in his, spits: "I think there are more important things to talk about than Julie Tinker's *chest*."

More important things: her subject these days is the Arkansas River, which we have just finished discussing for two hours at dinner. The fate of the river is critical; everyone agrees with her. And we took it seriously. But Christ, dinner's done, the dishes are cleared, everyone's drinking margaritas, we've solved the problems of the world over coffee, named a generation. Julie's breasts in the Alps of France are just as real as the fucking river and more current than Richard Nixon and at the moment just as important and certainly more fun for after-dinner talk. In my opinion.

But compassion, compassion. I certainly can understand what Madeline's going through. At least part of which is hormone therapy, let's not forget. The outburst is just an outburst, and tired is just tired. And Madeline's ready to leave. And I'm ready to leave with her. I'm tired, too, and I've had my own angry moments tonight. I mean, I admit it, Baldwin can get me going anytime, anyplace—he's just got to say anything at all about skiing or hippies and I'm climbing into the ring. Anyway, it's after eleven.

I stand and Madeline stands, clearly pleased I'm so willing. Everyone is gracious as hell, good night, good night. And Frank's up on his feet and actually apologizing to her.

She's got this power, has always had it. "Oh, Frank," she says. "It was a lovely party."

Another fast round of good-byes. Julie hugs Madeline, actually says she's sorry; courtly Frank's all over himself helping her into her fringed jacket. Baldwin says, "Those years were tough," conceding something about the earlier discussion, missing the point about our two generations entirely. Me, I'm the chauffeur, sad to leave this cheerful house. But it's time to go, time to go.

Roddy, however, looks profoundly irked, and is not apologetic.

Madeline has to pee so I'm waiting in the stone foyer there (Frank's house, man, it's all stone—a magnificent place, a fortress) and Roddy clomps up in her army boots, her hair a mess from tussling with Julie. She shrugs with that serious smile of hers and kisses me on both cheeks, one kiss tender, the next kiss rough, whispers right in the fuzz of my ear, "Come back later? I want to talk to you. Doesn't matter how late." She plunges her hands in her overall pockets, looks at me seriously, brown eyes shining. She shrugs and tilts her head, not smiling or frowning, just shrugs and turns around and clomps back to the stone den.

4

Shivering and exhausted at dawn, Coop tripped through the weeds at the side of the diner and back onto Main Street, Tyco. Not a soul. He'd expected trouble: parents' car at the gas station, Cindy still dancing, cops crawling everyplace. But nothing. For fifteen minutes—forever—Coop stood by a mailbox and watched the gas station, amazed. A different attendant was on duty, polishing the chrome parts of the pumps, some guy Hodge's age, maybe a little older, twenty-one or twenty-two. Coop watched him as the breakfast shift—three old ladies and a slouching Indian kid— came past one by one to the diner with sidewards glances each. A pickup crept by. An eighteen wheeler, roaring, speeding. Then a big stainless-steel motor home that slowed and waddled into the gas station. The enervating wind that had raged all night was silent now. Coop crossed the highway.

The guy at the pumps was big, in a clean T-shirt, severe crew cut. Coop said, "Hi."

The gas guy eyed him with genuine hostility, slammed the gas nozzle into the filler hole in the motor home. "Are you the run-away boy?" he said.

"I guess I am."

"Well, ha ha, faggot, your parents left you." He had started the gas pumping and the smell of it hit Coop along with the words.

"They left?"

"Said they'd come on back when you got you a haircut."

Coop stood heartshocked watching him, thinking what to do, whom on earth to call. Later, he'd figure out that the gas guy was lying; his parents would never leave him. In truth, they were in a bad motel not a half mile away and were frightened and furious and sleepless and completely concerned, as were the cops and just about everyone else in Tyco.

"They just left?"

The gas guy looked bugged. "Just a minute. Let me do this-here." The motor home took forever to get filled, but at length the attendant reached up to get money from its driver. "Eight dollars," he said.

Cooper couldn't stop it—tears welled up in his eyes, fell down his face.

"What's the problem?" the driver of the motor home said.

"Parents left him cuz he won't get a haircut," the gas guy smirked. How creative his malice! Much later, years later, in nearly a new century, Coop would wonder how the jerk managed to keep his mouth shut as the search intensified and the possibility of foul play was brought into the investigation and his parents were in the paper and on local TV.

"Just left you?" the man said. He turned to his wife and repeated the information, including the bit about the haircut.

Cooper heard her exclaiming, but couldn't hear the words.

He heard the man say, "You think?" then saw the same look of saintly love he'd seen on the faces of his benefactors in the diner: "Where were y'all headed?"

"Seattle."

"Well, you want to hop in? Maybe we can catch 'em up for you."

The gas guy turned to Coop with a falsely benevolent nod: "Go on," he said.

"We're going as far as Bozeman," the bald man said.

Coop didn't deliberate, didn't ask where Bozeman might be, just walked around the giant vehicle and climbed in.

5

At home Madeline boils: "Frank makes me *sick* sometimes," she says. She is pissed and steaming and she's flossing her teeth like she wants to saw her head in half. "He's just obnoxious, that's all, and you get with him and you're obnoxious, too."

"Well, Frank's Frank," I say. "I thought he was pretty nice tonight."

"'Pretty nice.' Fountain of booze, you mean. What's wrong with you? He's murdering himself and now he wants to kill you, too. Filling that house with girls . . . what will people say?"

"You've always liked Frank," I say. "And you've known those girls for years." I'm hearing Roddy's elegant analysis of the Arkansas River situation. I'm seeing Roddy's overalls strap draped down over her shoulder. I'm seeing the depths of Roddy's brown eyes across from me at dinner. I'm hearing Roddy speak in my ear, smelling her gently boozy breath. I'm thinking so hard I can't even defend Frank Kobil as I should. He's fighting to get me the best job I could ever hope to have and my wife's calling him obnoxious, mostly because years back he *was* obnoxious. Probably, she's on the attack because she feels what I'm thinking: Roddy, man. It's Roddy. I'm not sure what to do with myself. Our house is not spacious like Frank's; there's nowhere to go. I pace up and down along the wall of packed bookshelves, thinking, musing, doubting, remembering how in the team bus up to Big Sky a month ago Roddy and I talked ten hours without her ever once saying anything was wrong with me, though the subject was exactly that—what's wrong with Coop?

Roddy, it turns out, is the one person besides you, bro, that I can talk to. And she can talk to me: Claudio's a bully, treats her like a little girl. He's gorgeous but full of himself. He's shallow. He's vain. He can be incredibly tender, soulful, generous, kind, but it never lasts past his getting what he wants. And if a pretty pair of legs go by—watch out.

Reasonably I say, "Maddy, why would two perfectly intelligent and successful young women like Roddy and Julie, with all the choices they've got, choose to stay at Frank Kobil's house if he's such a pig?"

Ducking the question with practiced skill, Madeline says, "When are you going to grow up?" She says, "When are you going to get past these ski bums? Haven't you had enough of the public eye?"

"The public eye? Is that what this is all about?" I'm just walking back and forth, half potted as I have said, pulling this or that book out of the shelves very calmly, making a stack of stuff to maybe read when I'm in Maine for fall training, which is coming up fast. I can't quite answer her, of course, because she's not entirely wrong in her instincts. In some ways—Frank's deadly drinking, the attraction of the young women—she's entirely right. I stand there trying to think how to say this, how to concede without getting back into the argument about fame—the head coach job is highly visible, is what she means. The head coach job will invite scrutiny, perhaps even questions about my past, not to mention that I'll be in charge of dozens of people like Roddy and Julie.

"Oh, Mad, you're tired," I say when I should just be saying *You're right.* I try humor: "You don't really hate me." She is not amused. I say, "These are not ski bums. I mean, it's the U.S. Team. This is not bums." What I don't say is, *You are right. Frank drank maybe a quart of booze over the course of the evening. And suddenly I have a crush on Roddy, who has just kissed me. I'm even contemplating going back over there to see her. The job? The job will definitely invite scrutiny.*

"Frank Kobil is not the U.S. Team," she says.

"Frank Kobil is the only chance I've got," I say. And that, at least, is true.

"Well, Julie Tinker is certainly not the U.S. Team," she says.

"She won the World Cup in freestyle just last year," I say.

"Roddy Manor is not the U.S. Ski Team," says Mad.

"Roddy certainly is."

"Not for long with that limp," says my wife.

"That's getting mean," I say.

She marches into the bathroom, doesn't shut the door. She runs the water to brush her teeth, calls out: "I just want to know when you're going to grow up."

"Where is that book on ants?" I say. "It's called *The Ants,* I think. It's huge."

"You lent it to Frank." Toothpaste in her mouth.

"I *am* grown up," I say, just quietly. And what I take as proof that I am indeed grown up is that I don't get mad at all, that I just calmly keep pulling down books, that I'm not yelling back, that I see clearly all the ways she's right.

Madeline chugs into her room, and I admire her even in her fury, admire her hopelessly. I give her five minutes, then I'm in there to kiss her good night. She's half asleep, her blindfold in place, her earplugs in, but not too asleep to say, "You asshole," just as I kiss her lotiony forehead. But I hear the affection there. I hear it plainly and say gently, "You're an asshole, too." She knows what I mean, that I admire her steadfastly.

Good night, good night.

I sit in the living room and read a distracted half hour in a tattered old book of hers or maybe mine called *Daily Life in Ancient Rome*. All of them struggling with their marriages and their mothers and all the other crap that must have darkened their lives: diseases, sieges, anonymous death.

I'm reading the words but I'm thinking of Roddy. Her hair touched my face when she kissed me, her soft hair, smelling sweetly. I'm thinking guiltily of the gape of her overalls, the rise of her T-shirt's hem as she battled Julie, the quick flash of the band of a plain pair of white underpants, skin of her skier's belly, bone of her hip. I like the way she gets shy in conversation, the way she sits up tall to speak. I'm guessing how her skin might feel. I'm wondering what my going back to Frank's will mean. I'm telling myself not to go.

Roddy on the bus to Big Sky (a whole month ago when we were still coach and skier and not whatever we are now—flirt and crush, I guess) sat sideways in her seat, a coiled spring, her knees up to her chin and the landscape rushing and gray in the window behind her (no, not coach and skier anymore even then, but genuine pals), she searched my face with those brown eyes. She said if I was feeling so explosive I had to figure out why, not just hold the lid on. She said if I looked back across my life and thought a little bit, I'd figure it out. Her toes in silk liner socks poked under my thigh and their touch, the slightest wriggle, was good news.

"Remember your life," she said. "Do not romanticize it. And don't make things up. Just remember it plainly. Then maybe you can let go."

"I've already let go."

"You can't let go of something you don't have hold of, Coop Henry." Roddy has got this wisdom.

I said, "It's the summer I turned sixteen."

"So you already know what it is."

Roddy has got these toes. My thigh tingles, remembering.

I get my jacket on again, look blankly into the refrigerator, then creep out the front door quietly, slip into in my rusting Subaru wagon, only slamming the broken door closed when I'm safely out on the road. On the way back down the valley to Frank's I'm seeing myself ditching Mom and Dad in Tyco, remembering it clearly, like I've never remembered it before, my night of remorse alone on a high ridge of ranchland, remembering with supernatural clarity the strings of lights that were towns along Highway 87, remembering my quaking, my resolve. And it's the same kind of quaking and resolve I'm feeling now, or the *same* quaking and resolve, unchanged and uninterrupted. Quaking, resolute, I pull up to the one stoplight in Basalt, wait there for nothing and no one as it changes to green, then yellow, then red, then green again, a dozen changes through the sequence before a pickup comes up behind and I'm forced to go. I head on to Frank's house, thinking hard.

I really ought to turn around.

6

All of a black night in a barn full of shifting creatures Coop cursed his adventure, sleepless. But in the morning he breathed in the air of Montana and looked out over a million miles and mountains not far and snow on the mountains and the sky like a gray sea, no rain. He was going to find Hodge. The night's remorse fell away from his heart; the night's nearly physical homesickness was as nothing in the light of day. Call his parents at the first phone? Coop knew what Hodge would say: *Fuck that!* Even if he knew where they were he wouldn't call! Coop was a boy who slept in barns! A boy who could take care of himself! He wouldn't even call Grandma. He wouldn't call anyone back at home. He wouldn't call the FBI (as he'd decided in the night). He'd hit the road like Hodge, and join Hodge, and who could stop him? He'd find Hodge if it meant barns and bad nights for years to come, for the rest of his life!

Ahead he saw a town, couldn't say if it were five miles away or ten. He put out his thumb to the first car that came along, watched it stop, cloud of dust. A small man in a brown suit waved Coop into the car impatiently, and after a mere minute of driving looked at Coop hard. He said, "You're a boy? If I'd a knew you was a boy I wouldn't have stopped."

In town, anxious Coop walked till he found a store, a blowzy grocery on the straight main drag. The lady behind the counter was very tall, with glasses. She looked up from a pile of coupons with a beautiful neighborly warmth that collapsed completely when she saw who'd come in. Her fear gave Coop fear.

"We don't serve hippies," she said. Her hands were very long and shook on the coupons she was shuffling.

Coop smiled the best grandson smile he could and said, "But I'm not a hippie!"

On the street he opened the bread she'd finally let him buy with his fifty cents and swallowed four slices fast, thinking how Hodge would know what to do. He popped open the extravagant soda, too, drank it fast. Now he was dead broke. Still no one was around. At the end of the strip there was a post office, silver letters on brick:

DARBY MONTANA

But no money for a postcard or stamp, and really, no one to write to. Coop kept having a positive thought, that he'd get allowance on Friday—two bucks—but, of course, he wouldn't. He flipped through the fat post office directories, the fear rising up in him as if flowing from the cement floor, flooding up from his legs into his breast. He inspected a bulletin board near the door, waiting for someone to yell at him. Hay for sale. Dogs for sale. Backhoe. Beautician. Then, neatly written in big pencil letters on an old envelope:

WANTED: CALF HELP.

ONE WEEK TOPS.

SEE TAD THOMAS AT LAZY K RANCH BEFORE SUNDAY.

FAIR PAY.

No phone number, but then again, Coop had no dime. Timidly, he approached the clerk: "Do you know Tad Thomas?"

"Don't you, young lady?"

Coop didn't correct him, just listened to the directions: head west up the Lolo Pass road.

"Think you can handle the calves, do you, Miss Elizabeth?"

Back in the street, Coop hid his hair in the collar of his shirt, marched toward the mountains, toward this Lazy K, his only idea. He walked maybe four miles, growing thirsty, before a young-looking teenager in a pickup stopped. Meek Billy Fortune drove very slowly up the straight road while Coop bragged and lied about adventures he'd never had, but that Hodge surely might: cops kicked in the nuts, bales of reefer, Mick Jagger at a party.

By the time Billy dropped Coop in front of the timber archway of the Lazy K, the kid's eyes were wide, his life changed permanently. Coop gave him his first soul shake, called him brother. When Billy drove off, Coop was so alone he actually moaned. But he pulled himself together (a Dad command that he gave himself sternly), marched across the rails of the cattle guard and up the long driveway. He'd ridden a horse once or twice, silly prancing horses at his sister's riding camp. He imagined hard men leaping off horses to tackle bellowing steers. He saw snakebites and fist-fights and long pulls of whiskey. He saw himself bouncing and beaten for a hippie and dying in the dust with his hair rudely cut, alone. He walked.

The silos were tall and blue, shiny new, surrounded by easily a dozen well-kept sheds and barns and shacks. In the middle of these Coop crossed a tidy patch of yard to the blue door of a plain two-story house that needed paint. He knocked. Nothing happened. He knocked again, breathing hard.

Presently, a girl answered the door. She was a little older than Coop, was certainly taller, and didn't seem surprised in the least to see him. She wore big mild glasses with pale pink rims.

Coop attempted a swagger: "I'm here to do calf work," he said.

She raised her eyebrows. "Well, good timing, cowboy. Daddy's gone to Red Lodge till lunch. You can come in and wait." Coop made himself bowlegged, followed her into the living room—pliers and hammers and two coils of rope, piles of books on three separate tables, real cowboy boots next to tattered easy chairs, a loose pile of logs and sticks on the hearth, on the walls big seashore paintings, out of place. She'd called him cowboy! He sat on the couch, shrugged manly at his host.

"I'm Tricia," she said.

He meant to answer, but didn't.

"Your hair is kinda stuck in your shirt there," this Tricia said, helpfully. She was all hard edges till you looked at her, and even then not soft. She went to the kitchen and got Coop a glass of water without asking, dropped it with a splash on the worn table in front of him, clomped to the stairs in her cowboy boots. "I'm writing poems," she said, matter-of-factly. She was amazingly tall, and there was just something Coop liked about her. She said, "Don't be so *uptight*," laughed at him and disappeared.

Coop sat politely on the couch for an hour, exhausted by his very first step on the road to Hodge. He read in the magazines lying around, none of which were at all familiar or cowboy tough. All, in fact, seemed to feature poetry. He read poems with uneven lines, graphic talk of bodies, no rhymes, general weirdness, read till he got too comfortable in the soft worn couch and fell asleep.

7

Frank Kobil's house is dead dark, the forest all around it dead still. The front door is purposefully ajar. In the stone foyer—the foyer of two kisses—I shed my coat with deliberate rustle and flourish so as not to startle Roddy.

Who is in the living room still, her legs under her on the deep couch. She's gazing out the grand windows at Frank's Olympian view: mountains limned by stars, moonless night. My heart opens when I see her—she's but a silhouette—my heart opens and pounds in my neck, my face. She doesn't turn, not when I stumble over her tossed army boots, not even when I bump the great glass coffee table, not when I'm standing right there at the end of the couch. She's cradling a melted margarita. Her eyes are wide open in the dark; she's looking at the stars.

"What are *you* doing back?" she says.

"You asked me."

"Did I?"

"You did."

"Oh, Coop. I'm so nervous."

"It's just me."

"And me."

"And you."

I think she smiles. Frank's clock collection goes off in a staggered ensemble. It's midnight and you wouldn't believe all the noise, how long it goes on. Roddy and I are pretty well frozen in place, statuary. We've come this far, which is probably far enough.

After the last clock stops, Roddy says, "I promised myself this morning that I'd get you alone." She hasn't taken her gaze from the window for one second. "But now, I'm not so sure. I'm thinking about the question of historical returns. Does art advance as a screw turns? As a spiral into the future? I've been reading Hal Foster. 'How does *re*-connection with a past practice support a *dis*-connection from a present practice?' It's the oldest question in art history. And not a bad one for you, now that I think about it."

"Could you ask again?"

"You sound like the Mysterious Eight-Ball."

"And you sound like Encyclopedia Brown."

"I'm not as young as you think." Silence. Then subtly she turns to me. "What I'm saying is, you need to act. You need to do something." In the dark her hands are pale, her face obscured. "You have been unhappy, even miserable." She smooths her jeans, seems to watch me. She says something in Italian, then translates: "You are a frozen sea." She's quoting somebody. Who? Her delicate neck is as pale as her hands. I want to see her better. "I don't want to be the axe here, Mr. Henry."

I want to light the candle that's appeared on the coffee table, but Roddy's right, I'm frozen. I'm standing there awkwardly at the end of the couch among her shoes. Nothing in Roddy's manner invites me to sit. Nothing invites me to move. There is only the abstraction: *act.*

She says, "I've been unhappy, too." She puts her hair behind one ear, then the other, as if to listen better. Her dark eyes search my face in starlight, barely any light at all. She raises her eyebrows ever so slightly, skeptical. She's set this sweet trap for me. "Now, answer the question."

I make myself move, seize the matches off the coffee table, strike one quickly and light the candle, light the air around us in a flash, cause a glint of flame off the huge tequila bottle sitting there, off two of Frank's nice water glasses, off the shiny covers of Roddy's art theory books. Always studying, our Roddy.

"Oh," she says, blinking. The light seems very bright. Her lips are not so full and plain pretty as Mad's and I'm aware not only of Roddy's mouth but of the comparison I have made. Her mouth appeals in some other, more businesslike way. Her teeth are nice in candlelight, that's how closely I'm looking.

"I guess I just want to talk," I say.

"Talk? Then why do you look so ardent?"

She wants me to act. So I sit on the couch in the candlelight close to her. I sink into the deep leather beside her.

She leans away from me. Her eyes are vivid, bright: "You have evaded the question, Mr. Henry. So let me give my own answer: You came back here because that night coming back from Big Sky has been on your mind a whole month now. Yes it has. It's been on my mind, too." Then very softly, "You came back because of some changes you have to make."

She has hit some spot inside me. Tears start to my eyes. I do evade her, avoid her, haul her back down to earth: "You kissed me, Veronica Manor." As best I can, I make this funny.

Roddy says, "I only kissed your cheek," funny too. She leans forward intimately, looking at me steadily. I'm awkward with her looking in me that deeply so I cast my eyes down and see in the gaping scissored neck of her thermal T-shirt and only slowly realize that seeing means I must be looking. I'm looking at the delicate white bra and freckled cleavage of one of my skiers, a tomboy who's grown up in front of me, this former charge, this kid, my friend for years, her many charms hidden from me by something unseen, some obscure part of myself that Roddy sees clearly, despite all. And she is right. I do have to make some changes. I just don't know what they might be. I put my forehead on her shoulder, just that.

"Don't say anything about love," she says softly.

I put a hand on her breast, just firmly on her breast over her shirt and over the buckle of her overalls.

"I'm not going to kiss you," she says.

And I act. I kiss her neck, I kiss her cheek, tenderly, dryly. I kiss her cheek and then I kiss her lips. I kiss her lips and hold her breast and she sits there unmoved, unmoving.

"Because you are married," she says at length.

I kiss her and this time she kisses me back and we keep kissing, she smoothing the cloth of my jeans on my legs, I lightly holding her breast, I kissing her, she more allowing the kiss than joining in, her mouth tasting agreeably of margarita and faintly of the two cigarettes she must have smoked today, breaking training. We explore the kiss a long time, making soulful sounds, and the whole thing is as natural as stepping through a stream to cross it. Your shoes get wet. You keep hiking into the forest.

Roddy says dreamily, "I skied right up to you at my first time trials, the year I didn't make the team, and I said how I'd seen you win your Bronze at Sapporo." She tucks her chin in, swaggers her head to imitate me back then: "'Oh, *ahem,* that was all luck, little girl-thing.'"

"Come on! I was very nice."

"'*Luck*'!"

"Well, it *was* luck."

Roddy yawns, stretches, gets out my grasp, slides away from me, regards me coolly.

"The snow was bad," I tell her, as I've told a thousand people before. "Shitty weather, my God. The top guys crashed and burned. I was always an ice boy—it's the New England training."

"You didn't do it? It just happened to you?"

"I just skied the course."

"Coop, you won an Olympic *medal!* That's everyone's *dream.*"

I seem to have a ready reply, lots of words about luck and ice (I've said them those thousand times) but I've heard what she's saying and what she's saying makes me hear what I'm about to say, makes me not say it. Instead I say, "Can we have a fresh drink, you think? Or are we already too bombed?"

"Don't start saying you're here because we're drunk, Coop Henry. If you're kissing me just because you're drunk you can go kiss Frank Kobil."

"Never too drunk to take responsibility," I say.

Roddy rather likes that, smiles with one half her mouth. I lift the jug of tequila and take a swig. Not as awful as I would have thought. I take another. That race comes back to me whole, one millionth time, my suicidal crash through a hundred yards of deep ice ruts after a freak rain, clear, thick ice all the other skiers avoided by slowing and taking the gate way wide. Not I, nineteen years old, eighty miles an hour (Frank figured), eighty miles an hour with no car around me and the air like needles in my face and no concession to the ice or the curve or the million forces of nature, none at all, ski it or die, fuck it, with the object not so much to ski it, come to think of it, skiing it impossible. But through sheer force of rage and fear and guilt and I guess youth I stayed on the course (yelled in terror through the ice, pushing everything into those edges, full tuck), stayed on the course and made third best time, .016 seconds and .024 seconds respectively after the two Austrian boys who'd got the luck of the draw and skied before the cloudburst, the race delay, the temperature plunge. No one more surprised than I. Have you seen a kid fall at eighty miles an hour, bro?

I asked for it and didn't get it, at least not that time, that time like passing a speeding semi in the face of another speeding truck and squeaking back in line just in time. One sweats, one sees the crash in one's mind, one hears it, feels it, and then it doesn't happen. There's the empty road ahead, just empty road, no death after all, big smile, big screaming smile.

Roddy pulls the bottle away from me, hefts it to her lips, chugs, shudders, plunks the bottle down on the glass table, clank, resumes her smoothing of my jeans on my legs with her strong hands. We sit in that relation a long time, gazing at each other. Something more is happening than maybe we'd thought. Something maybe quite a bit more. The drink makes a warm spot in my chest, another in my head.

She says, "I spotted you at the committee table at my first eliminations—Park City—and skied right up boldly and told you I'd *seen* you. Remember this? I'd been to Sapporo with my folks before they split up, when I was like eight. I told my mother I wanted to *marry* you."

The sunny day of those eliminations enters my mind in a flash, the dazzling dry snow in Utah. This kid skis up—just barely seventeen years old—this basically gangly kid skis up with her handsome bright face and her freckly sunburn and broken goggles and says she's been planning on marrying me since she was *eight.*

Roddy wants to think I don't remember, but I do. "I was thirty," I tell her, but I don't say the rest: I had just been married to Madeline.

Mad's image enters Frank's living room now, sits as a cricket up in the great pinewood beams, chirring ominously.

"Put your hand back on my boob," says Roddy.

"Are you really saying that?"

"Act," she says, frowning.

I push the strap of her overalls off her shoulder, again hold her breast, which fits insistently in my hand. I hold her breast and look at her eyes, then lean into her and kiss her lips as her nipple rises subtly into my palm.

She lets the kiss happen, not quite joining in, then leans back, looks at me hotly. She says, "Tell me a secret."

She seems to want something specific. But the secret that first comes to mind isn't quite cooked yet, isn't quite ready to come out: I've only been smitten in this sudden way once before. "Tricia Thomas," I blurt. "A cowgirl."

"That summer?"

"Yup."

"You roped her!"

"She roped me."

"Hot in here," Roddy says, disappointed. She says, "I'd sure like it if some cowboy came along." She shrugs and wriggles such that the top of her overalls drops down around her waist. I think of Frank—light sleeper—what if Frank comes in? I think of Julie— no worry there—Julie has famously slept through towel fights, car crashes, terrorist explosions, world wars.

Roddy—this strong, sweet, brainy woman, this fearsome competitor—Roddy sits beside me on Frank's warm couch. "Your turn," she says. I put my hand on her belly, stroke her, pull her to me, doing my best to ride into town in a cloud of dust. Wild, wild West. We kiss hard and touch each other and say assenting syllables. Her hands press my back, smooth my jeans. But then she grows still, settles away from me, won't look at me.

At length, guessing at her thoughts, I say, "You're practically married, yourself."

Roddy leans back into me, puts her face on my shoulder, thinks awhile, says, "Claudio won't touch me anymore. He turns away. He's bored. He's tired of me. There's not enough between us, I think is the thing. Never enough between us. I think it was all passion, Coop, I think it's gone. The charm has worn off."

"You are manipulating me," I say.

"I invite you to respond in kind."

We betray our partners with sentences, first, then with our hands, then with our whole skeletons. Frank's clocks chime one o'clock, then two. We're taking a long, long time, all right. We're like the tide, low and high, swell and subside. I tell her about Connie Kirkbridge, for some reason. I tell her about Mom's detective, but not too much. I tell her about Tyco, Wyoming. I tell her about the Lazy K, and as much as I can about Tricia without getting all the way to you. I tell her that Mad and I are living like old roommates, really, which is dead true. I tell her how badly I want this coaching job that's coming. I tell her more than I've ever told anyone but you, brother. And though you are at the edge of all confessions, I manage not to say the second word about you—no betrayal there, not yet.

I say, "My father lost his job just about the time I was born." I say, "I wouldn't even know except my mom gave me the story as a bootstraps kind of thing when I was flunking college." I say, "Poor old guy. For a couple of years there he was the only dad in America not making the grade. He even lost our house."

Roddy holds up a finger. She's got a serious look on her face. "*Il faut que je piss*," she says, and I laugh. She untangles her overalls, pulls them up around her, pads off down the stone hall holding them up. In the silence I have twelve visions of you, Hodge, you and Dad pushing each other, shouting, engorged red faces, spitting fury. Why this, now?

Roddy's back. She wants me to go on about Dad, watches me expectantly.

"Can't remember where I was," I say.

Roddy sweetly says, "It's okay," knowing I'm withholding something, then whispers to me in the candlelight, tells me stuff I don't know about her. It's delicious, this talking, our faces so close. Her own father—industrial heir—left the family broke when Roddy

was six, left her mom, sailed his yacht till he drowned in some
swashbuckling mishap that may have had to do with running bales
of pot. Next phase for Roddy was a kind of hippie farm in
Pennsylvania, loony and distant organic-beans stepfather, good
snow at a little rope-tow mountain nearby, skiing every winter day,
reading every winter night (art books, art biographies, art cata-
logues, art theory, the same stuff she's still absorbed by now), trips
to Pittsburgh and Philly and D.C. for museums (art again, all art).
New York, of course, but later on—Paris, too, later yet, and Rome,
and then the world.

The tide is in. Roddy and I kiss and neck and pet and then we
don't talk anymore—the pitch and rhythm has changed. Her shirt
is pulled up high, her overalls are off, she's sunk in the leather of
the couch with her underpants askew. She likes to be touched. I'm
in a T-shirt only, her hands on my shoulders. She likes to be kissed.
She's all muscles from physical therapy and cross training. Her
thighs are smooth at my cheeks, her fingers kiss my face, her feet
cross behind me, she squeezes. I reach up to touch her mouth with
my own fingers, touch her teeth. I touch her tongue, which she
moves at first to mimic mine, then to instruct. We're stretched out
a length and a half across the couch. She's all rhythm as I heed her
teaching, pulls at my hair, then she's more rhythm yet, squeezes
me hard, her solid legs, then clench and freeze, pushes my shoulders with her hands, pulls my shoulders with her hands, pulls me
up finally to kiss me roughly and then we're all rhythm together
and I've got to say: it's great. For a long time afterwards we're a
redolent tangle. "This is who wants you, old wreck," she says. We
breathe together and touch sweetly and say what we say—no more
teasing—and kiss a half hour, an hour into the night, who knows?

Abruptly her kisses stop. Some thought has crossed her mind.
She goes defiant, recasts me as coach. I feel it immediately. She
says, "I'm going to quit the team. Back to school. I've had it. I'm

tired. I'm not going to end up on the Europe Cup circuit. Just not. The new girls are killing me. I'm quitting."

"Oh, no. Not yet, you don't," I say.

"Maine," she says. "I'll see how I do in Maine. But listen, Mr. Henry: I've already told UVM I'm back."

She's on leave, as everyone knows, from the University of Vermont. She's a student in their small but big-time doctoral program in art history, I don't need to say. And okay, I do know she's a genius. And I do know the degree means a lot to her. She'll be Doctor Roddy, curator in residence, worldwide renown. That's all coming, for sure. But I do not want her to stop skiing. Not just yet. She shouldn't stop skiing, and she knows it. School she can go back to after the season's up, maybe two seasons. She's in great shape, healing from her fall perfectly; she's the best we've got, no matter what she says. All at once, she's tense, I'm apologetic, our wet faces only a couple of inches apart. We're coach and skier, embarrassingly naked. The candle is more than half burned. We have a moment of disjunction, pull the little afghan off the back of the couch, struggle mildly over its coverage. Suddenly the sexual dampness of us is chilly. Roddy skootches herself up on the leather. I can only follow. We rest our chins on the back of the couch and look out Frank's grand window a long time. I hear how condescending my thoughts have been. I correct them: Roddy should do what she wants. The black sky behind the Maroon Bells has come a shade blue in advance of the dawn.

"Maybe you'll come with me," she says, going soft. She means Vermont. "Oh, wouldn't that be perfect?"

We are lovers again, kiss with renewed ardor, get all the way naked fast. We're thinking about the same thing, which is that in less than a month we've got fall training in Maine. Again Roddy stiffens, stares. She says, "But first we must get single. Both of us. You and Madeline. I'm serious. You've told me how bad things are for you more than once! Me and Claudio. Done."

In the dark of night and naked in her arms I am inspired, her logic seems perfect. I mount a small protest in any case: "That kind of thing takes more than a month!"

Very slowly, very quietly: "Oh, Coop. This can't be an affair. I won't do that. This is bad enough, just this we're doing now. In fact, it's despicable. I'm serious. Think of Madeline. No sneaking around for me. No more of this. We stop right now. Madeline's so brilliant. You'll stay with her. For my part, though, for me—just for me—I will tell Claudio tomorrow. Claudio, the Roman! And you, for your part, just for you, you do what you must. But I'd say it's time for you to *act*. You told me as much on the team bus. You did. And that was way before . . . this." That *this* is so complicated: our two skins, our deception, our conflicted hearts and minds.

"This," I say.

"*This,*" she says, and it's as good as declaring our love. We're quiet, then, drifting on our own thoughts, multiply intoxicated. A future newly imagined—never before even faintly possible—a future opens out in front of us. I contemplate the continued absurdity of living with Madeline.

But such clarity has one trait only: it fades.

8

Tricia's father, Tad Thomas, lifelong Montana rancher, wore pink-framed glasses like his daughter's, loose dungarees, an ironed shirt, walked fast, talked slowly, a word at a time, as few words as would do. He didn't smile. The sudden arrival of a grubby Eastern kid was as nothing to him. After the quickest conversation about money—one dollar an hour—and after a standing lunch (big strips of beef on white bread, no mayonnaise, no lettuce, no nothing else, that and a certain pork chop Coop's first meat in six months, and good), Tad said they had best get to work. He called for Tricia twice, didn't get an answer. He said, "On our own, it would appear."

Fuzzy from his nap and still bowlegged, Coop followed Tad out behind the silos to a large corral. Four horses came immediately to the fence. The biggest went straight to the rancher's hand, nuzzled it.

"Miles," Tad said. "Miles, boy."

Miles was enormous. Coop made himself touch the velvet nose, patted it and looked into the horse's huge eye as the others gathered up close along the fence.

"That's Coop," Tad Thomas said.

Tad and Coop walked to the barn. The horses followed on the other side of the corral fencing. Tad let Miles and another horse through, put halters over their heads, said, "We're weaning spring calves."

Coop nodded. To him, the horses looked dangerous.

Tad saddled Miles and the smaller horse named Seven-Up, took his time, motioned at last for Coop to mount Miles. Coop didn't think, didn't fret, just moved, foot in the stirrup and pull yourself up.

They rode at an amble down a draw and through a gate into the sparse range land that was the Lazy K. A ridge of craggy mountains loomed in the near distance. It all seemed so easy, a boy on his own, a rancher on his land.

Pretty soon the cowpokes came up on a barbed-wire fence, and down the perfect line of it Coop saw the feedlot, high wooden rails that made a big corral (many animals in there, milling, jumping up on each other), this attached to a weathered barn. The bellowing of the weaned calves reached him now, plaintive and loud, lots of calves, all of them making noise. Pressing against barbed wire at the edge of the scrub, the mothers called back.

Tad Thomas went in the barn through the little door trailside saying he wanted one calf led in there. He pointed. Coop didn't pause, but climbed into the corral the way he'd mounted Miles, all phony confidence, playing brave as if Tad Thomas were Hodge Henry, and found himself among the animals. They weren't little veals, not at all. One minute and the great door to the weaning pen rolled open.

Coop breathed and stepped toward the bulk of the young herd. Those nearest eyed him, stamped, stepped away. He stepped closer, and closer again, watching the stubs of horns on a particular beast before him, a scruffy blond-brown thing that wouldn't move. Five or six other calves bolted past, got behind Coop, backed up against the fence. Large brown eyes everywhere, scared of him. "Ha," Coop said, too quietly, and flicked his hands. He thought of the rodeo clowns on TV, the bronco busters, the calf ropers. "*Ha.*" Louder. The calf before him bucked, spun, kicked its back hooves in the air harmlessly, twisted, bellowed, jumped past. Coop fell to the dirt and rolled, wildly waving his arms as he got back to his feet. Calves thundered by until but two had got around him. He breathed a minute, feeling the mass of animals behind him but staring in the eyes of the two he'd cut out. He cried "Ha!" and waved his arms. Abruptly, both calves turned and leapt straight into the darkness of the barn. The door rolled shut behind them.

Coop laughed out loud at his success, then stopped, killed the grin, let himself into the barn behind the calves, serious and sober as Tad.

In the barn, gentle Tad rump-patted the animals with a broom into the chute that led to a kind of giant vise. The first calf charged straight to the trap with great noise and kicking. Tad lifted a handle, squeezed the beast immobile. He said, "Cooper Henry, could you move that heater over here?"

Coop did, wheeled the rocket-shaped heater close. Smell of kerosene. He jumped when Tad lit it. It burned blastingly, a fat live flame roaring from the forward vent. Coop didn't understand, didn't ask, didn't have to when Tad handed him two branding irons, a backwards K and a backwards 4, both with long handles, home forged, well used. "If you'll lean them on the block there," Tad said gently.

Coop leaned the irons on a scarred stump of wood so that the number and letter were in the big flame and though it wasn't a campfire in a ring of stones and though no one had thrown a rope or leapt from a moving horse and though the hot irons were going to be painful to see used, Coop's chest puffed. He saw himself clearly: a teenage boy about to brand calves, working his way in the world like an adult. He wanted to tell Hodge, would tell him first thing when he found him.

Tad lifted the tail of the creature in the vise. "Heifer," he said quietly. The heifer stood still, staring ahead. Tad pulled a syringe from a kit, filled it with a bluish liquid, gave the heifer her shot, speaking quietly, calling her girl. Next, Tad took up the tattoo gun, caught the heifer's ear and squeezed inked pins through the thinnest flesh, leaving a number. She shook her head hard, once, as if she'd been stung.

"Still rustlers out there," Tad said. "They use trucks, now." In a log book—the tattoo registry—Tad wrote the number of the calf, noted the shot he'd given, guessed at her age. He was calm and businesslike, felt her coat, checked her hooves, looked into her eyes, inspected her nostrils and teeth. He loved her, anyone could see that, but it was the love of a mechanic for a good car.

Tad turned the K in the fire. When the glow was evenly red he picked the iron up and poked it into the heifer's hide, high on her rump. She bellowed and tried to leap, shook and rattled the vise, flung saliva from the sides of her mouth. The other calf backed up against the barn door. A terrific plume of smoke rose from the heifer's flank and soon the smell of torched hair and well-done steak came to Coop's nostrils. The brand left a nice K, sideways. Tad did the same with the 4, right-side up.

Coop thought of his parents, felt a wave of remorse.

"Here comes the worst," Tad said. He picked up the horn shears, put the business end quickly over one fuzzy horn, opened the long handles to close the steel jaw, twisted it like working a posthole digger, collected a nubbin of horn from the very skull of the calf. A fine spray of blood pumped from the wound. Tad cut the other horn and opened the cattle vise. The heifer bucked and ran, spraying blood from both sides of her head. She made her way bucking to a corner and stopped, staring.

"All right?" Tad said.

"I'm all right," Coop said. But what about the animal?

The next calf was a heifer too and got the same. She joined the first calf in the darkest corner and huddled. The air in the barn was all burnt hair and kerosene fumes. Cooper went for two more calves, had no trouble separating a couple out and into the barn. The first was already in the vise (Tad calls this the squeeze), already pressed immobile by the time Coop followed it inside. That stray thought of his parents faded into pure interest in the work at hand.

"Bully," Tad said.

"Why do we have to take off the horns?" Coop said.

"Well, we poll them, it's called, so they won't hurt each other when the horns get big, or hurt you or me, either. And also because they look better."

"Who says it looks better?"

"People just say. I mean, why does a man shave?"

Cooper shrugged, held the vise tight while Tad gave the bully his shot and tattoo.

"Want to try the brand?" Tad said.

Coop said sure, took up the hot iron and pressed it high to the bully's hip. He could feel the flesh sizzle through the hot handle of the iron. Lazy K, 4.

"They don't feel it like a man'd feel it," Tad said.

Coop took up the de-horning shears, thinking about why a man shaves and what a man feels.

"Wait up," Tad said. "We're gonna steer this one, I do believe. He won't make much of a bull."

Tad lifted the tail, pressed it down along the calf's spine. "Hold that there. That pinches off the nerve." He climbed around to kneel behind, pulled a scalpel from the case. "I'm getting awful good at this." Tad slit the big scrotal sack of the calf, up and down, then slipped the purplish testicles out into the air. They were the size of small fists and covered with a delicate lacework of capillaries. The calf didn't so much as twitch. Cooper's own testicles rose.

Tad slid his fingers up the vas deferens and the testicular cord (Coop had learned these terms in biology, at the time finding them so hilarious he'd been yelled at). When Tad's fingers were well up inside the sac he slit the cord and the testicles came free in his hand. He threw them in a galvanized bucket, then swabbed the empty scrotum with kerosene. The operation was bloodless. "Dinner for two," Tad said, not really smiling.

Coop let the tail go, then Tad let him do the horns. Coop didn't do it so well, not getting through on the first couple of bites. He waited to get yelled at, but Tad only quietly took the shears from him and finished the job. They let the steer go. Spraying blood, it stepped gingerly out of the vise, took two steps, wobbled and fell with a boom on its side into the dirt of the barn floor. Coop looked at Tad, alarmed.

Tad said simply: "The bullys sometimes faint."

Coop saw the spray of blood across Tad's face, dots of blood on Tad's glasses. They waited. Soon enough the steer rocked itself and rose unsteadily to its feet, joined the heifers in the corner.

They did one calf after the next, faster and faster, Coop gathering them, Tad squeezing them up in the vise. Of fifty bullys Tad spared but three their testicles.

Coop asked many questions, learned the method of artificial insemination, learned that a heifer was a cow once she'd calved, learned that all the cattle here were pure Swiss mountain stock called Simmentals, learned that if the heifers at hand produced good calves they'd live for twelve or fifteen years as breeding stock. After that they'd go to the rendering plant and be turned into glue and shoe leather and fertilizer and smoke. The steers would live to a thousand pounds, a weight they'd reach a few months hence in the stockyards down in Denver. Tad praised Coop quite a bit, said he had an eye for cattle, said his curiosity would serve him well and cause him trouble, said he learned faster than any boy he'd ever worked with. And Coop had to admit he was doing well. Tad teased him about staying on at the Lazy K and becoming a ranch-hand, but never asked once what Coop's story was and never said one word at all about the length of Coop's hair. There was something not fatherly about all the approval, something almost chilly that made Coop lonely.

Tricia rode down late in the afternoon, petulant about being left behind, as if Tad hadn't tried to rouse her. With her help the calves were in and out of the vise in five minutes each.

"Tricia's the Valedictorian of Gallatin Regional High," Tad announced in the smoke of burned hair.

"I'm going to Stanford," Tricia said flatly.

"Full scholarship," her dad said. "She's a whiz like her mother was."

Coop said, "Wow," though he'd barely heard of Stanford.

They worked past dinnertime. Coop watched Tricia when he could. Her legs were the tallest part about her, longer than her dad's. She wore cowboy boots under her jean cuffs, and wore her beat-up jeans pulled way high on her waist, cinched in around a frilly blouse. And her glasses made her eyes big. She did look smart, now that he thought about it.

Coop asked a question that had been burning him all afternoon, asked in front of Tricia, asked when the last calf leapt snorting from the vise: "How do you tell which one's a heifer just by lifting the tail?" He knew it was dumb by the way Tricia rolled her eyes and looked away, walked off so her dad could answer.

Tad shook his head in the almost dark, rubbed his grizzled cheek distractedly, tried to find words. "Well. You lift up the tail and if it's a heifer there's a . . . well, there's a . . . it's a *twat*."

9

I haven't had friends so much as brothers, various attempts at replacing you, Hodge, attempts always fraught, of course, fraught with the fear of loss, for one, fraught with something else, too (fraught is her word—Roddy's—loss is her word too: it's Roddy who's got me thinking), this sense of smallness: you were always a foot taller and five years older when a single year was eons.

Frank Kobil, of course, Frank is a proto-brother. He's older and wiser and taller, too, has been my coach, refrains brotherly from giving me unsolicited advice though whatever advice is there always shows in his face and sounds in the tone of his voice as he asks how things are going. And things—goddamn it—things are going poorly at the moment. I've looked forward to this trip to Vail for some weeks, this chance to think.

I chug over the high mountain passes thinking, all right, thinking of you, bro, for sure, but considering Roddy too, Roddy's body, just night before last, Roddy's kisses, Roddy's talk, some languorous thing she said in Italian toward the end of the night, something she teasingly wouldn't translate for me till I was on the way out Frank's door at dawn: "Lovemaking the only earthly time beauty enters every portal of one's perceptions at once." Beauty is right. Jesus, what of Madeline?

Thank God for Frank—Frank I can talk to, and unlike you, Frank will answer me back. The two of us trainer-administrators (they seldom use the word coach anymore) are going to share a condominium on the very slopes of Vail, prime real estate. Frank and me, we're the ski team, and we're meeting with the money people. Frank's invited me along to help cinch my big job, introduce me around. I get there an hour late, park my bomb next to Frank's spanking-new, forest green Mercedes, "The biggest one they make," he says. I climb the flights of stairs to our weekend lair, don't have to knock, because Frank's right there at the door. "Been watching for you," he says, and he's my brother, all right.

No one looks more at home in a condo. Frank's been here just an hour and already the fridge is full of food (not that he eats—he just likes to feed the rest of the world); the gas grill is fired up; there are five kinds of liquor, two cases of assorted foreign beer, cherries and olives and limes, bags of ice. If there's a party, Frank's ready. On the mantle over the fireplace (concrete logs blazing merrily, gas hissing), he's already put out framed photos of his poor dead wife and his devoted daughters. He travels with crates of belongings. His world comes with him.

He inspects me carefully, hands on my shoulders, kneading my bones after our hug: "You look like shit, boy. Get yourself a shower. A nap. I hesitate to offer a drink."

"I need a priest," I say.

Frank gives me a generous laugh (it's a form of coughing, his laugh), shows me to my room, gives me two bulky towels, pastel, his own from home. He's a natural host. Yes, I shower. The scars on my knees are pale in the bloody heat-lamp light; they're like long fat caterpillars.

I take the drink Frank puts in my hand before I'm even dressed, drink it down between the work of getting my clothes back on, sit at the dining table and eat the huge steak he's cooked me, sit back afterwards contentedly, looking out the window at the grassy slopes of Vail, the brilliant aspens, clattering yellow leaves, chill fall day.

"Let's not talk about the meeting," he says, knowing exactly what I'm about to say.

"How's it look?" I say, despite him.

"We're going to do this thing for you, Pardner." Frank leans back and looks at me. He's tall even sitting down and tanned like leather and his blue and watery sun-bleached eyes penetrate. "You got to learn to trust to fate, Cooper boy."

"What's Mrs. Stone saying?"

Frank just grunts and stands—he's not allowed to say a word—wanders into the kitchen, where he pours us both drinks, rare un-blended scotch with tiny splashes of soda, his own crystal glasses, two ice cubes each. Frank loves a ritual. He says, "I saw Julie off Friday. She's going with Rick to Washington to plead funds, then they're off to some fluffy island he likes to go to, for a break before Maine."

I don't say anything, because as usual I'm about to insult Richard P. Baldwin and Frank has mentioned him just to have one more chance to say a few things about being classy when I get the job, about working with Rick, about how Rick Baldwin's ideas are going to save amateur ski racing in America, about how there's ski-ing and coaching and then there's business, how Rick Baldwin and I are going to have to learn to work together, are stuck together at the hip and permanently, now that the U.S. Ski Team has merged with the U.S.S.A., the all-new, all-improved U.S. Ski and Snow-board Association. No sense longing for the old days. This from Frank I've heard before. I keep quiet, making the arguments in my head, keeping my face gently composed, looking out and up, sunset obscured by the ridge of Vail, instant night, a thick steak inside me, whiskey in my hand, Frank beside me companionably.

"All right," he says, closing the subject.

"All right," I say.

He gets up, clears the plates. He's barely dented his steak, but tosses it in the garbage with the other trash. More drinks, mine smaller yet (he watches out for others, Frank does), and more drinks again, waiting for some folks Frank met at the powwow earlier. He calls them folks and says it was a powwow. He's talking about some annual regional meeting of supporters of winter sports—big bucks—mostly skating fans, meetings that before long I'm going to have to take part in. Frank slides open a great glass door and the two of us sit outside on a tidy and tiny wooden deck perched out over the view, cheapo lawn chairs.

"So what else?" he says.

Well, this: "My mother's writing letters to Madeline, now. She says she's going to hire a detective, Frank. The one who found Jimmy Hoffa!"

"Be generous," says Frank, but he's laughing. His eyes are warm and serious; he holds my eye to make sure his advice sticks.

"What she doesn't know is, my brother's not going to turn up."

Frank clears his throat, looks me over, taps each foot once, decides he's reaching me, so proceeds: "What I want to know is how this got to be your affair in the first place. If the guy doesn't want to come out of the woodwork, that's his problem, not yours. You give your mom his phone number, his address, whatever you got—quit being a dupe—so she can make it *his* problem. Get out from between them, boy."

"My own fault." Out in the autumn night the aspen leaves shake and rattle and invisibly fall. The stars are strong tonight and the ridge of Vail Mountain is sharply outlined, sharply foreign. For a second I think I'm actually in Frank's home, such is his comfort here. He grunts at my taking blame, won't dignify it with an answer. I've got to tell him: Hodge is dead.

He says, "How is Morton?"

Our little brother Morton, Hodge. You and me, we used to call him *homo,* not knowing. He's lost his lover. I say, "Do you want to know something? He's on a new program, and his T-cell count is up. He's eating again. He's on his feet again. He's going back to his apartment, if it keeps up."

"A miracle."

"It's these protease inhibitors. But it's not all cheerful. His memory's better and that means his grief for Larry is back."

There's some kind of explosion down in the valley. We cock our heads and listen to the echoes, then the silence. I go on: "And credit cards, the poor fucker—he's run about twenty of them past their limits thinking he was going to be dead. We're all chipping in to get him out of debt."

"Your poor mother, all this trouble," Frank says.

"All right, all right. I hear you. Generous. I will be generous." *Frank, I've got something to tell you.* Something like that. *Frank, I've been lying to everyone, I need advice.* Like that.

I'm this close to confiding in him about you, bro, when he shoots his chair back with a plastic snap, stands steady as a sea captain, grabs my glass out of my hand, heads to the condo kitchenette to freshen our drinks. He wants me plowed, I guess, when the folks from the powwow arrive.

Roddy's voice comes into my head, then the feel of her strong hands, then the taste of particular kisses and the goosebump skin of her neck, a draft of airy pleasure out on this cozy condo deck before further guilt descends upon me.

Madeline wasn't yet awake when I crawled home with the Sunday *New York Times* as a prop under my arm. When she did get up I was trying to read the magazine section and gentlemanly not doing her puzzle, just sitting there like a perfect turd, reeking variously, half drunk and sleepless but energized, trying to appear to have got up very early and gone to get the paper.

And Madeline said, "I'm sorry for last night. I must have been drunk." She brushed her hair with her head tilted and looked at me so seriously, trying to be light and sweet, trying to smile. She is not good at lightness, sweetness. "In fact," she said, "I'm hungover as hell." Hungover? She had maybe half a glass of wine. "Change of life," she added.

I tilted my head to match hers and smiled my own sweetness and light (turd that I am), said, "Mad, forget about it. And, anyway, listen: you were right."

Frank's back. I raise my eyebrows at the size of the drink he's poured himself. Half a big glass, no ice. I raise my eyebrows and shake my head to let him know I see what he's up to. The drink he's made me is small, a half finger of scotch lost in ice.

"Life," says he. And drinks. We fall into our melancholy companionable mode, together in silence on this deck under a mountain, a scene we've played many times.

Many times. After Tricia's "accident" (large bottle of Seconal, neat pint of vodka), I couldn't make anything work but plummeting on skis daily, medieval drinking otherwise. Add enough blow to keep wide awake and ready to go. Cocaine: we skiers hid it from Frank but kept brave and sharp with it in those days before urine checks. Fast, bro, fast was all I had. But Kakame Minimazawa was faster by miles. And Timmy Runche, too. And then a new one every year, guys who stayed in shape, guys who lived clean, guys whose knees were tough as old tires, guys whose shoulders touched the gates every time, whose edges cut, whose ankles held.

Where am I supposed to start, all the stuff Frank doesn't know?

I grope for words, get it wrong and sharp: "How did Rick Baldwin get himself in the running for Alpine Director?"

"Oh, Lord," says Frank.

"He'll make me snow coach or equipment czar, something tricky. Won't he? Something exciting and new that he can call a promotion. That *Brady Bunch* fucker. I'll look bad when I refuse."

Frank stays mum, though he smiles at the Brady Brunch reference, recognizing his own joke and liking it.

My brother is dead. That's what I want to say. *Hodge Henry is dead. He's been dead since August 2, 1969, dead since he was twenty-one.*

"Life," Frank says again. Time passes. We are silent what must be a whole hour, watching, drinking.

"You sure are staring," Frank says finally, like he's not staring, too.

"Nice view."

"Listen, Bud. Something to say. Every goddamn job looks good before you get it. But in the end they're all the same: you got to make your gritted teeth look like a smile."

"It's not the job," I say.

"We make our own trouble," he says.

"It's something else," I say.

"Do you know Billie once knocked me over the head with a tent pole? Lord. I had got visiting with some neighbor ladies camping, and my girl of girls just struts down and clobbers me, wraps that thing right around my head."

I'm going to tell him, brother. I'm going to have a friend. This about Billie, Frank's never told me. And this is the first I've heard him speak about her since the funeral. Frank and I, we can do this thing: be friends.

After a good long listen to the valley he says, "She was fifteen when we met. Shocks you? Well, I was fourteen. She's the one filled out my application to Colorado State, goddamn backwoods kid, I was. Finished high school, got married, went to State. Billie gets the credit."

"Billie," I say fondly.

"Surely the only woman who ever liked *you*," says Frank. He lets the silence build. Even in a forest of condos the valley looms before us, and the sky is above, the clarity of the atmosphere tonight intoxicating past all booze. At length Frank says: "Getting misty." He means himself. "New subject?"

"I do have something on my mind," I say.

"Shoot," says Frank.

I construct one sentence then another in my head, bro, the real thing, but my lips will not open to betray you.

"Speak," he says. He looks at me, his mists cleared. His posture is perfect, no matter what he drinks. He looks at me squarely, warmly, amused at my reticence.

I'm this close, bro, but I blow it. "Slept with someone," I say, adopting his curt style.

"Oh, Lord," says Frank.

"With Roddy, actually." I say this trippingly, trying to make the admission adequate to the emotion I'm feeling and must just now have shown. But about Roddy I'm cheerful. I feel the weather clearing. You, Hodge, you recede.

"Oh, Christ on a stick," says Frank. He's a decent Catholic; I've never heard him use this expression.

"Yes," I say, trying to stay downcast. But cheer rises. "At *your* house the other night."

"Oh, Coop, Lord. Not at my place. Ah, Coop. Thirty-three years I never once. Ah, Coop, Christ." He stands out of his chair, goes to the railing. "Pardner, Pardner, you guys were *pals*. There goes another happy friendship. What'd you tell her? You were going to leave Madeline? You lie to the poor kid? Ah, Coop. What about Madeline, boy? What were you thinking? You're way too smart for this."

"Frank, I."

His shocked eyes find mine and he holds the gaze long, trying to see inside me: "All for what? Oh, Coop, what'd you tell her? Your wife doesn't understand you? Is that it? That poor kid. Now what's she going to think? What's Claudio going to say? How are you going to work with Claudio?"

"What do you mean, work with Claudio?"

"Oh, Coop, Jesus Christ on a stick. There's been talk about Claudio coming to work for us for a year now! You *know* that. And now look. Oh, Jesus bloody Christ on a stick in hot weather. Coop. Oh, buddy, you and that pecker of yours."

Frank can't look at me; he's shaking his head, leaning against the deck railing, rubbing his chest. Roddy's like one of his daughters, like Kate and Linda, both of them anesthesiologists back in California, both around Roddy's age. You don't speak to a man lewdly of daughters.

"Frank, come on. She told me Claudio didn't understand *her*. It's just the opposite of what you think."

Frank isn't buying. He drinks down his drink, rubs his chest harder.

I say, "Plus it was nice."

"Oh, nice, Christ."

"Plus, Frank, I believe I'm in love with her."

"Oh, love. Oh, bloody heavens! Roddy's way too smart for this! I'm sick!"

He's serious. We drink our drinks. Frank's scandalized. Which shouldn't be a surprise to me. I've heard him talk fidelity for years. He tromps inside, comes back fast with yet another drink for himself. Nothing for me.

"You've had enough," says he. He's genuinely angry.

We're quiet a long time. Frank can't sit down, stands at the deck railing. He can't look at me, can't even sip his drink. I'm more cheerful yet, having got yelled at: "Frank, Christ, it's love, what am I supposed to do?"

"You sneaked over in the middle of the night? Is that it? This is love? What about Madeline?"

Yes, what about Madeline? I lean into this question with all my might, trying to come up with just the right answer: Madeline I admire, Madeline is my trusted friend, but Roddy I'm in love with. I want to tell old Frank about my struggles with Madeline, and hers with me, but keep my mouth shut, can't say it. Frank wouldn't buy it in any case. He stands at the rail, unable even to pull at his drink. He's puffing with outrage, now, and we're back in our old roles: outraged coach, debauched skier.

I open my mouth to speak as the door buzzes. It's the folks. The folks from the powwow. Two older couples (guys and gals, Frank calls them) with long stories of a recent trip to Cairo and Giza and on and on. Frank gets thoroughly engrossed, laughs and coughs, makes rounds of drinks.

Me, I'm ready for bed.

Their hilarity follows me into my plush room, and hilarity reigns as I brush my teeth. Laughter comes in gentling bursts as I drift off into sleep. It's like our parents' cocktail parties when we were kids, Hodge. Incomprehensible gaiety. A kid can't keep his eyes open.

Four in the morning I awake to a gentle touch on my arm. It's Frank. "Turn your lamp on?" he says solicitously.

I sit up slowly, nod, a light sleeper since the day I turned forty. The bedside light comes on with a click. There's Frank, looking poorly.

"I'm not feeling so goddamn good," he says.

"What do you expect?" I say fondly.

"Damn booze," says Frank.

"That it?" I say. I'm tender because Frank seems so vulnerable, and it's not drunk he looks.

He stands up, shrugs, looks closely at me. "Hell," he says. He shrugs once more, like trying to get a weight off his shoulders, turns and shuffles into the hallway. I get up, put my pants on, thinking to keep him from pouring himself a drink, if that's what he's up to. Frank is in the living room by the time I get to him, heading for the door to the deck in a shuffle unlike him. He opens the deck door in peculiar haste, shuffles out, turns to look at me beseechingly. It's such a haunted look, and I misread it completely, thinking it's remorse for all his drinking, or some kind of preamble to a confession.

"Oh, Pardner," he says clearly. Then he lurches forward, and before I can make one move to catch him, he falls hard on the straight new boards. I scramble over to help him up, then realize he's not getting up, turn him over brusquely, start in with all I know of CPR (I've learned it four times in class with Search and Rescue but have never had to use it), thinking how the fuck I'm going to get to the phone while I'm pumping his chest and breathing breaths into him. My idea is to gradually bring him into the condo, *pump pump pump and breathe*, pull him a few feet, *pump pump pump and breathe*, drag him a few feet more along the smooth floor, *pump pump pump and breathe*, drag him in increments till I can reach the phone and punch 911, all the while working his chest. I keep going during and then after the interminable discussion of the problem and my location with the woman who answers, but I know it's too late: Frank Kobil has left this planet for better things and Billie.

Frank Kobil is dead.

Chapter Two

1

I can't get a feeling. I keep thinking the basest thoughts: what about that *job?* The medical examiner in Vail has released Frank's earthly remains to his daughter Kate and the Murphy-Kolwitz Funeral Home, grim. Frank is on his way back to Aspen, last trip. Turd that I am, I'm glad it's not me. The thought keeps coming, unbidden. Along with the way *you* looked dead, bro. Madeline's gone to San Francisco despite Frank. She was visibly surprised if not particularly saddened, wanted to take back anything unkind she might have said about our man. She cried perfunctorily and I held her the same. She'll be back in time for the funeral, Monday afternoon.

I pumped his chest and kissed breaths into him for ten minutes there on that dismal condo floor—but nothing. The ambulance guys didn't even try when they came, just wrapped him up.

The last call I make—every bloody name in Frank's tattered address book—is to Italy. My heart pounds to talk to Roddy, but it's Claudio who answers, barking happily in Italian. First thing he says on hearing the news: "There fly away our coaching jobs."

A Saturday alone looms ahead of me. I have this idea, not a joke:

I'm going to perform a cleansing ritual. This sort of thing is pure Madeline, of course, Ms. Flower Power, she of the owl wings and flaming sage. She also of the tender stomach, of the migraine, of the hives. A ritual to honor Frank, a ritual to honor you, too, bro, a ritual to acknowledge and therefore release me from all the events and relationships and memories that keep me molten, a ritual like, say, washing a corpse, as people used to do, wash that corpse and handle it intimately to acknowledge what has happened before putting what has happened in the ground forever.

Madeline loves rituals and loves to create rituals and talks eloquently about the need for ritual and the lack of formal ritual in modern American life to the point that the talk is a ritual itself. And people argue with her: What about the Sunday *Times?* What about my haircut every three months? What about football on TV? Also long discussions about the rituals of corporate life or family life or travel. But what Madeline means is something quite different. The ritual for her is mystical, some formal activity that can't be said to have a practical side at all. No information gathering. No moneymaking. No logic. No burying anyone. Just a very formal and usually ridiculous exercise that brings its own benefits in its own way, always unsayable.

The day we moved into this house (this plain little house made for families, this wooden ark alongside the Frying Pan River, this nervous house, this yard and barn, this windy corner under giant mountains, this wreck that takes my hours and fills my heart, this monkish lair, this hundred acres of rock and tree, this patch of stars, this blue of sky, this progression of clouds and seasons and years, this troubled Colorado home), Madeline worked up a special rite of possession in the truck, just whispering all the ways we would try to drive the bad spirits out and all the ways we would try to keep the good spirits in, ardently laying out an involved ceremony, which absolutely had to happen before our furniture could go in.

In this house there'd been some awful people, we knew. The father was in the newspapers on and off for months on his way to jail. He was a bully people knew in town, a hard drinker who right in our house had beat his wife's face into a stiff mask. He'd regularly sodomized the kiddies, too (in fact it was the distended anus of his second boy that first alerted Doctor Kellogg, who cared enough to turn the father in). He'd shot three of the neighbor's milk goats, run over cats on purpose, hung dog hides on his fence.

This is one way to get a deal in real estate. In fact, when we first looked at the place (with our broker, cheerful-vicious Bonnie Hairspray McDuff), the mother was hiding out in the barn with a bloody nose and a jug of Popov. And across the river was her new man, glaring at us, a Yeti dripping wet from wading off to hide. The real-estate lady pretended she hadn't seen a thing, that there was nothing whatsoever to see.

"We'll start in the basement," said Madeline. "We'll ask the good spirits of the ground to come up the stairs with us and chase the bad spirits of the rooms away. We'll burn seven pinecones in the kitchen. We'll dance in the dining room. We'll blow blue smoke from wands of sage into the corners and closets. We'll ask the house for its graces. We will kiss every rafter in the attic to call good spirits down from the hazes of heaven to fill the house. We will stand in the living room and command the evil to go. We will be polite with the evil, but firm. We will walk backwards through the barn. March 'round the yard three times. Throw nine rocks in the river, thrice. Spit once each into the mailbox. Keep a pebble from the driveway in each car, a chip of wood from the porch in our pockets."

We did all of the above—Madeline at her best—a whole emotional and somewhat humorous evening's worth, then slept on the living room floor in blankets, unloaded the truck in the morning. The place despite my scoffing felt safer and more empty, as if the last lingering molecules of the bad man had gone off to prison to join him, as if there were no longer a foothold for hatred or misery or meanness, bad spirits indeed.

Yes, I'm leaving something out. I'm purposely but helplessly not saying anything of the dance Madeline did upstairs, the dance in our bedroom for fertility (we'd tried everything else, God knows), this dance that successfully called up the last vestiges of our lust for one another. She was a Hindu Goddess, she was Aphrodite, she danced without irony, she unveiled her long body, she called me into the dance. We christened every room with subtle moans and sweet human moisture.

But, no fertility descended into this house. The pinecones in the kitchen smelled nice, at least, smelled nice for weeks. We never made love much again, not like that, and lately very little at all, like cars going in for service: lube and an oil change.

Cleansing. I know the whole idea is nuts and I'm embarrassed to even tell you about it but I have to do something, bro: I'm at the end of a nasty run. I have to act.

Inescapably my idea is to do something useful (I don't want to find myself boiling bat wings or dipping my head in the river) so I decide I'm going to finally wash the trim all around the house. I'm going to wash the woodwork: it's mildewy near the ground and mossy higher, and flaking everywhere, and needs to be scrubbed and scraped before I can repaint it, which is why for eight years I have not repainted it. This ritual, I figure, is perfect. Each doorway a metaphor, every window. Plus when I'm done I'll have a major job accomplished. Madeline's in San Francisco, as I've said, giving a talk at a conference: "Pro Bono Lawyering in the Age of Greed." She's leading workshops. She's the star of the show. She's even staying at the Western Star Hotel, a palace. I've got the long weekend to think about what to say to her about our life together, and what to say has fled my mind completely; the clarity of my night with Roddy is gone. This is our home. Why would I leave it?

We don't have a proper bucket, so as the first part of my ceremony I drive down into Basalt to Merck's (people have started to call it the True Value, which annoys; before the chain came the place had truer value in every sense). I drive down the valley to town, hard on myself, down on myself, losing the thread of the cleansing idea, thinking of Frank intensely, the futility of this game, the taste of his mouth, actually convincing myself that I had something to do with his death, then moving from that to full reproach, my heart sinking in my diaphragm, my breaths shallow, full blame, all tied up somehow with Roddy and Madeline and even Tricia, even back then. All tied up with you, that is, a thousand bloody thoughts racing on top of one another as I race down the hill to town, thoughts all tumbled and interlaced into a prickling blanket lying heavily upon me. I'm thinking what a world-class turd I am and can only lighten the load by thinking how it's a good damn thing I've got an idea, here: I'm going to cleanse my soul. Simple, effective, appropriate, the exact gesture needed, absolution, purification.

I firmly believe, driving slowly. I'm getting into it. It's going to work. Push all judgments aside. You call the front door of the house the gate for life to come, and wash it, prepare it. You call the back door the exit for bad spirits and bad luck and all bad faith, and wait to wash it till everything bad is gone. You call the trim around the roof linear memory, and wash it down. Each window you call by some familiar name: Mother, Father, Francis Connelly Kobil, Roddy, Maddy, Morton, Tricia Thomas, Robert Hodges Henry—Richard P. Baldwin, too—and cleanse each completely, scrape and wash and lay bare the soul inside there, ready to paint.

I'm going to Merck's to buy the best bucket they have, the most expensive sponges. Excellence is required. You can't do a ritual with budget tools. In the hardware store I breathe and stand a moment, centering myself, making up the protocol as I go along. The cleansing is already working. One starts with the bucket. This is written. One pictures the bucket, breathes, repeats the word till it loses meaning. Bucket. Bucket. Bucket. And no plastic bucket is good enough for these ablutions. Bucket. Bucket. I'm enjoying the humor of this at the same time I'm beginning to believe in it.

No metal bucket is on display. I see old man Merck in the corner of his newly corporatized place (sold out by his own sons!), go to him as to any elder. And Roger walks me back very slowly into the deep wooden storeroom, holy and ancient warren of shelves—plumbing parts from Noah's time, lag screws the size of your leg, stove pipe in every length and diameter ever made—all untouched by the modernization. Solemnly in the farthest corner he pulls down a gorgeous galvanized-steel bucket, size large.

"Now that's a real bucket," says Roger slowly, his eyes atwinkle.

Amen.

I ask about sponges and he walks me back into the fluorescently lit store, hundreds of yards, shuffling, to the opposite far corner of the Merck domain. There I pick out an enormous overpriced thing, put it in the bucket. I ask about scrapers. Roger scratches his neck and walks me all the way across the store again, and it's like he's showing me the place the sun will rise on the solstice; he's so dignified, so quiet, limps so pathetically; he's sage and shaman and doesn't know. I eschew the plastic scrapers, the knock-off scrapers, the cheap tricks, the equipment of amateurs, of altar boys. There's a stainless-steel bevel-headed razor/peeler that goes for thirty bucks. I don't even blink, picking it up. I get two less exalted tools—a sanding pad and a utility knife (the very best they have, of course)—a trinity of treatment, and I'm done, writing a check at the counter.

Roger says, "You say howdy to Madeline," and I'm reminded that they sing together in Community Chorus. One hundred voices: *Glory to God in the Highest!* He retreats to his office in the storeroom, slowly, stately. He's a very old man, nearly ninety. When he goes they'll knock the walls down, get a twenty-yard dumpster, haul all that shit he's gathered to the transfer station, make room for microwaves.

The kid at the counter is a snot teen with *have a nice day* written all over him. "There's cheaper buckets over there," he says. "And the plastic don't rust," he says. "You sure about this scraper?" he says. "No one buys these anymores."

I'm sure, goddamnit.

At home I set up the ladders, taking my time. One starts with memory. Memory, of course, is the hardest, for to cleanse it you must interrogate it. Also, it's second-story work. I'm setting up, getting the hoses out, thinking of you, Hodge. Thinking of our days as kids, thinking how I've brought you with me in definite ways wherever I have gone, a corrected and polished you, to be sure, one who would never slug me or invent cruel games or know the many names of ammo.

I fill the bucket, give it a couple of splashes of Mr. Clean, fill it fast and sloshing, then watch it drain. The sudsy water just pours out. The seam is split invisibly, never got welded, just metal folded on metal, pouring water. I watch till my bucket is empty. Bucket. Bucket. I start to hum. Bucket. Bucket. I kick that bucket hard, then chase it. I kick it again. Bucket. Kick it. *Bucket.* I kick it up the hill through Madeline's rock garden, then down, kick it to my aging Subaru (a gift of the manufacturer from when they used to give gifts instead of fat endorsement deals, from when I was a skier still and not a turd of a conditioning coach with bad knees and wobbly ankles), throw it in back, making noises in my throat, growling.

Back in the car. And back downtown, fast as hell, weaving that prickling blanket of memory and pain. And back in Merck's, humming furiously with the grass-stained bucket flying behind me, irony lost to fury. That teenager's at the counter, staring into space.

"This bucket," I say.

"Plastic's better," says the kid.

"The weld is no good. I need another."

"You have a receipt?"

"I just want another bucket."

"You have a receipt?"

"Kid. Young man. I do not have a receipt. But I bought this bucket an hour ago. From you. As you well know. My check is in the cash register, right at your belly." I'm thinking, Bucket, bucket. Thinking how of course this must be part of the ritual. Obstacles. Unbelievers. I say, "So what I'll do is just go on back and get myself another."

"I think you'll need a receipt," he says.

I make a noise at him, an actual snarl, trying not to say any words. I snarl and thrust the leaky bucket into his hands, march back into the timeless storage room, back to the dark corner, ancient home of venerable buckets. I manhandle the next one in the stack, check the weld, check it twice, march the bucket back to the counter. "Thank you," I say, sweeping the old bucket away. It rattles and pops and rolls on the floor.

"No way," says he. "You dented the heck outta your first one. You think Charlie's going to take it back?"

"Listen," I say, and let out a loud speech that I don't so much hear as see: the kid's face goes from smug to alarmed to afraid in the course of this sentence I seem to be saying. I'm telling him loudly that he's fucking with my cleansing. I'm weeping and shouting. The blanket is upon me. I'm leaning over the counter and my hands are holding his shirt front and I'm pulling his face into mine and I'm telling him he's a disrespectful imperious fleck of shit and that he cannot stop my rite and that the new bucket's coming with me, coming now, walking out the door of Merck's with my hand on its handle, coming along with me no matter what he says.

I let him go in such a potent way that he falls into the cheap-ass new counter behind him and knocks it over. This smashes the glass of the case on the other side and leaves him spraddled head over asshole in shards of glass and maybe a hundred high-end router bits, also a pile of Timex watches. I'm out of there, walk stately to the new double doors, hugging my fine new pail.

Charlie Merck, craven sellout, Roger's fattened second son, an old man himself, materializes in my path. "Jesus, Coop," says he. "What on earth's going on?"

"Bucket," I say. "Split bucket."

"Hey," he says, and suddenly has the new bucket over his head and I'm dancing with him, bro, dancing him right through a cardboard True Value man and into a great rack of work gloves. The bucket protects his head as I push him through the store window; I'm just, well, just observing, peering through the weave, listening to my own voice saying *Bucket* and *Bad faith* over and over, watching that safety glass break into ten thousand slow teardrops, ten thousand valueless jewels, watching poor Charlie roll into the gutter with the bucket still on his head. I'm smelling pine and exhaust, hearing a distant air hammer and close chickadees, watching Charlie struggle with his bucket, feeling my shoes on my feet, my feet on the ground, tasting blood as a pair of mean-looking cowboys grab hold of one of my arms each and begin to pull and shout. Quickly we're all waltzing and tugging and staggering down the sidewalk, me shaking those ranch hands like fish on lines, losing one, losing the other, leaping to my car.

People are coming at me from all sides, and I'm turning the key and stepping on the gas and backing into parked cars and laying rubber, screeching out of there without my bucket. That's all I can

think about: *I need that fucking bucket.* Once around the block con-
fuses the crowd. Now they're all gathered around Charlie Merck.
He's got a cut on his face and he's bleeding like a fountain of punch
at a bad wedding and looking faint. More important, he's got my
bucket at his side, and there's no way I can get to it through the
crowd.

So intent are they on Charlie that no one notices my old Subaru
as I come creeping round the back of the store. I drive very slowly
through the new True Value doors, which part nicely to admit me,
car and all. The teen is still sprawled in the router bits, doesn't even
look up as I drive past him to the back room down an aisle too
narrow for even my little car. The mirrors strip the shelves. I've got
light bulbs coming in the windows, tubes of caulk, Lysol.

The plaster board of the new back wall is as nothing, and I get
far enough through the shitty metal studs to clear the driver's door
such that I can climb out. Bucket. I march to the bucket shelf, pull
one down. I'm checking the weld when the police start turning up.
They point those guns right at you, Hodge; you know how it is.
They point the guns and shout and shake like nervous brides. I'm
just standing there blinking and surprised, holding that old (but
brand-new) bucket—the last steel bucket they'll ever have in
stock—holding that bucket in front of me like a shield.

2

In a towel after a boiling hot shower Coop felt a buzzy crush over-come him as Tricia dragged him into her brother Tim's big closet and found him some clothes to wear, insisting he try on shirts in front of her. He liked her hay smell, her long legs, the way she spoke in sentences and paragraphs, like a book. They found him a seer-sucker shirt that fit and a pair of big blue jeans with ironed creases.

Tad said grace at dinner, invoking his sons: Terry, who had come safely home from Vietnam; Tim, who was still there; and Toby, who had enlisted and was about to willingly go. Tricia gazed solemnly at Coop through the whole long prayer, trying to crack him up.

They were supposed to eat the testicles of some of the bullys they'd steered that afternoon. Coop sliced his, and pushed them with his fork, but never tasted them.

"I find it sickening to eat an animal that's still walking in the calf pen," Tricia said, but ate.

"Do you have any brothers or sisters?" Tad said, apropos of his prayer, and in a way clearly calculated to launch tonight's conversation, get it away from complaints about the food and ranch life.

Coop held forth, tried to make it interesting: "Four. Older brother is Hodge, then my sister Cindy—she's younger than me, I'm second—then there's Morton, and Jeremy who's just a baby." Tad was really listening. Coop said, "Hodge was King of the Prom. He was really nice to everybody. He quit the football team because the coach was too hard on the fat kids in gym." Now Tricia was listening too. "And then half the rest of the team quit to join him, and they lost the championship. He's a good skier, too, but I can beat him anytime." The subject of Hodge was going over with his listeners, so Coop turned it on: "He worked for Miceli Paving in the summer doing road work, laying asphalt, driving *steamrollers,* and had to take salt pills because it was so hot. He was the best employee and got a raise his first week! He got four A's and one B his last term at high school. He was going to go to Williams College, but he has strong *beliefs* and decided it would be *wrong* when other people aren't able to go because of *poverty* or whatever. So now Hodge is away. I can't say where." Coop spoke faster: "I don't know where, because he's not allowed to tell." Faster yet: "He's undercover. CIA. That's all I can say. Somewhere in the States."

Tad's eyebrows lifted.

It was an awful lie, preposterous. But hearing no objections, Coop went on: "I'm looking for him. I'm going to find him. I'm allowed to say no more."

"Righty-o," Tricia said.

They ate, Coop concentrating on the potatoes and peas. He couldn't believe what he'd said but couldn't have said the truth in this house: Hodge was a draft dodger, and maybe worse.

Tricia said, "I was reading this afternoon how the brain is divided, right side and left side, and that the two function differently. One is logical and cold, the other is creative and warm."

"Oh, honey," Tad said. Coop could tell he'd heard a lot of crackpot theories from Tricia.

She said, "What we think of as head and heart is really left brain and right."

Tad eyed her: "And where did you read this?"

"Like men and women," Coop said.

Tricia said, "That's an insult."

"He means men and women are different," her father said.

"Oh, thanks, Daddy. But I don't buy it. What I'm saying here is that brains are the same, male or female."

Silence. Then Tad: "Your mother thought that a little of the man was in the woman, and a little of the woman was in the man."

"My mother is dead," Tricia said, turning to Coop. "Daddy tells people she was sick, but she killed herself, right in the horse barn . . . "

"Well," Tad said to stop the flow of his daughter's confession. He wasn't angry, though, didn't turn red, didn't stand and shout. He just stared off toward the corner of the ceiling. And Tricia seemed maybe embarrassed, undefiant, just stared, too, a different direction.

Tad Thomas didn't let the silence get too long. He turned brightly to Coop, sudden as clear weather, popped the table with the flat of his hand, said, "So what do you think of the Lazy K?"

And Coop held forth again, praising mountain and horse and bull and barn, filling up every possible silence and taking up all the possible room for embarrassment and grief, wishing Tricia would listen harder.

After dinner Tad rose and stretched, announced he was going to bed, asked Coop kindly if he wouldn't care to wash a few dishes.

Tricia cleared the table distantly. Coop made jokes, but the girl had drifted off somewhere, utterly preoccupied, didn't acknowledge him. Coop felt his crush turn miserable in his chest as Tricia clomped off into the living room, cowboy boots and dirty jeans. He washed silverware, cleaned dishes, banged the dented pots around. Inexperienced, he scrubbed each pot five minutes, trying to get every bit of black off, every ancient stain. Eventually, he got done.

In the living room, he found Tricia on the couch reading in a book of poems, swaying her head and moving her lips as if she were hearing music. Coop sat in an easy chair, picked up one of her strange magazines and found a poem. He read it to himself, swaying his head and moving his lips as if he too were hearing music. The poem rambled without rhymes through a lot of nonsense about the legs and pregnant belly of some woman. What he understood just seemed mortifying.

"You could write a better poem than this," Coop said, slapping the book down.

Tricia smiled but continued reading. He watched her boldly. He liked her hair and her mouth and her glasses and her shoulders. She had an air about her.

"And how would you know?" she said finally, not looking up.

"I can tell listening to you talk. It's like a song when you talk."

She looked at him over her glasses, seeing how to take such flattery. She said, "You better go to bed—darling Lothario, dear Lothario, dread Lothario—you're getting tired."

Now he needed a dictionary. He yawned and stretched, got up, examined photos on the fireplace mantle a little, sauntered to stand near her, looked over her shoulder at the long poem she was reading but couldn't think of a word to say or an excuse to sit down. So to the stairs.

"Good night," he said.

"'Night," she said, not even looking up.

In Tim's room, Coop stripped out of his borrowed clothes, got naked into bed. He started thinking of his family, how completely furious Dad and Mom must be, how worried. He thought of the way it was when Hodge left—how Mom had tried to be so tough, but how she'd sat by the phone daily for a month, how she'd exhorted the cops in New York, how she'd exhorted Dad, how they'd taken trips weekly to the Village to look for that face: Hodge. How they'd lectured Coop about letting his brother go, as if Coop had anything to say about it. Coop himself had never cried over the matter—you didn't cry over the heroic actions of heroes, even crazy ones. So now what? His folks, they were probably frantic. Though if they were so frantic, why'd they just go on to Grandma's? He'd better get to Seattle before they left, that was sure. He thought of Tricia's off-center smile and replayed the ways he'd made her almost laugh. He clicked the light out, but even tired as he was, he could not sleep. Dad was going to massacre him.

After a long half hour, Coop heard Tricia patting up the stairs, bare feet. He heard her brush her teeth. He thought how she'd have to take her jeans off to get in bed, thought of her peeling them off. Long minutes of night went by in perfect silence.

And then, as if by force of his thoughts, the door opened. Tricia slipped in, stood there in the dark. Coop heard her breathing, felt her straining to see. He played dead, tried to make his own breath smooth as sleep.

"I know you're awake," Tricia whispered.

"Well, you're wrong," Coop said.

"I just wanted to tell you one of my poems." She floated over and sat on the very edge of the bed, a ghost in white flannel. The mattress compressed, rolled Coop subtly toward her.

Coop said, "Huh."

Tricia took a breath and rather formally spoke something that sounded like regular writing, not a poem. He didn't hear a single rhyme, but he began to listen to the words and enjoyed them quite apart from the stimulation of her presence. The poem was about a trapline, about animals killed in the traps, and about the trapper. There was no sentimentality about the animals, just the story of their deaths. The poem was long, and she knew it all, said it all easily, whispered through it without a pause.

"That's a poem?" Coop said, when she was done. Somehow he couldn't find a compliment.

"You like it?"

"The animals seem so stuck, like they're resigned, like they gave up."

"It wouldn't make sense for them *not* to give up, would it?"

"They could at least chew their leg off, or something."

She didn't laugh, said, "Your hair's so pretty." The air around her seemed charged with light, the room itself with lightness.

"Aw. That's what my father likes to say."

Tricia shifted a little, seemed to hover over him. He could feel her warmth. She said, "You know there was a hippie hitchhiker in Livingston and he ate the rancher that picked him up. And when they caught him, he had four fingers in his pockets for snacks!"

She was there above Coop in the dark. She shifted her weight, let her fanny press coolly against his hip. She smelled of soap. Just quietly they stayed like that for a long arc of night, then Tricia Thomas took her head full of poems and slipped out of the room.

3

Hodge, help. I'm in jail, this handsome old cell out of a cowboy movie: brick walls and iron bars, a good galvanized bucket to piss in, a tin cup to drink from, Larry Forrest—our jailer on call— coming back every fifteen minutes to find out if I'm okay. Larry and I have fished near each other often in the Roaring Fork and Larry likes to ski, in fact is a ski bum from the old days and thinks of me as famous. He brings yogurt, brings me news from the hospital: Charlie Merck is okay. Thirty stitches to his cheek. The counter boy is worse off with a broken arm and a loose tooth and a fairly serious concussion. Hodge, I've hurt this boy in a half-sardonic quest for a goddamn bucket, and I've hurt Charlie, and Frank Kobil is dead, and I guess you won't have any trouble imagining how depressed I am.

Since I refuse to use the phone, Larry's been trying to call Madeline, but I know he won't get her: Madeline's in San Francisco. I have refused my one call, have refused, actually, to say anything at all. I'm just standing in the corner of my cell, three hours, then four, Larry's gifts of food and pop piling up on my bunk. I'm silent. Everything silent as the bottom of the sea, except for Larry's pacing in the office up the hall. I've got him worried. He's got my belt, my change, my shoelaces.

Suddenly, voices. A lot of voices. Hodge, there's an assembly coming through the front door of the jailhouse and into the office, just down the hall, just out of my sight. Ancient Roger Merck is the main voice. He's exhorting the old boys: District Attorney Swanson, Judge Anstedt, Sheriff Miller, three or four state troopers, Hapless Chief Box of the Basalt Police, the fire captain—Boynton, I think his name is. One by one they drift back to get a look at me. They say lugubrious hellos to my back. I know them all from picnics and singalongs, from rummage sales and ski classes, from Madeline and her work. I keep my back to them, keep silent. I'm ashamed, it's true, but there's something more, some little edge of rage, something boiling hard in me, just at my throat. I keep thinking to call Frank. He's the only one I want to talk to.

Roger Merck has the floor. He's quietly explaining that he fails to see my actions as any kind of crime. "He's an awfully good fellow," he keeps saying in his feathery voice. "What he needs is a solid night's sleep and then a good looksee by Don Kellogg."

"Could be a brain tumor," Larry says, unhelpfully.

"That's not going to pay for your store," says Sheriff Miller. "That's not going to heal Charlie boy's face."

"I'll not press charges," Roger says gently. He holds a lot of sway with these men. They go silent, considering their options.

"There's plenty *we'll* charge him with," Norton Swanson says, at last. Norton has never liked me and probably never Madeline, either, though he pretends.

"Now what would be the point of that?" Roger says.

A voice I don't know says something about drugs and Judge Anstedt says "Christ," meaning how stupid that idea is. You don't steal a bucket for drugs.

"The man's obviously in serious pain," Roger says slowly. "He's obviously not well. What he needs and what our little Rocky Mountain town needs in this case is compassion. Think who we're talking about here. It's Coop Henry, folks. Think what he's done around here. Think about the children's ski program, for land's sake. Think about the Rivers Council. Think about Search and Rescue, for *land's* sake. Think about that. He's the one skied in for the Dorset twins when they fell. He's the one brought those little girls in. Who on earth else could've done that?" More silence.

"You heard about how he was asking for Mr. Kobil," Swanson says.

"I did," Roger says. "Exactly my point. Something just isn't right by him."

A long silence, very long. They're all thinking hard. Hodge, brother, what have I done?

"Remand to Valley View," says Judge Anstedt solemnly. Decision reached. And everyone stays silent with his wisdom.

4

Always after Coop would think of any big breakfast as a Montana breakfast: four eggs each and piles of bacon and a mound of sausage along with a half loaf each of toast and a leftover Rocky Mountain oyster for Tad, who ate with the veins of his arms straining, one of the thinnest yet strongest men Coop had ever seen. No Tricia in sight. Tad and Coop rode back out to the feed lot, where the calves they'd worked over yesterday were not glad to see them. Fewer of the mothers were standing in the wailing corner, but those few bellowed and strained at the barbed wire, listening for the cries of their calves. At the other edge of the pine trees behind a stouter wooden fence where they had not been yesterday stood five impassive bulls.

Tad said, "They've come to see what all the commotion's about."

Coop dismounted, jogged over to admire the bulls up close. They were big enough to look over his head, didn't immediately shy back from the fence as he approached, the way the cows did. When he said "Ha!" they edged away disdainfully, and when he said it again they didn't move at all. Coop pretended he was a matador. Standing erect, he looked into their eyes, holding his cape. They were much bigger than bullfight bulls. He twirled his cape, bowed. The bulls watched him, still impassive.

"Let's hop to," Tad said. "See if you can find some shade for the horses."

Coop tied Miles and 7-Up under pine trees. The sensation of Tricia's cool fanny pressed against him kept rising up. He worked like an old hand, wheeling out the ancient scale, a cage similar to the squeeze, into which each calf would be chased for weigh-in. They set it up at the barn door, moved fence sections to make a divided chute, one path for the heifers (who would join the cows), another path for the steers and the three bullies (who would join the big boys in the pasture behind the pines).

After an hour, Tricia drove up in the pickup, climbed out truculently, marched over to her father. She'd set her hair, plainly spent a long time at it, though it did nothing for her looks. Coop watched her hair goofily bounce and thought of the sound of her voice saying the poem in the dark. But she didn't give him the slightest glance, went straight to Tad, said imperiously, "Why didn't you wake me?"

"I never wake you," Tad said.

"Well, how are you going to separate calves with only two people?" She pointed at Coop, flung her hair back over a shoulder: "Especially him!"

Tricia's job was to stand at the weighing platform, squeeze each calf as it came and enter its weight in the tattoo registry. Tad stood at the barn door and patted calves out one by one to the scale. Once the first three or four had gone the others wanted to follow, and the work grew easier and faster. "Five hundred fifteen pounds," she'd call, and "Six hundred ten." Coop watched Tricia's efficient weighing and recording, watched her hands at work, watched the way she stood, her weight on one foot like that, hip cocked in his direction.

Coop's job was to stand at the fork in the chute and send each heifer to the cows, each steer to the bulls. As Tricia opened the bar of the scale she'd shout "Heifer!" or "Beef!" Faster and faster the calves came, some racing straight where they belonged, some pausing, unwilling to go near Coop at all, still others challenging him, trying to duck down the wrong path in pursuit of the calf before. One balky steer, or possibly one of the bullies, just stood in front of him, head lowered, stalled in fear. Coop pretended not to look at it, stood nonchalantly in the chute, hoping it would walk on by. But Tricia sent another calf: "Steer!"

The second steer refused to pass the first, or to go back. They looked at Coop with big untrusting brown eyes and snorted. Then Tricia cried, "Heifer!" when she should have waited—she could plainly see the situation—"Heifer!" when Tad was in the barn and couldn't see, "Heifer!" and the sprightly young cow came barreling down the chute, crashed into the steers, who leapt and bellowed and charged past Coop. He dove in between the second steer and the heifer, trying to stop her, but she knocked him out of the way, in desperate pursuit of her cousins. She bucked wildly, kicking him sharply in the thigh as she passed. Coop went down in the dust, heard "Steer!" and hard hoofbeats. The next steer managed to leap over him forelegs first, but the hind hooves caught him, one a kick to the neck, the other a solid, weighty footplant on Coop's stomach.

"Shit!" he cried, rolling out of the path of the next beast, and "Whoa! Tricia! Whoa up!" He got to his feet with a hand to his neck. "Jesus, Tricia, stop a fucking minute."

"'Whoa up,'" Tricia said, mocking him.

Tad stepped out of the barn. "What's happened?"

"Coop let a heifer in with the bulls," Tricia said. "And now he's cussing."

Tad didn't look the least disturbed. "Oh, my. Coop. Well. Let's get after her before the old boys do. Coop, you'll go in on foot."

And soon Coop was among the bulls, shouting and leaping and falling and running, sending the old giants and new steers past Tad and Tricia on their horses, keeping the heifer in her corner, cutting out the boys, shouting and leaping, falling and running in great fear and excitement and pride and humiliation until the heifer was alone and the riders could guide her to the chute.

5

In bed, Valley View, a pleasant place and clean, everyone is nice to me from receptionist to ward nurse, station by station till I'm alone on a large cot in a little room, door open to the hallway, unnecessary suicide watch in progress, bedtime. Plenty else to think about, I'd say, but what I think about is you, dead boy.

First memory: varnished grain of wood, a blue leaf of paint, headboard of my crib, a living memory with warmth and nose and strong emotion attached and the hands of this other-than-parent pressing my head staring into me so close he's cross-eyed and it's just two of us and he is me, even as he tugs me by the arms over the bars of the crib and even as he holds me up by the armpits for jealous inspection and a little shaking, and I'm in the unsafety of these hands smaller than Mom's, these tough small hands slippingly grasping my forearms and swinging me in circles getting faster.

Next thing it's bulldozers in the old pastures up the street from our house—dinosaurs, we called them—and we'd play on them when the workers left, jump up on those heavy treads. Steam shovel was a brontosaurus, steam roller was a triceratops. We threw rocks and smashed the windows of Tyrannosaurus rex, vanquishing him, smashed his windows and stole his teeth—gearshift knobs unscrewed—a blast! We stole the beast's teeth and were started on the bulldozers, when the guard showed up in his yellow car and leapt out yelling and chased us into the woods and of course nabbed me, little kid, and dragged me back into the pasture. He seemed like the very angel of death, or seems like it now, and he's lecturing me and dragging me, and then *wham* and he's falling down holding his head and we're out of there screaming with laughter. You, you asshole, you nailed him with a two-by-four from our stolen cache of treefort lumber! And of course the police are at the house by suppertime. That's all I've got. I'd ask Mom what happened next, but I guess I can't really talk to her about you, not at present.

Nor Dad about when you drove the Studebaker out of the A&P lot. We got as far as the post office—pretty good for children six and eleven—and only knocked over the blue row of mailboxes and a couple of street signs. Dad had to be *restrained* when he turned up. You were in trouble daily, always rumbling with Beaky Johnson and the Bernardo boys and all the worst you could find. You guys, oh man, you burned that barn at Jackson's orchard. I loved this: you painted the door of the police station pink and left pink footprints down Main Street, uncaught. And you and Beaky taped Chuck Calligan to his locker upside down (he had some kind of foaming seizure because of it, right?) and rolled a tire down Maple Avenue through the front window of Tate's Store. But you helped people, too. You saved Timmy Monahan from the cops that time— just pulled the cruiser door open when they looked the wrong way and dragged him out by his shirt and ran, the two of you. And you were a brain in math—I could always go to you, always, and you always told me how. And sports, every team: Hodge Henry the star,

Hodge Henry getting the coach to put the fat kid in, Hodge Henry refusing to play if the coach made Lionel Washington chop his Afro. We were the football champs with the hair coming out of our helmets! You were every kid's hero! You were Robin Hood, at least! God, how I loved you!

I wet my bed a lot in our room for awhile there, didn't I? You were kindly about it, I recall, helped me resent Dad's solutions (he'd wake me twice a night, he'd withhold all liquids from dinner onward, he'd wrap me in the wet sheets and make me wear them to breakfast, later he'd spank me and slap me and berate me mornings and call me Pissy Girl all day). So the one night I didn't wet the bed you were as excited as I. You said, Go get Dad, go get Dad, show Dad! And I tore off to get him, pulled him away from Sunday coffee. Back in our room my sheets weren't dry anymore—my sheets were *soaked down* in piss. Your piss, but Dad didn't know that, and I didn't tell him, you fucker.

God, how I loved you, and love you still.

6

Tricia was quiet at dinner, and Tad's conversation was all beef: the weights different breeds could reach in harsh climates, an article in *The Stockman* about the new concept of artificial insemination, the trials of calving, the stock sales in Denver. After dinner Coop washed dishes unasked. Tad seemed to want to stay up, kept talking about how it was Saturday night, how in the old days you'd have a dance in Horzendruber's barn. Tricia just read poems, lost in a fat book of them.

Eleven o'clock and Tad finally stood out of his chair. He yawned and stretched, said, "Yes, kids, she rode that mule backwards straight to town." He laughed with himself, said, "Good night, good night," terribly pleased with the universe, and to bed.

Tricia put her book down, bang. "Let's play cards!"

On the living room floor they played gin, and Coop found Tricia's gaze significant. She'd done something more to her hair. Coop's kicked butt felt good in a way: stiff and sore, cowboy stuff. On the bridge of Tricia's nose were unexpected freckles. Her teeth were perfect white but didn't meet center to center. Her chin didn't seem too pointy at all anymore. Her neck was strong, her shoulders wide. She wasn't what he'd ever thought of as pretty before now, but after this and for the rest of his days, she would be what pretty meant to him.

She started a ruse of loudly speaking out the plays in the game: "Discard!" and whispering what she really wanted to say: "Do you ever like to kiss?"

Coop said, "Four of clubs!"

She said, "Let's kiss now."

Coop said "Ha" like he'd been socked in chest. He waited for something to say, whispered: "Your hair."

"Stupid game!" Tricia cried. She slapped her cards down, put her hand on Coop's knee.

"Cheater!" Coop said. He put his hand on hers. They listened for a full minute for Tad, then leaned forward across the cards and pressed their lips together dryly. Coop thought of Connie Kirkbridge. Coop thought of Tad. After a minute of awkward but companionable kisses, Tricia unbuttoned Coop's borrowed shirt three buttons and placed her hand on his chest.

"My neck," Coop said.

"Oh, tough luck, cowboy," said Tricia.

Coop opened a button on her shirt, slipped his hand in, contrived to touch her plain white bra.

Tricia trapped his hand in there with her own. "I've got a Ouija board," she said.

Quietly Tricia got the game down from a high coat-closet shelf. "You know my mother wouldn't allow this kind of thing in the house. Witchcraft! Uncle Burl gave it to me after she was gone." They got the board out quietly, put their hands on the pointer. Immediately it began to move. Tricia put on an eerie voice: *"But what's funny is now Mom talks to me."*

The pointer went letter to letter and spelled HELLO. Then some gibberish. Then: HEAVEN IS SWEET.

"See?" Tricia said passionately.

The board had a lot to say, letter by letter, word by word, and Tricia spoke each word as it was completed. Coop didn't much believe it was her dead mom, but to sit in the dark in whispers with Tricia was heaven indeed and sweetness itself.

"Ask her a question," Tricia said spookily.

This didn't take much thought: "Where is Hodge?"

The pointer went to four letters: "W-H-E-N."

"Now," said Coop.

"T-R-O-U-B-L-E," said the board.

"What kind of trouble?" said Coop.

The board said "K-I-S-S." Tricia leaned hard and kissed Coop on his flushed cheek. He kissed her cheek, too, twice and three times gently. She turned her head a little for each kiss so that the fourth met her lips. They kissed in a deep way new to Coop, kissed a long time across the Ouija board, upsetting the pointer, leaning awkwardly.

Again Tricia trapped his hand in her shirt, never letting go their kiss, touching his teeth with her tongue and then his tongue with her tongue.

"You better go to bed," she said, at great length.

Coop leaned toward her—not yet, not yet—but she wouldn't kiss back. "To bed," she said.

Coop stood and spun quickly away from her, his pecker caught up embarrassed in his pants like some blunt dumb animal, turned away and up the stairs, good night.

Naked in bed, Coop tried to think calves, think homework, the conjugations of French verbs: past perfect, conditional, subjunctive.

Finally, Tricia slipped into the room. The air changed with her presence; the sheets heated where she sat, right at Coop's hip. She put a hand on his chest roughly, suddenly told him another poem, about the way an older Indian's black braids had attracted her in town and how that attraction had made her fearful and also aroused her and filled her dreams at night. Coop couldn't believe she would admit this stuff to anyone.

She lay down along his side, just the sheet and her nightie between them. "You're so short," she said.

"I'm not," Coop said. "It's just you're always wearing those cowboy shoes. I bet we're the same."

She forgot to whisper, said, "Five-ten."

Coop shushed her, said, "Five-eleven," though he wasn't quite that. With no false start he got his hand to touch her back, ever so lightly on top of her nightie. This stopped his breathing. Then Tricia snuggled in, kissed his neck, ducked to kiss him on the chest, got shy or anyway stopped.

"You've done it a lot," she said.

"Nope," Coop breathed. Not even once, if fucking was what she was talking about.

"I'm not a perfect beginner," she said, enigmatic.

They kissed profoundly, and slowly she sent her hands under the sheets to touch his back and bruised butt and slowly with his half-trapped hands he worked her nightie up, and at length the charged tips of his fingers brushed the silken hair of her pubis. He backed off at her sharp breath.

"Okay," she said.

And they kissed like drowning, and Tad was in the same house, and they kissed ardently but quietly, and not one wisecrack only kisses and with his fingers he touched her, delicate dips, long pauses. He'd heard about how wet. Trish said "Okay," and "Okay," again, then she rather flung the sheets away from him and climbed on him and pushed at him with her legs closed, rolling on him while they kissed.

"Okay," she said, seeming to tighten every muscle. "Okay," she said, letting the clench go. "Heavens," she said, "this is just fine."

Coop wriggled too and Trish made sounds like crying almost, like a baby and everything about him seemed to gather and grow tighter in one hot place and he made a sigh in her ear and she pushed against him and he against her and even as he tried to hold back in shame everything about him let go. He panted his own name in her ear; he didn't know why; how numb could you get: "*Coop.*"

"Ick," Tricia said touching her stomach.

They held each other in a breathing silence.

At length Trish said, "Tomorrow you're just going to leave."

"No, I'm not," Coop said.

"Yes, I've seen the future. Tomorrow you go. But I know something else, Coop Henry." She was kidding, not kidding. "No matter what you do, I am going to see you again." Tricia sat up fast, wiped her belly with the sheets all businesslike, hopped off the bed and stood, letting her nightie fall in place slowly enough that Coop saw the dark damp strings of her pubic hair, a vision that along with her shrug would be available in his memory forever and arrive at the front of his thoughts unbidden at odd moments till his last day.

7

Ho, Ho, Ho, Bro. They've put up a Christmas tree in the TV lounge here at Valley View though it's not yet Thanksgiving. Later with some of my new pals I have to decorate it. We're sewing popcorn right now.

I haven't seen any psychiatrist or psychologist or social worker. There's a little man here they call the Counselor. I had to talk to him for several hours last night after my dramatic arrival (fast ride in the Basalt ambulance, Larry Forrest at my side, loose handcuffs on my wrists), and an hour this morning.

The Counselor has asked me lists of questions that I know are tests. He has thin black hair colored with dye and combed over his flaking dome. I answer the questions quickly, as he has instructed. Many of the questions he repeats, but they come so fast you only have time to notice that it's the same question going by or a question very like one you've answered and you worry that your answer won't be quite the same in some way that will show how nuts you really are. His name is Mr. O'Dair. He does not look Irish.

There's a morbid silence about the place. I have pumped the

floor nurse—Sally Kline—for information about my status. All she'll say is what O'Dair has already said, and in the same language: one of three "Visiting Mental Health Professionals," someone important and of whom both Ms. Kline and Mr. O'Dair seem awfully afraid, someone who knows what's what, will drive on over from Denver or Boulder on Monday to assess me.

Valley View. Clean as a small-time airport and as good for the soul. The men on my locked hall are perfectly pleasant, wear street clothes, don't yell, mostly look like people on a subway car: unfocused, drugged heavily, huge black holes for eyes, going where the train goes. They are not turds. They have genuine, debilitating, heartbreaking illnesses.

And wait, what's this ongoing turd stuff? Jesus, I've got to get hold. In the pay-phone room under a staircase, I make my first call since the . . . the *debacle* . . . and it's not an attempt to find Madeline in San Francisco, which it goddamn well ought to be. Hodge, I know it ought to be. Instead, I call Frank Kobil's. I get his machine, just listen to the jovial recording—it's still him; he'll call right back. I want to leave a message; I have the strong feeling he'll get it, but what am I going to say? At least I don't feel like yelling anymore. "Frank, good-bye," I say, knowing his daughter will hear it and think less of me yet.

I dial San Francisco. The desk lady at the Western Star Hotel says no one by that name is registered. I try again, get a man who says the same thing, politely. This is how far apart Madeline and I have grown—she's changed hotels and not even felt it important to tell me. Or worse, she's told me, and I have forgotten. In my heaviest businessman's voice I say, "If she turns up, please let her know she can reach her husband at Valley View." I call our home answering machine, leave a calm description of events.

The tree's trimmed, the calls are made. I watch *Star Trek* with a puffy man named Edward and two other gents in the TV lounge.

When old soft Ed falls asleep I rush back to the phone room, leave a message on the machine at Mad's office. I call Buck Holander, her sometime law partner, but no one's home at his house, and what message am I going to leave? I hang up, call directory assistance in San Francisco: hotels with Western in the name. Hotels with Star in the name. The operator is unbelievably helpful, completely helpless.

And then I start to sink. *Star Trek* makes it worse. I'm starting to believe that what Judge Anstedt did was not meant as a favor: it was the only thing he could do with someone insane as I am. Fighting that thought I get up and turn the TV off. No protest from Danny or Boris or Pete, though all eyes remain glued to the set. With the TV off I realize that there's been a quiet radio on as well the whole time—light country hits. Some fellow talking about the lightness of the hits they play. So I turn that off and a deep silence is in the room. This wakes Edward.

"Do you have permission?" he says. And he repeats this several times as I fire up the old console-stereo record player someone's donated. In the cabinet are hundreds of venerable albums, and right away I find Miles Davis playing ballads. And to "Autumn Leaves" I sit down and worry.

"You didn't ask," says Edward.

"Sally Kline said it's okay, Edward," I say gently. "She told me to tell you to relax and listen to Miles."

"Oh," he says. And relaxes, and listens.

I play the LP over and over and force myself to think of fly-fishing in the Frying Pan River, but what's really coming up is the struggle with Madeline—where is she? I think of a particular boulder I like to sit on in the center of the tailwater below our house. I think of the summer sun, the river rushing past, but the problem of Madeline pushes in. I must act, make a choice: stay or go. I slump into the couch and listen to the dulcet trumpet and try like hell to think of fishing in the sun and nothing else. But every fat fish my imagination pulls in is another worry.

Late in the afternoon—lunch is done, nap time is over—I'm staring out the TV room window as if I know I should be watching for her: Roddy. And roaring up the long and curving drive comes that brand-new and ever-giant Ford pickup (endorsement deal, garaged forever at Frank's), Roddy's red F250.

She's come back from Europe to help bury our friend Frank; somehow in the dusk of mourning she's heard about me. When she climbs out of the truck I'm surprised for the first time: it's really her. It's her all right, dressed in modest grays, tweed suit, stockings, looking exhausted. Seeing her I feel how completely, painfully sane I am.

I'm allowed to see her in the milk room, they call it, a crappy linoleum lounge with two milk machines and the smell of old milk, the exact smell of the lunchroom at Johnson Elementary, Hodge, if you want to call it up. Sally Kline brings Roddy in, is already fond of Roddy, gives me a look that means she's going to allow us just as long as we want, screw the rules.

Roddy looks at me hard: "I hear you need a bucket," says she.

I'm so sheepish I can barely smile. We sit at the table in there, opposite sides. My hallmates slip in the room to get a look, pour milk, slip out. My friend Edward comes in three times, then just stays, tries the candy machine, dropping the same bent quarter endlessly into it, saying *dag* at each failure.

Roddy says, "Oh, Coop."

"I'm okay," I say, since that's what she wants to ask but can't.

She looks at me a long time, unpitying, a little severe in her exhaustion. I can't see what made me like her mouth so much, can't see her clearly at all. Brightly, she says, *"Un uomo in una donna, anzi uno dio per la sua bocca parla, ond'io per ascoltarla son fatto tal, che ma' più sarò mio."*

I keep smelling the institutional shampoo I used in the communal bathroom this morning.

Roddy pokes me, goes all playful: "Do you just hate it when I speak Italian?" She's trying to cheer me up: "No, no, you just hate it when I don't translate. You think I'm a show-off!" She eyes me—she's just doing what she can to make conversation here. "It's Michelangelo," she says, no translation forthcoming. She pulls a pen out of her big purse, pulls out a pad of green paper, writes the quotation out for me, hands it over. We've got all the time in the world. "Did you know he wrote poems? To Vittoria Colonna, a woman!"

Edward drops his quarter, listens.

"A woman he couldn't have." Roddy studies me, wishing she hadn't said that, I can see. She hurries on: "I'm writing a paper on their so-called friendship. It'll be controversial. You are *required* to read it. You'll need to learn Italian, though."

I remember kissing her mouth. I look at her mouth and remember everything. And I know what she's avoiding, so I say it: "Poor Frank."

In her Frank Kobil voice, the old imitation, she says: "He's off to heaven, as he's long planned." There's light in her hair, and her eyes are tired, and even if she's not saying it clearly, I can feel it: she's said no more to Claudio than I've said to Madeline. And worse than that, looking in her burning eyes I find the whole story: our night has led to one of those long arguments that clear the air for a couple and rekindle regard and bring back the passion.

Has Frank's death become somehow the death of Roddy's and my chance?

"I killed him," I say.

"Oh, Mr. Henry." Suddenly I can see her heart in her weary brown eyes; that hasn't changed; still, I can see that she thinks she killed Frank, too, that she's had the thoughts I have. She's glad it wasn't she who died, but of course it's you I'm talking about. I killed you, Hodge.

I let the thought pass. I say, "They aren't going to let me out for the service Monday."

She puts her hands on the table out of reach of my own. "You'll need a lawyer," says she.

I find her eyes. "That was sweet the other night," I say, though it's not the time.

"Yes," she says, no smile, only her serious eyes.

That thought holds us a long time. Finally I say, "Luckily, I've got a lawyer in the family."

"Yes, you do," says Roddy.

Between us the possibilities have become impenetrably opaque. "But I can't find her," I say.

Roddy rises quickly to come around the table to my side. She takes my head to her strong shoulder. "Shh," says she.

"No physical contact," says Edward mildly.

The TV, the stereo, the radio. Sally Kline loudly on the phone at the distant floor desk, talking to a friend ("You cannot *wear* that dress and expect . . . ").

"You're a mess," Roddy says.

She's right about that.

8

Sunday Breakfast—Tad and Coop alone—was cereal and milk and two piles of toast and a hot dog each, since a couple of dogs were left over from Saturday night.

Tad said, "You want to go to church?"

No seemed like the wrong answer, especially as Coop had decided to spend the summer here, maybe the rest of his life. He'd sleep in the barn; he'd earn a little money; he'd get to be great on a horse. "Sure." Then a little warily: "What church?"

Tricia came down with her hair all awry, eccentric multiple ponytails. She didn't look at Coop, just walked right to her father's side, pointed at Coop, said, "He has to leave."

"Now, honey," Tad said. "Go ahead and get something to eat."

"That boy has to leave. He came in my room last night and bothered me."

Tad didn't get it at first, looked with equanimity at Coop, smiled a little as if at the oddness of women, shrugged, said, "What? Trish? Honey?"

"Coop came in my room last night and kissed me and tried to touch me."

Tad rose quickly. "You did what?"

"No I didn't, sir."

"You did *what?*" Tad's face like he'd been punched.

"Nothing, sir. Nothing at all."

"Nothing at *all!*" Tricia wailed. She ducked into her father's arms like a little girl.

"You get going," Tad said quietly as ever, holding his daughter.

"Can I get my stuff?" Coop said.

"Forget your *stuff.* You just get up and go, cowboy. Get up and move."

Coop went. Out the door, down the long driveway to the high gate and cattle guard. There he stood, looking up the road toward the mountains, down the road toward town, trying to think what he'd done. He started toward town then turned and thought and walked back toward the mountains. He saw Tad stepping hard, coming at him down the driveway. Coop didn't run, just stood waiting for it, figuring whatever Tad did, it couldn't be worse than the kick of a heifer, or anything from Dad.

The rancher stopped on the other side of the cattle guard, let that define the gulf between them, tossed a bundle across it at Coop's feet in the dust: Coop's clothes and what was left of his pitiful loaf of bread. "I tried to help you," Tad said.

"I just want you to know that I didn't do what she said."

"She told me what you didn't do."

"No, Mr. Thomas. Really. I thought we were having fun. I thought we were in love."

"You're lucky I'm a civil man. And you're lucky this fun of yours didn't get any farther. And don't tell me about love." He reached in his pocket and found a neat roll of one-dollar bills, tossed that atop the clothing. "Put it in your pocket," he said. "That's your pay."

"I didn't do anything to hurt her."

"That girl's going to Stanford in September," Tad spouted, as if such a plain truth should have protected her.

They stared at each other across the cow guard till Coop looked away, west toward the mountains.

Tad said, "God is always watching you," then wheeled and ran back up the driveway at a lope, as if he were going to get his elk rifle or call the cops or the Marines.

Coop stood a half hour and watched the house, but Tad did not return and no policemen came. Worse, there was no signal from Tricia. Some joke, if that's what it was. At great length he collected his clothes and the money—sixteen dollars, more than he'd earned—collected the partial loaf of bread and began to walk. He took step after step until the walking was mechanical, and step by step he headed toward the mountains, toward Seattle.

Chapter Three

1

Talking, Grandma Vanderhoop showed her true age, Coop thought: sixteen. But she lived inside a large and tremulous old body, was soft like her feather pillows, smelled of lilac and not Shalimar (Connie K.) or cowshit (don't ask). Grandma moved her hands in concert to make her points; she gazed into him with her wise blue eyes; she pulled him into her firm orbit furiously. Coop basked in her anger.

She made a large point (both hands, in fact, pointing, though she was driving) of having taken the day off to come collect him at the bus depot on First Street, Port of Seattle. She drove her new Impala very slowly, lecturing him and squeezing his neck with furious affection at every stop. Coop watched the rain, happy to be contrite.

"You've given us quite a scare, Anthony Cooper Henry. And destroyed your family's vacation, just that simply. And here we are praying for *your* safety when all the while you are simply carousing with who knows whom!"

Coop softly said that he wasn't carousing (and might have added that Grandma was supposed to be an atheist), but knew that nothing that crossed his lips would alter her course in the slightest:

"And since I can't have the whole family I have insisted that I get you for the week. It's signed, sealed and delivered, young man. I've talked to your father. Deprive an old lady!" She squeezed his neck again, hard. Coop hadn't seen her so worked up since the week she babysat while Mom and Dad were in Europe and she'd caught Hodge (openly her favorite of twenty-seven grandchildren) naked in his smoky bedroom at dawn, ripped on some kind of mushrooms with two naked neighbor girls more Coop's age, all of them smeared with peanut butter and Cindy's finger paints: four colors smudged to brown. "All of us emotional wrecks! Your father with his distrustful phone calls at all hours! Which reminds me: he's going to call this evening at seven o'clock, precisely. You are not going to go unpunished!" Again she squeezed Coop's neck, as if affection were punishment.

He began his defense: "Well, he's the one that left me in Wyoming!"

But Grandma seemed to disappear into herself, began a familiar muttering, the thoughts in her head leaking out of her lips, mumbly but furious, so clearly articulated that a person could hear the topmost workings of her mind as she drove, though to listen was embarrassing. The downy and intricately wrinkled skin of her cheek shook: *"That man an ant. Anti-ethos. Ethiopians. Wretches! Working for their destruction, selling wretched weapons to wretched countries to kill wretched innocents in the fields of their wretched farms. It's sinful, I've said that often. Criminal. And his business trips!"* To Coop: "How many months was your father away this year?"

"Not so many," Coop said. Even when it came to Dad, his instinct was to protect.

"No wonder you children disrespect him so! No wonder you find yourself in *jail* in *Idaho!*"

"I wasn't in jail exactly," Coop said, but Grandma didn't hear. In fact, the cops in Idaho had been rough with him, had flung him handcuffed into their car headfirst only because he wouldn't talk to them that freezing four in the morning, had ripped the pockets off his shirt yanking him back out of the cruiser, had been chastised by their sergeant, the good man who'd uncuffed him and talked him through the night and called Grandma for him.

She drove an indirect route—more time for their chat—stopped to fret in front of every puddle, waited through green lights, alternately muttering and talking, wound her way to the Seattle Arboretum, pointing out favorite trees and the low bridge under which she'd once hopelessly jammed a rental truck—famous family story. Coop spied some wet hippie kids on a deeply green lawn, three of them, a pretty girl and big boys throwing sticks for a frowsy dog, a gang laughing and shouting, having a blast.

Catch cold, muttered Grandmother.

By the time the old Impala reached the huge house on Boylston Street the little matter of Coop's running away had been wholly put aside. Grandma squeezed his neck one more time, and Coop gave her an awkward hug across the seat, held her longer than he had ever held anyone but Connie K. and now, he guessed, that other one, Tricia Thomas.

Grandma's house was three stories tall, a stately cube with a mansard roof. The peeling paint was at least partly hidden by roses and lilacs and ivy; instead of a lawn she had blackberries, a thicket so dense one no longer saw neighbors. The couch swings on the front porch hung, same as always, but looked unused, unswung. An old wreath sagged on the blue front door.

〰 "You may dispose of *that*," Grandma said, seeing he saw it, "and *someone's* got to paint the porch steps," then began a long muttered list of the woes of the house.

Inside, books: musty multivolume sets on law and medicine and literature and philosophy and economics, thousands of novels old and new, shelves upon shelves of leather bindings and obscure dictionaries and phone books from strange places, hundreds of books cracked open and stacked on tables and chairs, paperbacks interlayered with magazines interlayered with atlases interlayered with textbooks and serious novels and mysteries. Coop went to the full shelf of joke books immediately, remembering what he loved best at ten, only a few years back, really, only five summers ago, one-third of his life: *The Big Book of Jokes, Riddles and Puns.*

Hodge back then was a teen hellion, Coop's age now; he guzzled Grandma's booze, stole her car, brought actual biker girls home, stuffed homemade pipes with hash he bought at the park and sticky globs of opium he got somewhere more dangerous, definitely did other stuff Coop didn't know about but heard the noises of. In Seattle back then Hodge just dumped Coop, called him *Boy Scout* and *Shrimp*, hung out with that big, growling ape Boyd Friendly.

> GHOST: Please let me join the marines.
> RECRUITER: Why?
> GHOST : I want to fright for my country!

Grandma led Coop around her castle, assigning chores, pointing out ancient books in which he ought really to get interested, plants she particularly esteemed, photos she most cherished, familiar shots: Hodge's first birthday, Hodge in his football uniform, Hodge with Missy Kirkbridge. Then some unknown photos: Hodge in some kind of peace march, Hodge with a handsome girl Coop did not recognize. And then, on Grandma's nine-foot grand piano, just one amid thirty nicely framed portraits, Hodge as Coop had never seen him: beard and short hair, glasses.

So Grandma had a secret. Coop clutched the little photo in its silver frame, gazed at it. His mission swelled in his breast, renewed. Grandma came up behind him, murmuring placidly to herself alone, or to Grandpa. Coop slipped the photo of Hodge frame and all into his pocket.

"Time, darling, for a little nap," Grandma said. "You've made us weary, young man."

Nap time was formal with Grandma. Coop knew the drill, played his little boy's role perfectly, carried the tray with cookies and books and milk, walked behind Grandma up the grandly curving stairs, saw her into her room.

"I'll tell you the truth," she said. "We were never worried about you at all." She sat on her bed and looked weary indeed. "You Henry boys are exceptionally self-reliant!" With that she lay back—no cookies, no milk, no books—lay back and arranged the towel over her eyes.

Downstairs, feeling his exceptional self-reliance, Coop deconstructed the months and months of opened and piled mail that kept Grandma's rolltop desk from closing. A half hour into the heap (letters from England, letters from Vietnam, letters from Spain and France and Guatemala and Brazil, letters from China and Iceland and India and Chad, bills from every store in Seattle, letters from grandchildren, letters from half the Democrats in Congress, letters from Coop's mom and all his aunts and uncles, letters from the Vatican, the White House, the governor of Washington), he saw the familiar handwriting, his own almost. With no compunction, Coop read:

Dear G-mom. What's happening? Did you win that fight with Mayor Shitstone? Why do you fuck with those people still? No, really—you should set him up for a lesson—get a couple of monkeys to beat him with pipes or something. Electrocute him in his Shitstone shitbath! And no lectures about my language, please—fug that. Just kidding. Thanks for the cash money! A beautiful $100 bill. It made it through the mail all right and I bought two shirts very dressy as you wanted and two dinners out, as you commanded. You know I listen to my old Grandma! You said I should have a date, so I did. Two dinners, two girls. One I met at Geoff Street Collective. Very uptight. One I met in the park Sunday. Very not uptight. No I don't miss Missy. She's got a boyfriend at Amherst and I'm in so much trouble anyway I think I'll set him up for a lesson. Couple of monkeys with pipes! Firebomb him in his math class! Kidding, Grandmother! I know you hate that. No lectures, okay? Just send money. Kidding again! Still plenty change left from your gift! Also, your wrong, Mom and Dad do not mean well. They mean a bum trip sure as shit. Last time I talked to them was last winter and Dad said it would be best to just face the music. Do you hear me? So don't tell me I should try to communicate more. And meanwhile what kind of music are we talking about? I'd as soon kill HIM than any Viet Cong. Your right when you say I AM serving my country and principle IS more important than blind obedience. But you say SOMETIMES more important. I say always. So you see of course I think for myself. Why would you say I don't? Your supposed to be one of the good guys, GV. But don't even bother sending me money if you can't support me. You say nonviolence, I say think for YOUR self, Grandma. Fight fire with fire, I say. Kill the pigs. Make a list. Get them each one. I thank you for believing in me, Grandma, when nobody else will. My vow is to fight the power. By any means, as the CIA says. Oh and I bought oil paints (no canvas—$$) but I paint on pieces of plywood (easy to find), I don't know how you do it, it's really very hard I tried to make a painting of Missy, looks more like Mayor Daley (who should be tortured, too, and not just killed—and I don't mean a wet towel in the shower, either). Very hot days here. I don't want to take all your money, but if your university idea works out in Toronto I think maybe we should talk more about that loan. Yes I will call you on my birthday, you old FLAPPER. But remember, your too uptight! *Peace, Love, Hodge.*

No envelope, no return address. A strange, scrawled postscript said *Very sad today* in different ink. Coop perused the sacred document ten times seeking clues. Not much to go on, and Coop found himself jealous of Grandma's attention to his hero. He wedged the offensive letter back in its place, leaving the desk just the mess he'd found, occupied himself with a snoop around the familiar old castle.

He peeked into what Grandma had always called the little-girls' room, two bunk beds dressed in pink, then into the little-boys' room: crib and bunk bed. In the two adult rooms there were double beds, and nice dressers, and more and more pictures: kids in their graduation gowns, kids on bikes, kids at summer camp, kids with their parents on mountain outings. A lot of pictures of Hodge, more Hodge than anyone else. Looking at them, Coop felt his face go hot.

Up the steep steps to the attic Coop crept, up into the familiarly hot and dry, dusty and promising dark. Here you played Risk and fort, Monopoly and doctor; here you retreated to escape the adults—aunts and uncles with booze on their tongues. In the attic you could spy through the cracks in the pine-plank walls, see Hodge and Boyd Friendly kiss girls and with luck see the girls partly bare. And you could play. Because up there under the eaves lurked crates and trunks and boxes of Grandpa's stuff, untouched by Grandma since it was packed by family friends in hasty grief, and Coop knew all of it: diaries and bow ties and cufflinks and keys, diplomas and inkwells and postcards and rocks. Grandpa had owned a Malaysian machete, too, and a 30.06 hunting rifle. Also a heavy .45 pistol hidden in a box—all the cousins knew about that gun, and played with it. World War II, mostly, or *Dragnet*. Also this, Coop's secret: a little handgun hidden in two socks inside a jacket pocket, an almost dainty .32 with an opalescent shell handle and the words *Little Pal* engraved along the stainless-steel barrel in quaint script.

Coop just stared at the boxes.

Where was Grandpa now?

2

So, brother, my little ritual takes me to Dr. Prenci's office. The tests are done and I'm not nuts and so am completely responsible for my actions. Fortunately, I'm married to Madeline. Madeline has made deals all around: there's no trial coming up, but still I go around imagining it. You know, me in the witness box looking up at a fat judge and Mom and Dad and everyone in the gallery looking stern and banks of lawyers and Jimmy Peek on crutches (that's the kid clerk from Merck's, the kid I harmed—turns out he's Ellie and Carl Peek's kid, the most forgiving people I've ever met). And on the evidence table: buckets. Lots of galvanized steel buckets, and photos of my car wedged into the back wall of Merck's True Value (plenty damage, and Aetna refuses to pay, since they say it was no accident). The jury is composed of women, Hodge, women suspiciously like Mom, and I can't tell if they're on my side or not. And in this phantom courtroom are great boxes of transcripts of my talks with Dr. Prenci. And videotapes, which the jury gets to look at.

Dr. P. is very chilly and distant but you can tell she's interested in this case. On the stand she says how cooperative I was in her office. She clicks on the video.

"Well," says I, looking not at the camera nor at the doctor, but at the floor, hands clamped tight between my knees: "Funny how it ended up here, huh?"

"Could you explain?" says she.

"I mean, funny that I'd go to those lengths in pursuit of a cleansing. I meant to . . ." Long pause.

"To what, Mr. Henry? Can you articulate what it was you wanted to clean?"

". . . well, the house, of course. The woodwork of the house. But the symbolic thing is. The metaphor was to clean out all the . . . "

"To clean out all the . . . "

"Bad spirits. I guess you'd say."

Silence. Doctor Prenci lets it last, then: "Now, earlier you mentioned that your friend and mentor Mr. Kobil had just recently passed away."

"Dead, yes. Just the other night."

"Could you talk about that a little?"

"Well, he'd been heading for it."

"Would you say your emotion at his death accounts for what happened the other day?"

"I don't know. Would you say so?"

"Did you fight in Vietnam, Mr. Henry?"

"Please don't call me Mr. Henry."

"Did you fight in Vietnam?"

"No Ma'am. My lottery number was 102. I sweated it, but in 1971 they only got to 97. Nixon had started his program of so-called Vietnamization. Why?"

"Well, sir, I am someone who believes in causes. Anguish like yours probably does not arise spontaneously, though it may be triggered by a shock—your friend's death is a good example, of course. But the shock isn't what we're looking at here. The state of mind that determines your response to a shock is what interests us. This state of mind, let us call it, is an effect, whose causes lie not in the present, but in the past. Let me be direct: do you have an incident you could point to? Some trauma? Some terrible loss? An accident? Are your parents alive?"

"Ahm. Trauma?"

"Some devastating incident?"

"No." Yes.

"No?"

"Definitely not." Definitely yes.

Long pause. "Do you remember your childhood?"

"Sure. Of course." Not entirely.

"Of course. But are there any periods you do not clearly remember?"

"Whole years?" One whole summer.

"No, Mr. Henry. Just any time at all. Are there any blanks in your memory. Blanks you've come to notice?"

"No. No, no, no. That's the problem. I remember all of it all too well."

"'All too well.' And what is it that you remember 'All too well'?"

"That's just a figure of speech."

"Tell me about your youngest years, your memories."

I tell her about the crib and my big brother flinging me about, as if I had no doubts it were real.

"Tell me about first grade." And I do, then second grade, and third, fourth. The courtroom of my mind is full of old acquaintances and our oft-pregnant mother and our siblings and Dad heading to the train station every morning and Mrs. Loomis teaching math and reading and geography in third grade and how her son played the guitar.

"What was junior high like for you?"

Well, Connie Kirkbridge and Chester Tanay and that tough kid Beetle, and the Beatles on Ed Sullivan and the appearance upon my pubis of hairs and dances in the gym at the Y and ski trips to Vermont and ski racing and winning those races and suddenly finding a place in that way—yes skiing is crucial to my story, Doctor P., skiing, skiing, skiing, but not only skiing—there's lots more, including regrets: I could never manage to kiss girls even when it was plain they wanted to be kissed.

"What about your summers?" says Dr. Prenci. She doesn't care about skiing or regrets over girls; she's noticed that I've said not a word about summer. Summers: I manage to give Dr. Prenci a catalog of family trips and summer camps and team sports and beach parties. There's only one year I can't remember much of, the summer I turned sixteen, of course, your summer, which would be 1969. The same summer as Woodstock, though we were far from Yasgur's farm. Same summer as the landing on the moon, though we were even farther from that. Same year as Altamont—getting closer. All of it overshadowed (as was everything at that time for any young man) by what we echoed the soldiers in calling 'Nam. Yes, overshadowed by Vietnam, by the prospect of our brothers or our heroes or our friends going there, by the prospect of having to go ourselves, by the awful and just barely subliminal message that our fathers wanted us *dead*, that presidents and senators and congressmen—proxy fathers all—would see us *dead* in stupid and wasteful violence, make us pay for their own bad trips in World War II.

And it's that summer that Dr. Prenci and I talk about for the full second session and into the third. I can barely get to it, Hodge. Don't want to get to anything, as you might expect. And so I lie, give her a summer, a nice family trip to Maine, a winning Babe Ruth League baseball team, dates with Connie K.

The people in the court of my mind who aren't yawning are

examining me closely. They know something's amiss here. They know it just by looking at me. Even on the tape you can see it. This guy's pure turd, an enormous stool, sitting on a stool, head bowed, dunce cap.

Third session:

"So you'd say you'd got through life till now, till the death of your friend, without suffering any other particularly important trauma or loss. . . ."

"I'm not sure what you mean by loss. I guess that's the problem. I'm not sure what you mean by any of these questions. I'm not sure what you're getting at."

"What do you imagine I mean? What do you imagine I'm 'getting at'?" She says this so kindly; you can see her face change; you feel like you're talking to an old friend or maybe Mom when we were little. She's Mom after the punishment's over. She's Mom when you're feeling rocky. We sit in perfect silence and the tape just rolls, my face placid, the turmoil inside me invisible.

To evade the question I find a way to misunderstand it. I take the meaning of loss to be defeat, as in downhill, as in giant slalom. Loser, winner. Second place, third. Then I seem to be regaling myself with a series of ridiculous childhood incidents: the twenty-dollar bill Dad entrusted to me at Disneyland, lost; the huge striped bass that flopped off the jetty at Norwalk after I'd reeled him in and unhooked him (no one believed a word of that), lost; the bicycle I rode to the edge of the ice at Miller's pond before I crashed through, lost, gone forever. And then I'm thinking of Tricia, of Tad Thomas's equivocal and apologetic and tragic letter ("your friend Tricia has had an accident"), of how clearly—thirty-two Seconals—there was no accident: every poem a suicide note, once you thought about it, once you read the book. And now every schoolgirl buys that book. Forty plain poems. And even unfinished the poems are taken very seriously: Ph.D. dissertations, quotes as epigraphs, phrases in songs and in titles and in the most casual talk.

I remember first lines: "Downhill to California / The desert paints my heart," and, "I am impervious to your insult / but not to your lewd shrug," and that most famous one, a long narrative thing, which starts something like: "Mother left me horses / father cleans the barn," and the person talking is in her bath with a knobbed butter knife whose one end is a little sexy, the other just dangerous. I can't even look at the book anymore. But the poems really are good, well regarded, pretty serious. Have you seen them where you are, bro? Something like seven web sites devoted to her. How are the Internet connections in Hell?

Finally to Dr. Prenci I say, "I had a girlfriend who died. But that was years after I knew her."

Long pause, as at the height of tide, before the cresting water turns and again flows seaward, the actual turn undetectable but soon a current rushing.

"Anything else?"

Word by word, distant, high voice, small, I say, "Well. My brother. My brother disappeared when I was thirteen." That's as much as I can manage.

"Disappeared," she says.

We sit a long time again. "Yes," I say. "Thirteen." And all can see in my face that I'm holding back, that I am trying to carefully manage the appearance of emotion, that this man on the tape thinks—really believes—he is feeling nothing, thinks the only problem is that the therapist is too prodding, too prying. And at the cusp of confession the turd pulls closed the last curtain: "He was avoiding the draft."

Dr. Prenci waits a long time.

The cryptic turd is composed, will say no more.

"That's a terrible loss," says the doctor, deeply and truly compassionate.

My face looks the same, just blank, but then there's a tear, and then another, then I'm quietly weeping, trying not to show it, just sitting there with a blank face weeping, then the hands go to the face and the man, the turd, is sobbing, crying, wracking wretched tears for a whole half hour, well past the end of his session. Dr. Prenci just sits compassionately and watches, nodding her head almost imperceptibly, sliding the box of yellow tissues near, nodding her head. She seems pure benevolence and the man pure despond as he blows his nose and weeps and makes pitiful noises.

Eventually he's over it. She says, "I see no indication of mental illness here, Mr. Henry."

The next afternoon they're letting me out. I've missed Frank's funeral. Missed it clean. Our mutual people have the sense that I freaked out seeing him die—a shock indeed—but they don't know about you, bro, the anguish that came long before. Old man Merck won't press charges. Madeline has talked to absolutely everyone since she got back yesterday—spent all her time, despite the call of her huge caseload—and everyone has been understanding to the point of saintliness. She solves all the problems, makes all the deals, attends Frank's funeral, explains to one and all what's happened to Coop Henry: grief.

Tuesday, she drives down to get me.

On the ride home she's driving stiffly, hot over missing yet another day in her office, a day that after her trip she can't afford. She says, "You were drinking."

"That wasn't it."

"And what on earth was Veronica Manor doing at Valley View?"

"She was just concerned," says I.

"And how is it that she came to have this concern?"

"She heard I was in the nuthouse. She heard about Merck's. It was on the news, I'm afraid. She was in town for Frank's funeral. She didn't want me to be alone. Is all."

"Signed in as your wife?"

The turd: "Madeline, darling. I was alone in that place and desperate. They wouldn't have let her in otherwise."

"How much Scotch did you drink before you got in your car and wrecked that store?"

"Why didn't you tell me you switched hotels?"

"Don't change the subject."

"I wasn't drinking, Mad."

I wait the whole ride for her next words, but that, bro, is the extent of our conversation, one full hour in the car, I holding back from correcting her: I drink bourbon, if I'm going drink whiskey, and she should know it.

But thanks to Madeline I'm off the hook. The terms are all arranged—no court date, no jail. I just have to do the fall plantings and miles of raking and the spring cleanup and litter patrol in Tremble Cemetery and along the Frying Pan Road into Basalt. My little cleansing ceremony ends with 150 hours of community service, a suspended fine, no probation.

The cleansing, such as it was, seems to have worked. No more fury at the local merchants. Now I just weep. If no one's around I weep like a penitent, silently, thinking of Dr. Prenci's compassionate face, thinking of the mossy place you fell, the way the sun patterned the moss and how everyone froze and how surprised you were, really, how surprise was your last emotion. I remember and weep and empty my hollow self, wondering why I didn't just tell Prenci the whole thing. She knew there was more. She knew. Why not ask?

3

At six fifty-five, Grandma thought to plug the phone back in, and all was lost. At precisely seven it rang, and despite the fervor of Coop's hope, Dad spoke: "By God, son, it is good to hear your voice. You're all right?"

"Fine and dandy."

"Well, let's us start by saying 'Happy Fourth of July.'"

"That's tomorrow."

"So it is. Fair enough. Why not let's us get down to business? Nothing for our champion skier to report?"

Deep irony, sparked by Dad's officious tone and the complicated model for his approval built into the bit about skiing: "No *sir*, sir!"

"Then what's this about the police picking you up?"

"They didn't pick me up. You guys left me."

"Now wait just a minute, chief, we didn't leave you."

"Then where the fuck were you?"

"Watch your language, son."

"You left me and I decided to hitch to Grandma's and I just gave up, that's all, and went in the police station and talked to this nice sergeant and that's the whole story."

"That's not what the nice goddamn sergeant told me, Coop."

"Watch your language, *father*."

Rising anger: "He said you were picked up at four-fifteen in the a.m. roaming around Coeur d'Alene."

"So it was *early*."

"Your mother and I have had a little goddamn talk, too."

Coop knew what was coming. He said, "Why should I be punished? I've suffered enough. Haven't I suffered enough? You dump me off in some shitty town in goddamn Wyoming and now I've got to be *punished?*"

Dad went all calm: "Number one: You get yourself a haircut—first thing Monday morning. And Coop, I mean a goddamn flat-top. None of this Dave-Clark-Five stuff. Your grandmother knows about this. Number two: You are not to leave your grandmother's immediate sight. You are grounded, and I have told her exactly the rules. Number three: you are to do any chores Mrs. Keepnews might have for you. Number four: please, Coop, for the love of Pete, keep your wits about you!"

"Her name is Ms. Vanderhoop."

"Well, Anthony, that's her maiden name, yes. It's just something I haven't goddamnit got used to. I guess I'm just . . ."

"I guess you're just an . . . *asshole*." Coop said it, couldn't take it back, rose to the awfulness of it, said it again, voice cracking: "It's because you're a big . . . *farting asshole*." Coop hung up with a ringing slam. There wasn't another choice, after what he'd said. As an afterthought he unplugged the phone, then sat in the kitchen alone, breathing hard, stifling giggles.

Grandma let him steam and titter a half hour before she looked in on him. "Nice chat?" she said seriously.

"Delightful," Coop said.

"It sounded to me as if you two worked everything out splendidly." Grandma was funny when she wanted to be, but Coop wasn't going to laugh. If she was in on this haircut routine there was no joke funny enough.

"He just doesn't care about me," Coop said. "I mean, probably he's off on some trip next week . . . "

Grandma looked at him a long time wisely, maybe a little sadly, couldn't find the words she wanted to say. Abruptly she stood, changed the subject: "Let's read a book." Coop's stratagem had succeeded: Grandma hadn't ever and wouldn't ever take Dad's side in anything.

In the parlor in deep chairs amid books and under the eyes of Grandpa's sober portrait, Coop read the opening pages of *David Copperfield* out loud ("What's a caul?") till Grandma fell asleep, then read the book to himself an hour till she woke in a fog, asking him to back up a little, she'd lost the story.

The next morning was blue and brilliant as any morning in Montana. Across Puget Sound the Olympic Mountains were back, bigger even than Coop remembered them. At elaborate length, Grandma descended the front stairs all dressed to go visiting, a strange hat like a cake tied to her head with a red-white-and-blue scarf. She ignored Coop, marched to the console and put a record on: John Philip Sousa.

"Find the flag," she commanded, marching.

Oh, was she funny! To please her, Coop rushed up the stairs and to the attic like a little boy, fetched the formally folded and gargantuan Stars and Stripes, rushed to hang it on its familiar nails across the big porch in back. And once again as in years gone he enjoyed imagining that everyone in all the boats on Lake Union below and in all the houses and buildings in Grandma's glorious view was intently watching and cheering him on: Iwo Jima, Guadalcanal. Grandma, for her part, stood in the yard of brambles below the house and clapped her hands in pleasure as the old flag unfurled. Oh, he liked making her happy!

Which is why at noon, without complaint, he climbed into her car: they were off to Lake Washington Park for the speedboat races. Grandma had friends to meet, people from the Planning Board, lawyers from all over Washington, people from her days in office: Congresswoman Vanderhoop.

In the car she squeezed his arm repeatedly, kept reminding him: "You are not to leave my side."

Yes, right, Grandma! Too soon, Coop stood politely in the company of a bunch of old humans, who stood in turn amid an enormous citywide lawn party beside the lake, blankets everywhere and much shouting and singing and laughter and sport. Coop eyed the crowd, jealous of every free teenager. The only good thing was a blimp that motored floating back and forth overhead. A couple of Grandma's friends were dressed in black tie—dressed in black tie for a damn picnic!—hoping so hard to be noticed that Coop made a point of ignoring them. Two of the old guys had marched in the parade, and everyone had to listen about how tired their feet were and how the *governor* had seemed particularly surly this morning. Grandma accepted a martini in a nice glass and told everyone all about Coop. He played his part, stood and grinned and nodded, though he was *appalled,* as his mom might say. One younger guy named Theophilus (young enough for Coop to maybe hang around with today, but in a tux) said "Hey brother," and "Kind of a drag," trying to make himself out as cool, and gave Coop an overdone soul shake. Some soul. The guy looked more like an accordion player from the worst TV show on earth, Lawrence Welk. The other adults asked Coop questions, "How is your mother?", "Your Dad still with Dow?", but luckily got bored fast. Theophilus poured more martinis, slipped Coop an orange soda laced with gin. Well, all right. Coop drank it down fast, felt his ears glow red. He said loudly, "Of what city is someone named Daley mayor?"

Theophilus led the laughter. And Grandma entered in. Coop snorted too, when he saw they thought he'd made a joke. No one answered his question, they just made dumb jokes in return, about the mayor of Seattle, *Shitstone,* Hodge had called him. There was the best joke. But the old dorks spat with laughter, cried with it. Mount Rainier stood on the horizon to the south like a ghost, like a great brother (the Stillaguamish Indians called it that, Coop knew from Grandma's shelf of Seattle books) draped in snow, in distance. Coop drifted: dropped by helicopter, he skied the face of Rainier—not just skied but soared—leaving perfect sine-wave tracks in the untouched snow of the mighty glaciers; he leapt crevasses no man had ever crossed; he conquered cliffs; he roared down the hill, finished in a cloud of fine snow, gave modest interviews to the international press, starred at parties, got the girls.

Unnoticed, Coop the Champion wandered away from the picnic, not too far, not too close, climbed a tree. Up there you could make out the race a little, survey the crowd of families and picnics and senior citizens. Not a cool kid in sight. A cop car slowly cruised the road. Two cops walked along the waterfront. Coop settled into the tree, lounged on a thick limb, turned his gaze upward, studied the blimp a long time through dense leaves. He was alone in the world, drifted with the blimp till whoever was driving the thing decided to speed up and leave. The tree limb gouged his back. He thought of a certain bright cowgirl with pain. But then a raging, heart-stopping roar tore the sky hard above him: six fighter jets nearly touching each other, delta formation not two hundred feet up, streak and roar and gone—silence—then roar, then gone, then back again. Blink and they were gone. Blink and they were back, flying at each other, ducking, spinning, climbing, louder than thunder. Coop screamed with excitement, held onto his branch.

The fliers made spirals, made flowers of smoke. They disappeared, they came back, they were gone.

In the sudden silence a huge cheer erupted. The boats on Lake Washington blew air horns, firecrackers burst, people whooped and hollered and clapped. But within the cheers, Coop heard booing. He craned to see a big crowd of hippies who'd gathered on the hillside across the park road, hundreds of people, close. Coop made out guitars and headbands and blue jeans and passed puffs of smoke; he saw purple shirts and bare feet and giant sunglasses and big clouds of hair; at the top of the lawn there was someone making huge gestures, someone else throwing flowers. All of them booing and hooting at the sky.

Coop dropped fast from branch to branch to the grass. Only Theophilus at Grandma's picnic looked his way. Grounded and so what? Coop ducked and covered and ran like a commando, crossed the road in front of a bus, popped through the deep hedge. The crowd of *freaks* had grown larger.

From up on the hillside drums resounded. Coop headed that way, soon stood at the periphery of a tight, serious knot of people dancing. A freckly Black man in a headband beamed, handed Coop a burning joint. Coop didn't think twice but took a deep pull, quickly handed the thing off to a fat woman who laughed and puffed till the fire about burned her lips and dropped the butt onto the muddy grass just as a pair of cops sauntered up. They didn't do or say anything. They certainly didn't notice Coop, but oh, he felt a jolt in his belly: those cops in Coeur d'Alene calling him *fairy*. Coop knew what cops would do.

The Black guy said a cheerful "Shit."

That was the right word. That was funny. Coop laughed bubblingly and felt himself in important relation to the group of happy people and in important opposition to the police.

"Pigs," said the fat woman, just a little too loud, and that was funnier yet.

Coop slithered his way into the heart of the crowd and away from the *pigs*. He'd become aware in a rush of feeling of the hair on his head, how it grew from his *mind*. People shook and waved their arms, dancing. Fuck the cops! Two dark-skinned Black guys and a darker Black woman rocked at the heart of the session behind five tall conga drums. Two white guys with little beards banged expertly on upended trash cans. Coop got right up close, danced self-consciously, thought of Connie Kirkbridge in white gloves at Mrs. Johnson's Academy of Dance. The drummers bowed their heads, banged at the skins with taped fingers, slapped the skins, thumbed taut drumheads in the rhythm of a heart Coop suddenly saw was his own. Some younger girls had cowbells and shakers and sticks. The beat grew warmer and faster and more meaningful, the frowns of the players deeper. Someone pushed Coop's shoulder: the freckled man, grinning with two beers in his two hands, offering one to Coop. Coop chugged it, thought of Grandma drinking martinis with the stiffs in tuxes, banged his empty bottle on the rail of a park bench to chest rhythm, danced, yodeled timidly, then forcefully, got welcome attention for that from the people around him, shouted, hooted, kicked his legs.

A pale, big man with a partial bottle of cheap vodka squeezed into the crowd and watched. He looked tough and unhappy, lifted the big bottle and sucked it. Coop watched him. In fact, everyone watched him. He was the not-cop, their fearsome ghost. He was colossal in his way, his presence. In this he was like Hodge some little unexplainable bit. The rhythm of the drummers even broke for a moment as each in turn took note of this big brother of a boulder in their stream. At length the still, huge man finished his bottle, let it drop to the ground, fuck the pigs, fished in his baggy pants pockets for a . . . harmonica! . . . and over the Latin rhythm he burst in with a train of unlikely blues chops.

Coop heard himself playing like that, oh, he could and would if his own Marine Band harmonica weren't lost in the fucking police station back in *Idaho*. Tricia—he thought of Tricia in that moment, sinking. He listened hard to float back up, listened to the huge harmonica man, listening for the flaw but the guy proved over many verses just plain stupendously talented, standing tall, standing still except for his thick hands moving the instrument across his taut lips. Jesus, no way: Coop couldn't play like that in a million years. He puffed at a joint that came from a spotted hand. He banged his beer bottle, danced harder, shouted. The conga players subtly altered their rhythms to meet the blues halfway. The still man took the harp from his mouth and bellowed a phrase of lyrics, then blew, then alternated shouts with blowing: love was no more and a wail, love was no more and a cry, love was no more and *baby!* He blew answers to his own plaints. He wasn't performing—he was too drawn into himself for that. The bottle bangers and shakers of maracas moved to be closer to him; the crowd around the congas grew. Coop was part of it, at the heart of it. Joints came by in a rhythm of their own. Coop puffed. A hundred people clapped hands and clanged bottles and sang back to the harmonica man who blew a phrase and had it back, never moving his feet. Coop shouted with the rest, banged at the park bench, subtle rhythms that he hoped the titanic harmonica man would notice, oh, but forget all that, fuck all that: he was in the music and of the music; he was in time and in the heart of it, part of it!

Till he looked up and saw the pair of pigs edging in. *Kill them!* They edged close to the still man, the giant white brother, the singer of blues who blew with his eyes shut tight. Those cops edged close and stopped in the space that opened around them, stopped and impassively watched the big harpoon man. Yes, you called it a harpoon, a harp, and it was a weapon and heavenly instrument in the mighty hands. The cops stopped, the musicians save the harmonica man stiffened, faltered once more, but the harp went on, and so the others did, picked it up, pounding, shaking, dancing, hooting, singing louder and even shouting, wild. The harmonica man opened his eyes blue at the end of a phrase and saw the pigs. Nothing about him changed. He only blew harder into his harp, looking straight at the pigs over his puffing cheeks, a foot taller than either of them.

Kill the pigs!

One of the central players, an overweight and dark-skinned woman with a giant mushroom of hair, rose and began to dance with her drum. She writhed and dipped and quivered twice around the unsmiling pigs, then twice more, then froze and grinned and held her instrument up to them. Without looking at one another, without so much as a shrug, they both pulled out their night sticks. Separately they got pieces of the beat and, not quite smiling, banged the drum in rhythm with night sticks for a solid five minutes, never changing expression, never out of the harmonica man's downward, freezing gaze.

So a pig could be all right, Coop saw, and a song save the world. *Peace,* he thought. *Love.* But he was pretty fucking stoned, and there was violence in the music.

4

It takes Madeline a grumpy week to catch up her caseload after her long trip and my strange one. She works till eleven each night, leaves at seven each morning, and partly this studied absence means she's unhappy with me. I'm spending my days at home examining a certain summer—yanking it whole from my head— all while staring into U.S. Ski Association and U.S. Ski Team protocol manuals. I'm writing up some of my ideas—without Frank I'm on my own as far as the Alpine Director job goes, and given recent events I need to make it a strong case:

> We've got to be smarter in the way we develop these kids. We've forced today's young racers to spend too much time traveling and racing. That's not only expensive, it's destructive. These kids learn how to chase FIS points, but they don't learn how to ski. We should see to it that young racers get a lot more time to just ski, ski, ski, without worrying about gates. Free skiing top to bottom, getting a feel for all kinds of different snow and terrain. That's how a youngster becomes a complete skier and that, most importantly, is how he falls in love with the sport.

Oh, Christ, I sound like a fucking *coach*. *Carpe diem*, boys and girls! Ski, ski, ski! What I ought to tell 'em is how I did it: bolt your boots to your bindings, and do your best to die. If the coaches tell you slow through the glade, you tuck harder, go faster, strip bark from ashes. If the coaches tell you take no risks, scare 'em, fuck 'em, scare 'em all, scare yourself. If you haven't screamed a couple of times per run, if you haven't flipped into the forest at warp speed, if you haven't broken ten pairs of top-end skis and wrecked experimental boots and wrapped ski poles into pretzels around your own head at the crash end of impossible flights, get going! Blow it up! What've you got to lose, champs? A bone or two? Your life?

Grandma's attic, Hodge. I can't shake it. And I can't shake the notion that if Madeline cared, my hiatus at the nuthouse would more than *irritate* her. She's uncomfortable with strong emotion, maybe most uncomfortable with fear, covers fear with anger. Is my guess.

If I were still pretending to converse with my big brother I might ask him if he thought I should press Dr. Prenci to take me on as regular client. To which if my big brother weren't dead nearly thirty years he might say: Prenci lives in Denver, you fucking idiot.

I put the manuals away and quit my task of applying for the job I should have simply walked into, make an overnight solo to the Frying Pan lakes, a box-canyon trail, march hard between the ridges and rude peaks, entirely alone under the perfect, narrow dome of the sky, four hours hiking till I reach the first lake, a beaver impoundment so ancient that the dams have become pond banks you can walk on, fling your line. The floor of the valley is 8,600 feet above sea level, but I'm not puffing. The peaks right here are over 11,000 feet, a couple of them 12,000. I've brought my little three-weight fly rod and four flies only—two Adamses, two hare's ear nymphs—and with them I fish for food.

Mashed in my daypack with the sleeping bag is one hunk of bread and one large potato, so the stakes in terms of dinner are high.

In the crystalline water pouring under the gate of the beaver-works, the auspicious source of the Frying Pan River (which will meet the Roaring Fork, then the Colorado, then roll a thousand miles through the world's greatest canyons to the Gulf of California—if it gets that far after irrigation and other depletion), I can see six fish; that is, I can see the shadows cast by six fish, and see these shades feeding on something, maybe pond shrimp. The Adams floats over them perfectly twenty times to not the slightest interest. The hare's ear gets the two biggest ghosts to turn their heads, but that is all. After a couple of hours of this teasing and playing, this pure distraction, the sun drops behind the knuckled peak of Mount Turnbuckle, which the Indians called Fist. The sun drops and though it's only maybe four o'clock the day goes dark in the canyon and suddenly it is winter cold. Earlier I'd thought I'd swim, hard to believe now. Instead a fast hike around the ponds, dropping the Adams whenever I can get a clear backcast, or can at least roll a cast in front of the dense alders that make the shore away from the dams. Nothing. Hodge, do you remember days like this? We were kids at the gravel pit, we fished. You threw me in.

I'm famished. Back at the headwaters I can't see the six fish any-more. Their camouflage is precise and perfect, and now the sun won't give them away. I tease them with the nymph. Two of the bigger fish move at it; I can see their sides flash. These are rain-bows of perhaps a foot in length: not big, not small. One will do. Two will fill me up. They are coming to the surface irregularly, feeding on something I can't see, something traveling or floating under the surface tension. Back to the Adams. This I float just twice to no response at all. I get my knife out and trim nearly all of the hackle off the fly, leave the wings mostly intact, then soak the thing in the stream, let it waterlog. Now back over the fish, maybe an inch under the surface. Bang. Silver flash, set the hook, play him. He's strong, bro, he tries to hide in the sticks of the dam. I'm miles from disquiet. The fish comes in and I thank him before knocking his head. Next cast I've got the rest of dinner and two beautiful glistening animals to look at, spots above the lateral line, fading colors from sky and spring meadow. There's not a person in this canyon, not the sound or possibility of a car, not a contrail in the sky.

It's got cold, and clouds are blowing in heavily from the northwest. I get up into the trees far from the water and make an old-fashioned squaw-wood and pine-stick crackling fire in the old-fashioned and much-used ring of stones the NOLS people keep taking apart, sit there warm and happy while my potato gets baked. The fish I put on a hot, flat rock after an hour of daydreaming and firetending. Flip the fish, five minutes and it's dinner. It's dinner and I'm eating succulent fish and the fire warms me and I warm the fire and break the bread which breaks me and drink from Mad's water bottle which drinks me and poke the potato out of the coals, burn it with my fingers, taste it as it eats me up, taste it and know its satisfaction even as the light snow begins to fall.

And in my bag it's a wakeful night, a long but fairly tranquil night, four or five inches of snow, a soft sifting of memory, of impressions, Coop Henry under the snow in his bag, not moving, quietly in his thoughts: the job, the young racers, Frank Kobil, Madeline, Roddy (Roddy, Roddy), then Grandma's attic and the summer of you, Hodge.

5

Coop worked hard at Grandma's straight through the weekend. He painted the porch steps, sealed the basement floor, clipped the weeds, hacked at the supertwined blackberries, tried to reclaim something of the lawn with Grandpa's old reel mower. He was definitely going to stay too busy for a haircut, and Grandma seemed to know it. He fixed the hinges on her jewelry box and worked two hours with coat hanger and screwdriver to clear her bathtub drain. He was still freaked out about the hobgoblin Hodge, that stone-faced harmonica man, who didn't even look like Hodge at all.

Sunday morning Coop made breakfast for Grandma—a glorious tray—hoping for at least a small reprieve from his grounding. He wanted to find the drummers again. Grandma had bought two plane tickets. One for herself: her annual trip—her pilgrimage, really—to Japan. And one for him: a flight home on the tenth, next Thursday. The tickets perched on top of the pile on her desk, bracketing the end of his chance to find Hodge and, worse, a haircut in the making, even if he escaped every barber in Seattle. Coop did those chores. He worked hard.

Monday dawned gray, turned grayer, stiller, quiet and heavy, then the rain came. Some dopey cheerful guy called to cancel Grandma's groundbreaking ceremony at the new First Bank. So Grandma took Coop to her office for a couple of hours during which Coop actually enjoyed the bustle and enjoyed the spectacle of Grandma's importance. She had a big photo on her enormous desk of herself with John F. Kennedy and Lyndon Johnson, all of them grinning. At lunchtime she gathered some cronies and Coop found himself in a dense and fancy restaurant eating clams and sitting at the center of some meaningless fight about sewer access in some meaningless neighborhood in some meaningless ward of Seattle.

Grandma deftly made jokes of the opposing arguments, quietly offered her own arrangement of facts and figures, and before dessert was gone she'd won the fight without seeming to have joined it, without seeming to have made an effort at all. At home, though, she rushed straight to her room—no tea, no chat, none of the usual ritual—an early nap. Coop stood on the porch and stared at the rain awhile, wondering what the hippies did on bad days. He watched Grandma's ancient TV (breaking the rules of his grounding): a swamp-monster movie and part of a baseball game. He liked being alone so well that when the doorbell rang—nearly suppertime, a formal bing and bong—he leapt to answer it so Grandma wouldn't wake.

Whoever it was didn't ring again but was waiting, Coop could tell. Definitely one of Grandma's crackpot friends. He could act sullen and say Grandma was asleep. Or he could act super friendly and let whoever it was in and make hot chocolate and wait while Grandma woke up. Or he could be Grandma's smack-addict, black-sheep grandson, kind of shuffle around, rubbing his arm and sniffling. Or he could do a butler routine, announce that Madame Vanderhoop was not *in* at present. Coop chose the last option, stood at hard attention, leaned to turn the fat brassy-green knob, a whole hand to grasp it. He pulled his chin back, turned down the corners of his mouth, got ready to bow, let the door fall open. "Vanderhoop residence," he intoned.

A tall girl stood there, all wet, no smile, fogged glasses. Tricia Thomas. Tricia Thomas in a checked blouse with her mouth set and her father's Gooch Feeds cap and a little girl's suitcase and the same dirty jeans and the same tall cowboy boots: rodeo girl, vale-dictorian, warm woman in a nightgown, poet, liar.

"It's me," she said.

Coop just raised his eyebrows and looked, and she looked back at him, and it seemed like a whole night of verses they stood there before she let that smile touch her lips. Coop didn't crack at all, not even when Tricia let out a whoop and a laugh. He hustled him-self out on the porch and shut the door behind. Tricia laughed so hard he had to escort her down the walk and out onto Boylston Street. When her laughter ran out they were just wet, standing in front of Mrs. Milton's famous arborvitae hedge.

"The Ouija board was right," Tricia said, settling down. She expected to get yelled at, Coop could see. But he didn't feel like yelling, never felt like yelling. He just looked at her, looked away, waited for her to be quiet before he led her inside. The two of them slipped up the stairs, step by step past Grandma's door. Tricia's cowboy boots clunked loudly. In the attic she dropped her bag on Hodge's bunk.

"Soaked," she said too loudly.

"This is the attic," Coop said.

"Drowned," she said. She unfastened her shirt so that her bra showed whitely. "I think I need a towel or something."

Coop slunk downstairs. He could hear Grandma coughing mildly in her room, awake.

Upstairs, the liar Tricia said, "There're only three Vanderhoops in Seattle."

Coop watched her dry her hair. He said, "My grandmother's downstairs." He would make Tricia leave. "You can't stay." He made himself cold.

Tricia didn't notice, or maybe did. She said, "You were the first boy to ever really listen to me."

Coop sat by her. "Well, anyway, you have to go."

Tricia hugged him, got him wet with rain. She kissed his neck and suddenly buried herself there. She fired sentences: "I was so sad. Daddy thought you must have really. He said, *You are going to see Doctor Burke!* You were going to leave anyway, Coop. I didn't know what to do. What was I going to do? I mistook the feeling, maybe. I never felt anything like that before except in a *disaster,* a *tornado,* forty feet of *snow,* flood takes the *barn,* horses loose in *town,* fire in the *silo,* all that with my *mommy.* Here's a secret: I'm crazy, okay?" Tricia sat up, opened her shirt sleeves to expose bandages white as her bra. Coop looked away from them, too.

Grandma's door opened, her footsteps patted down the front stairs.

Tricia said, "I never was *in love* before."

They kissed a plain kiss. Tricia felt strong and big in his arms and her shirt was wet and her hair was dripping. She *loved* him. Still, Coop wanted her to leave. But he couldn't get it out, couldn't phrase it, couldn't get past the place in his throat that stopped him. So he took up her wrist, the other difficult thing: "What?"

"I fell in the barn. I fell through glass."

"Always lying," Coop said.

Tricia sniffed and shivered and Coop didn't at first know she was crying.

He held her gently and put his face in her hair and they were secretly in the attic at Grandma's where Hodge had done the same, put his face in her hair and patted her back and let her weep without saying not to, surprised he felt so much affection for her and so little lust.

Coop ate dinner with Grandma. Good thing she was grumpy; she wouldn't much miss his company tonight. In the kitchen after the meal he put together a hasty plate of food, then banged up the back stairs. He found Tricia lying on her stomach in Hodge's bunk, reading *Tess of the D'Urbervilles* so intently over her elbows that she didn't notice him come in.

He watched her eat—she really did eat like a ranch hand—pleased he could feed her. They whispered about how her father was going to slaughter her, about the three separate buses to get here. Coop said, "I have to leave Thursday."

"Thursday!" Tricia said, too loudly.

Coop thought he better go downstairs. Thursday would be fine with him.

He spent an hour with Grandma in front of the TV—yawning dramatically, stretching. When Ed Sullivan was over—early as that—he said good night.

Then lay with Tricia under the covers in Grandma's attic, clothes on. No one was going to go to sleep. No one was going to say anything. At length, Tricia took her boots off and pressed Coop's feet with her toes. The wind blew hard in the tops of the big trees on Boylston Avenue. Change of weather, as Coop's dad might say.

All but asleep, Tricia said, "You looked so scared and pretty coming up the driveway."

In the morning Grandma said twice how she trusted Coop. And he was in for a treat: Theophilus DuPont's family cottage in the Cascades. The two of them could fish and hike and if Coop didn't like Theophilus (and not everybody did like Theophilus, said

Grandma, though she herself did), Coop could easily enough go off in the woods awhile and contemplate nature, as Grandma knew he loved to do. Perhaps they'd see elk, or bear, or bobcat.

Coop twitched and wriggled listening to her. When she went to dress for work he gathered a breakfast for Tricia, trotted upstairs with it.

"I'm going with you," was all she said.

"You're going back to the bus," Coop said. He'd never been so forceful.

But Grandma left for work, and when Theophilus pulled up honking in his '57 T-Bird, both Coop and Tricia bounded off the porch. Theophilus didn't look ready to fish or track bobcats. He sported white pants and blue blazer like a kid off to prep school. His hair was shaved in back, long in front, combed high. He grinned when he saw Tricia, put his finger to his lips—our little secret. He said, "We've got one stop to make."

The one stop was to pick up one Helen, a girl only slightly older than Tricia and entirely different, her rich hair permed into ringlets, her nails polished red, eye makeup, lipstick, a loud barking laugh, a voluptuous build. "Greetings, greetings, greetings," Helen said, flouncing to the car.

Theophilus drove as if he were in a race: a hundred miles an hour on the freeway, fast as hell on the sharp turns that took them up and up and into the Cascade Mountains north and east of Seattle, drinking martinis all the while from one thermos after the next pulled from under the seats. Helen held her hair down and shrieked with delight at every drifting curve, daintily holding a crystal glass. Tricia laughed, too. She kept a hand on Coop's thigh (he a hand on hers, too), did not refuse the alcohol offered, shared Theophilus's extra martini glass with Coop.

The "cottage" turned out to be an imposing stone-and-log mansion in a huge meadow at the end of a long two-track trail. A ridge of mountain peaks loomed westward. Miles to the north an enormous glaciated hump of a mountain presided solitarily.

Gaily, mock tour guide, Theophilus said, "Mount Baker, ladies and gentlemen. One of our Pacific volcanoes. And I'd like to request some sobriety here; you are standing on holy ground, spiritual ground." From the breast pocket of his blazer he pulled a thick joint, lit it, said, "The ancestral reefer."

The cottage tour was at breakneck speed, pure proprietary boredom on Theophilus's part: hand pumps, elegant outhouses, two kitchens, two dining rooms, ten bedrooms—eleven if you counted the loft over the four-car garage. In the grand beam-and-stained-glass living room Theophilus put Jimi Hendrix on a hidden hi-fi, blastingly loud.

"Lunch," Theophilus said. He passed out small black capsules, large white pills. "Black beauties," he shouted over "Purple Haze." Helen ate her pills eagerly, began to dance.

"Black beauties is *speed*," said Tricia. But she ate the capsule, sipped from the new martini Theophilus poured. The white pill had *Rorer 714* stamped on it.

"Only way to stay awake in the woods," Theophilus shouted. "Don't worry. Quality material. Comes on slowly. The quaalude keeps the edge off the meth. Later we'll do some further downs if adjustments are required!"

Coop ate his pills, too. Geronimo, and what the hell.

Helen kept dancing, draped comically on Theophilus, who sat at the great kitchen table. Pretty soon he plunged his face into her big breasts, waggled his head, making her laugh. He came up for air, shouted, "Helen and me, youngsters, are madly in love."

"Coop and I, too," Tricia shouted over the music.

'Scuse me while I kiss the sky!

Theo shouted, "You two should hike on back to the guest cabin. You're guests, right?"

Purple haze!

Outside in the silence of birdcall and breezes Coop and Tricia walked briskly down a pair of tracks maybe half a mile to a small house. Theophilus had called it a cabin, but it wasn't a cabin, it was a miniature stone villa perched at the edge of a sheer ridge with a plain view of Baker and a jagged string of other peaks. They sat on rocking chairs on the cabin porch, rocked hilariously fast, jumped up laughing at once and into the moss yard, where Tricia eluded Coop's hug, ran.

Past the cabin the trail got fainter, headed higher, up and up. They sweated, marched, climbed up rocks, made a high ridge within a half hour, energized. The hard climb precluded talk, but when they sat at the height of the ridge and looked back out over the world (Rainier visible in the distance to the south, and Mount Adams farther, St. Helens farther yet, but Baker to the north so close you could spit to it), the whole glorious picture seemed reducible to words and the words came fast and seemed profound beyond possibility.

"It's very hot," Coop said. "It's very bright."

"I wish this moment could last forever," Tricia said.

And Coop said, "When I look at you, all I can think about is the way you told me your poems and how you were in bed with me and how I thought this was what love is like and how you fucked me up with your father."

"Do you want to see?" Tricia said. She rolled up her flannel sleeves and put her wrists, the adhesive tape, to her mouth, pulling with difficulty while Coop went on:

"I respect Tad and I just wish I could have ended up better with him because he taught me so much and there was no reason for him not to like me and you made up that bullshit and no matter how I think about it I can't make sense of it why did you tell him that? Last night you said because you're crazy but that's ridiculous.

Even if you're crazy as you say there's some reason you do everything so why did you do that? I think it's because you are afraid of me if you want to know the truth I didn't know this till right now but now I see that it was because you were afraid of being in love and thought being in love with me was such a powerful feeling that something must be wrong. I didn't know this till now."

"See?" And Tricia showed him her wrists. Not much worse than bad scratches, really. Five or six inches up and down her forearm, already well healed. "It's nothing much. I was just trying to make a statement, as my father said."

"What statement is that? I mean, since when is trying to kill yourself a statement of any kind?"

"He means like I'm trying to say how sad I am about things like about growing up without Mommy and having these brothers that are so distant and cold really and about how Daddy doesn't talk unless about his stupid heifers and about how I just want to be like Mommy . . . "

"But a statement is saying something, it's when you say something with your mouth, you know like, Today is a beautiful day. That's a statement and what you did wasn't a statement it was an act and you wanted to die."

"No, look."

"So you didn't cut very far. Still, who could cut themself like that who wasn't trying to do something very serious? Are you sad? Are you depressed? Do you think you are really crazy?"

"Sometimes I'm depressed, yeah, I think that's exactly right and everything seems still and hot and oppressive and almost sitting on my shoulders and the idea of doing all the things I've been thinking of seems impossible, you know, I can barely sleep and all night I'm thinking about how I'm going to organize my notebook and fix my room and write a letter to my roommate for college and ride Seven-Up all day and then the sun finally comes up and all I want to do is sleep and even that's not good enough and I think of riding and I can't even get the right clothes on and then I'm downstairs and Daddy's trying to get me to help him do something and the idea of just opening the door seems . . . "

"But cutting yourself, that's a pretty direct action, I mean, you can't clean your room but you can find razor blades and . . . "

"It wasn't razor blades it was a stupid butter knife or something so you can see I wasn't very serious and Daddy's right I just wanted attention. Till I got it, then I wish I never had to talk to him. And suddenly, I mean the wrists, you know, gave me total energy, total energy like now and I ran all the way to town and got the bus and just left easily as that. To come to you. So just shut up."

"I get really like that too sometimes, really not sad but frozen in syrup or something like that. It's fucking beautiful here. Do you feel anything from that black beauty yet?"

"I don't think so."

"I feel good, I mean really great. Like the way I want to be. You make me feel the way I want to feel."

"I'm not afraid of that either. I can't believe you said I'm afraid of being in love. I told you I was in love with you. I am in love. I feel good too. Don't you want to *do* something? Let's *do* something. It's the black beauties. Like horses inside."

They laughed at that and stood up and looked out over the ridge, threw pebbles endlessly off the edge of the earth, standing close, so their shoulders and hips touched, then turning so they were back to back, shoulder blades to shoulder blades, butt to butt. Then turning so the other sides were touching, then turning face to face, chest to chest, knee to knee. They made ten turns this way, kissing perfunctorily when their faces met, very seriously turning, very very slowly, as if performing an important rite. At last they stopped shoulder blades to shoulder blades, butt to butt and watched the world two directions and talked more and rapidly.

Tricia said, "Do you think love is from the past, like from a past life and that we were lovers before or friends at least? Is that love at first sight?"

And at the same time Coop spoke and they both just talked words with their mouths pointing in opposite directions hearing each other but both talking, answering each other's queries while hearing the next query or the answer to the last, two people back to back talking about the nature of love.

Then Trish said, "Turn." And they turned one quarter. Then "Turn," and they turned face to face. Then "Kiss," and they kissed, but not perfunctorily, long and deep and mouths dry.

"Drink," Trish said. And they never laughed though there was humor in it, but seriously hurried down the path to the brook they'd walked alongside and drank. They put their faces in the water and drank and it was so cold but Coop took off his shoes and put his feet in. Tricia took her shirt off and her bra and then her shoes and one sock and her white jeans and her underpants and stepped into the little sandy pool by Coop, shoulder to shoulder with him, hip to hip. "Turn," she said. Coop turned to her and though this was funny neither of them laughed but kissed a long time. "Turn," Tricia said. And they turned shoulder to shoulder, looking straight ahead. "Take off your clothes," Tricia said in the same voice, like the instructions for a job and Coop took his pants off and his shirt. "Turn," Tricia said. Naked butt to naked butt. "Turn." And "Turn" again. Face to face, kind of rigid, very funny, still not laughing, smiling while kissing, lips made hard by the smiling, then licking each other's lips and faces and finally laughing and then Tricia pulling him down into the moss and pine needles and feet in the water (she wearing one sock) they kissed and

Coop got for the first time ever with a girl a hard-on that did not embarrass him and Tricia pulled at him and he kissed her neck at her clavicle and they licked each other and kicked at the water and the thing was how much fun it was. She kind of climbed on him and pushed at him and his hard-on went inside her and she was wet-warm and tender and his feet in the water were cold and wet and his heart pounded through him and hers through her and met at their serious lips and he held onto her bottom and she slithered very slowly and like snakes they slithered till she said a noise and was breathing very hard and Coop pulled himself out and came in the boundary between them, her skin, his. And they kissed more till Tricia said, "Turn," but they were lying down so the turn put them side by side looking up at the sky and "Turn," she said again so they were butt to butt and "Turn" again so Coop was lying more or less on top of her and looking into her eyes, the darkest and most open he'd seen them. She said, "I love you."

And Coop said, "I love you."

And Tricia said, "Turn," and they turned a different way so Coop could kiss her thighs and kiss her where she was so wet and so she could suckle at him as naturally as a calf might its mother and said "Turn" and they kissed and fucked again and "Turn," when they were done. The joking was not the kind that hides feeling but an intimate joking and very funny without a single laugh.

They left their clothes and bounded back up to the high ridge and sat in a kind of familiarity neither had known before and looked at and touched each other familiarly and as they wished and talked seriously about love and the role of sex in love and the effect of love on sex and identified the new familiarity. It was very hard not to talk, to only look out at the mountains. Baker just there like a great being. And in the hot sun the two of them naked with crawly fingers and lips kissing and any number of times came and went that might have been the end and time to get dressed though if you didn't stop it was not the end of making love. "Turn," Tricia said, which had become hilarious.

But there was a way to laugh with your body, to communicate hilarity with each muscle, and that's what Coop and Tricia did while looking outwardly intent and deeply sober, face to face, watching the mountains two different directions, each over the other's sleek shoulder, tossing words like pebbles into the sky below.

6

The work I've done, for one thing: the path to the river, the grass in the front yard, the new big windows in the living room, the trees behind us thinned to aspens with trunks so white and straight it's like a chapel. I like beyond reason the bench we built from floor planks, I like the plants that live thereon and how the circle stains made by wet clay pots have intersected over years, how the sun falls there all day. The kitchen counter, stone, upon which I've rolled dough a thousand times. (Brother, when Mad and I moved in that counter was a sheet of plywood with contact paper layered on.)

The location, for another, this river that I know the miles of and the inches. The big rocks, the boulders, the black pool that changes yearly (though always cold to swim in), the way our long driveway turns at the boxcar rock. I'm going to leave this?

Madeline has beat her way through our bad week. Today she's in blue jeans and has her hair braided elegantly, strands of gray, strands of black, equal-equal. She almost smiles at me, lets me in again. We've had some good years together. I've done my community service for the morning, raked leaves six hours in the cemetery, got up early. And Madeline has just settled a big case—won it—with a single phone call.

After lunch she's got a leg over the arm of the armchair my sister Cindy gave us and she's lounging and looking at me simply again. I like her ease, the way her smile climbs one side of her face then the other.

"Come sit," says she.

And I do.

"Cripes," says she.

"Congrats," says I. We're talking about the work she's just put in, the six solid weeks, the upwards of *four hundred seventy* grand she just earned.

"That Milton Fairfield is a crafty, creepy lawyer," she says, nodding her head, then shaking it. "He's got this way of sneaking it past everyone even when one knows him. He plays the rube, pretends to swallow all one's bait, then in front of the judge this inarticulate, quivering, jittery mass for whom one's got total pity and to whom one has even made concessions out of that pity pulls himself up and makes a speech like Abraham Lincoln."

"There was snow back up in the canyon last night."

"I beat him back, knocked him down; one could almost see him deflate. And the beauty of it is, sweetie, that he didn't even know it till the middle of his bloody summation. Too late, Milt."

"Took two trout."

"Maybe now they'll clean up their act a little." She sits there in satisfaction and I think of all the years I've known her. She kicks her foot like a schoolgirl.

"Plenty to think about," I say.

"Though I oughtn't to gloat."

"Snowed on me."

"Did you even bring matches this time?"

"You can gloat if you want. You deserve to gloat. That's a lot of cash, Wonder Woman."

Outdoors the sky is crisp and blue. Soon there will be ice in the river and the booming of floes at night will commence. There's that, too.

"What shall we do with ourselves today?" Mad says.

"You feel like a hike?"

"I don't feel like walking as far as the kitchen, even."

"We could play cards."

With a smile: *"Never."*

"Go get some lunch in town? Go into Aspen?"

"Let's go to the Jerome!"

We look at each other briefly and laugh. It's our history we laugh about, Hodge, a certain hot afternoon seventeen years past, me sitting in the window of the Hotel Jerome in knee braces, drinking Jim Beam solo, only slowly aware that someone was looking at me through the glass: Madeline, whom I hadn't seen in twelve years. And let's make it very clear, brother: I'd not seen her since the day we buried you. Since Madeline and I and Boyd Friendly and Tricia Thomas and Bailey Shapiro buried you and stood there over your grave and held hands and made our pact: we would not tell anyone, not ever. We would beat the *pigs* that way. We would not tell and we would keep you alive that way forever.

I beg you, bro, just think of the emotion of this appearance on the street in front of the Jerome. Madeline. Bad Boyd's Madeline, fresh from law school, all on her own. There I was sitting drunk in that famous hotel window, furiously conversing with you in my head (you recall every damn word, I trust). And suddenly there was this tall woman looking at me, willowy Madeline, unsmiling, just staring at me from the bottom of her crafty soul, hardly even surprised. And then she was rushing inside, full of hot energy, newly a lawyer, scared to death they were going to find out she was party to your crimes, brother, and Boyd's. She blasted down to Aspen to find me, knew from reading tarot she'd find me easily, knew from reading sports magazines just where I was. And once in Aspen, where else but the Jerome? She floated inside on her cloud of karma and we talked intensely and hugged intensely and remembered in passionate whispering our day with you, our last day with you, your last day. I'd made myself forget all that. But Madeline was there, and now there was someone to share the horror of that secret. And it was the same for her, I think, the horror of our secret, the comfort of my company in that horror. Not love at second sight, as we claimed then, but support under horrific guilt, under the horror of our secret, which was horrible indeed, which was you, bro. We were two from the pact and we could talk about the pact and it was like lifting a stone from my chest, and like lifting a stone from hers (she said) very close to love, so close we named it love. Our history, bro, is *you*. Our love, brother, is *you*. We talked in the Jerome and pretty soon were walking home to my house and pretty soon again we were making love like two people in love, the great stones lifted from our two hearts and made into one, one stone.

Efficient Madeline: within a couple of weeks she nailed a position with the only truly national law firm in Aspen (Dipshit, Mugger and Ace, we called it), passed the Colorado bar first try, kicked ass from the start, within two years left that firm to go it on her own—less money, better cases—rented her little space above the Hennypen Diner in Basalt.

And always—always—she was afraid that somehow it would come out that she had run with Boyd Friendly and Hodge Henry, the Boeing Bombers. She came to Aspen to check on my loyalty, she did: she was accessory to Boeing and maybe worse in other cases I have never heard about, major felonies. Our love, then, was

never innocent, as love must be. I was her connection to a purely
romantic vision of herself as revolutionary. I was her protection
from censure by the bar. I was the Sisyphus who carried the rock
of her horror off her narrow chest, carried it off and off again and
off again and off again giving relief that felt like love. Or was love.

Frank Kobil approved of Maddy like crazy, thought she'd
changed me for the best. Suddenly, my coaching career was born.
One gets on a path like that and things start to seem pretty clear.
Frank as my best man (my only man) handed me a flask to drink
from before the *I do*'s, and Billie made us that elaborate quilt. This
quilt; we still sit under it nights, not safe from guilt or horror.

Madeline swings her feet. She says, "You know, medical records
aren't as private as they used to be."

"Is this a case you're working on?"

"No, but we haven't had a chance to talk, sweetheart. I'm just
curious about what came out in the evaluation down there. That's
all." She's talking about Valley View. She's talking about you,
Hodge.

I just look at her a long while, for the first time knowing what
our marriage is, really knowing. Our marriage is *you*. I say, "I got
awfully close, if you want to know."

She's gazing out the window, getting edgy. At length she says,
"How close is that?"

"Well. Unavoidably close. I'm beginning to see that it's Hodge
at the heart of all this . . . *struggle* I'm having. Maybe at the heart
of yours too."

"I'm not having a *struggle*." Her weather has changed.

Mine too. Outside the chickadees are bombing the feeder I've
set out after first snow: there's another thing. How can I leave the
birds of this forest? I say, "Well. You know what I mean."

"You had sex with Roddy."

She's a lawyer. Has done more work in court than most lawyers.

I'm on the stand, have been on the stand since she smiled and called me over to the couch. I say, "You sound like you're in front of Anstedt."

"When did it start?"

"I'd like to deny this," says I. What I should say is yes, *love*. We made *love*. Roddy has no basis in *you*, brother. Roddy I quite simply love.

"Does that mean you cannot deny it?" She crosses her arms in front of her. Her eyes flash in conquest, not anger.

Quickly I say something stupid in the nature of a lie. I'm overcome not by my wife's accusations but by this truth that has come over me fully articulated for the first time ever: Madeline and I are not in love and never were but are only united by horror, by Hodge Henry. I say, "We kissed on the team bus on the way back from Big Sky, I don't know, six weeks ago, and that's it." But Roddy and I did *not* kiss on the bus back from Big Sky, only talked. I'm lying and telling the truth at the same time, my great strength. What of the horror? I should speak of the *horror*. But that would be the truth.

"Lying doesn't help anything, Cooper."

"No, no. That was it, just that, an embarrassment, a momentary embarrassment. To diffuse infatuation."

"Did you use a condom at least? Two?"

"And it worked. We realized the error of our ways." I sound stupid, even to myself.

The prosecution changes tactics: "Don't you find her defensive and insecure? Isn't she always correcting you? She likes men a little too much, don't you think? Don't you find her a bit *brittle?* Isn't Claudio a baron or something? With *millions?* Isn't her hair bleached just a little too *blond?* She's too smart for you, isn't she? You think you have a cute little jock to *spank* or whatever queer fantasies you're up too, but that woman has an intellect—she's got designs." Mad hears herself getting shrill. She breathes, starts in again calmly: "Coop, what we've got in Veronica Manor is a slumming highbrow who'll soon grow tired of you." Then—forget it—she loses lawyerly control as she hears how wrong she is and remembers all the years of my Roddy-on-the-road stories: "Even if you do go with her to every gallery and grotto on every team trip to every little mountain city in the world!"

"Whoa, hey, sorry. Madeline, don't attack Roddy. It's me. It's you and me. It's the Jerome—do you remember the Jerome?" My God, I'm one foot poised over the abyss.

But Mad can't hear me now. It's like I'm talking to you, Hodge, the words, filled with their horror and truth, fall silent. Madeline switches tactics yet again, says, "Veronica Manor! She needs approval and it's not hard to get approval naked in someone's king-size bed! Aren't you abusing your power? Your *power?*"

"Mad, come on. It was a kiss, a silly little kiss on Frank's couch, a mistake. Let's speak of the Jerome."

"Frank's couch? I thought you said it was the team bus." Forget about courtroom aplomb: "And *what's this crap about the Jerome! We're not talking about hotels, Cooper!*"

And I lose my temper, too: *"Yes it's hotels! Why didn't you tell me you changed hotels?"* And thus do I skip past the truth I've discovered and land firmly and loudly on the petty.

Madeline floats to her elegant feet and glides so smoothly across the house to the kitchen it's like she's on wheels. Efficiently, she puts on the water kettle. I watch the birds outside at the feeders (Stellar's jay, junco, many sparrows, the chickadees, a cautious gray jay) and can't quite get my breath.

After a long silence Mad calls lightly: "Yeah, let's go over to Aspen for lunch. The Jerome would be fine, if that's what you want."

"Mad," I say. I get up and get near enough her in the kitchen so I don't have to sound like I'm shouting, no nearer. And loving my house and my woods and the birds of my forest and the stream and in horror of the truth I say the next lie: "I'm happy here with you."

"Happy," says she. She's putting a tea bag in a U.S. Ski Team cup, pouring water over it, stirring honey in, stirring, stirring. She's got big thoughts tracking in her head, but not the big thoughts in mine, the horror that is our love, that is you, brother.

We lean on the counters in silence, Madeline sipping her tea till it's gone, a long time, the time of a very hot cup of tea.

I say, "It's like this book I got from that book club in grade school. Scholastic Book Service. We used to order paperbacks by the dozens. The title of this particular book always escapes me. But it was about some boys and their time machine. There was a dinosaur on the cover, and a blond kid running away. And that blond kid was me, see. And in the book he had a big brother named Owen. I still recall that name: Owen."

Madeline gazes steadily at me, listening closely but thinking hard, trying to get a few more moves ahead of me—what's all this about childhood science fiction?

"And the two of them build a time machine out of old radios and egg crates. And they go back in time and have amazing adventures with the dinosaurs right to the minute Owen gets trampled and crushed and killed by one. I think that's what happens. And this kid, our hero, he rushes to the time machine and goes home upset as hell and all around him there's the same old house and home, but no sign of his brother. The kid's got their bedroom to himself now. He's an only child in this new world. And the worst thing is he's starting to forget about Owen, though he tries to hang on. Then he does forget, only gets twinges like when the principal of their shitty school says something on the P.A. system like 'Owing to inclement weather,' and the kid sits up in his seat and feels the loss but can't say what it is. Not anymore he can't, because if you get killed by a dinosaur before you're born you never existed."

7

Grandma yelled up in the morning that she was on her way, not to get up. But Coop and Tricia were wide awake already, up. Up and buzzing hard. Up and over the top. Tomorrow meant Coop's flight to JFK and then the drive home to Connecticut in a car with his father and that had been the subject of carefully stifled, ungodly loquacious, and tearfully poignant talk for the last four hours. Before that the subject had been comparative anatomy along with congratulatory analysis of their lovemaking compatibility punctuated by exercises and experimentation therein, lots of hard breathing and chortling and thumps on the floor that they hoped would not wake Grandma. The effect of Theophilus's killer black beauties had outlasted that of his Quaaludes ten to one.

They heard Grandma's noisy departure, heard the car leave the drive. Their nudity had taken on a certain chummy comfort, so naked they went downstairs, ate their first meal in twenty-four hours. And for the first time in all those hours there seemed not much to say. Thursday Coop would be home and Dad would be calling the barbershop and Tricia would be on the bus to Montana to get ready for college and both of them would be in maximum trouble.

"This is what they mean by *crashing*," Tricia said.

"Let's sleep," Coop said.

"I saw the greatest minds of my generation . . ." Tricia intoned, and kept going, though Coop ignored her. Upstairs they lay on their backs in a bottom bunk, hands familiarly upon each other, thin blanket pulled up.

"What else are we supposed to do?" Coop said.

"I could help you find your loser brother."

A long silence. Coop thought of his family in Connecticut, how every kid had cried when Hodge was gone. "He's not really in the CIA," Coop said.

"No joke."

"He's actually just a regular draft dodger."

"Don't worry, J. Edgar, no one believed you."

"My grandmother knows where he is."

They lay there looking at the boards of the top bunk.

Trish said, "We'll make her talk!"

"She'd never."

"What about that letter?"

"Aw, there's nothing in the letter."

"Have you looked in the trash?"

"He's not exactly that dumb, you know."

"But there's got to be a postmark, right?"

Some small portion of the hilarity of yesterday's romp in the mountains came back and Coop and Tricia raced and wrestled naked down the stairs to Grandma's desk. Coop stabbed at the thick envelope on top of the pile, opened it, pulled out Grandma's ticket to Tokyo. Then his own ticket home. Tricia snapped this from him, flung it fluttering across the room where it landed neatly on a wing-backed chair. Coop found the letter fast. Tricia read with a finger in her mouth, tousled hair. Coop didn't want to be apart from her again ever.

She said, "He sounds petulant and mean."

"He's smart."

"And he can't spell." She read carefully. "He sounds unhappy. He sounds dangerous and quite crazy, if you ask me."

"He's really dedicated," Coop said.

"I like him," Tricia said.

"He's no one to mess with," Coop said.

Tricia laughed. She said, "You dope, he's in Chicago!"

8

Kid-brother Jeremy calls from New York to tell me he's seen me in *Sports Illustrated,* calls to congratulate me. He's gleaned the wrong message from the spread (he also wants to let me know that Mom's glad I've been working on you, bro—this kid's almost magically uninformed and misinformed and disinformed about everything, so distant from all of us in age and temperament—Mom won't tell him bad news, ever; it was Cindy who told him about Morton's HIV, and I think in the same conversation Cindy who told him Morton is gay, ten years out of the closet, oblivious Jeremy). So I drive into Aspen, too embarrassed to show myself anywhere in Basalt, furtively buy *Sports Illustrated,* throw it on top of groceries.

And in the parking lot of the Food Supreme I search the bags for the magazine, whip it open. Jesus, Hodge. Baldwin with "the late" Frank Kobil, Baldwin with Roddy and Julie, Baldwin with the rising young alpine stars. Always there are skis in the pictures, though the pictures were taken in summer. The *SI* photographers set up every shot—nothing spontaneous about any of it. A quote from Kobil: "We're a family year-round." All the supposed candids of us supposedly playing softball. You think Baldwin ever played softball in his life? You think he ever fucking played catcher anywhere, with that face? Hodge, listen to me, they had to convince him to take his tie off for the ball game. He played catcher so they could get a shot of him behind every skier on the team, figure out who was hot when the rosters got announced, the jobs. But here's what bugs me: they knew who *wasn't* hot already, weeks before any adventures I might have had at the True Value. And weeks before Frank's fall and doom. The imagery is striking. I'm a scowling face in Baldwin's armpit. *New USST Alpine Director steps up to bat,* says the caption. And that's how I find out.

That evening, a Thursday, Baldwin calls me to congratulate himself. He's all friendly and bubbly and conciliatory, as if it's he who must concede, as if he's been handed something awful and ponderous he can't refuse because of his sense of duty. Like I'm the lucky one. "I'd like you to be my Conditioning Coach," he says after some mewling about Frank Kobil. "You know, go on over to Maine with the troops and get fall training underway."

"I'm already set for that, Rick," says I. "I've had that written in pen in my date book since I bought the thing last January, *Rick.* It's one of those *Month-at-a-Glance* deals. I've been looking at Maine right there in November for close to a year, *Rick.* I'm going to Maine, I was always going to Maine. As Frank Kobil's assistant I was going to Maine. As Interim Alpine Director I was going to Maine. My contract is up December tenth, *Rick.* Your contract, if you'll look above the bottom line, says December tenth, too, *Rick,* unless I miss my guess. So I'm good till then. You'll just need someone new for race season. Is all. Good night, *Rick.*" Or at least that's what I should have said, and not so loudly.

December tenth, Hodge. That's Mom and Dad's anniversary, too—small stinking world. I don't forget, because just mentioning the date to Baldwin makes the phone ring the second I hang up with him. I'm more than half out of breath from the tumult of talking to the guy, and it's Mom, set on stun. No hello, no small talk, just this: "Coop, what have you heard from Hodge?"

I tell her, "Mom, nothing." I'm breathing hard, like a horse in a cold river.

She says, "What are you huffing and puffing about? Have you been smoking?"

"Just came in from a run, Ma."

"What does Hodge say?"

"Mom, I haven't talked to him. Hodge is . . . gone."

"Well, then, that's it. I might as well tell you. Mr. Czako is already at work. He's going to find Hodge. All this trouble you could have avoided."

"What'd you pay for this, Ma?"

"Every cent will be money you could have inherited, believe me, Anthony. And Mr. Czako is at work already. I gave him all the photos he needs and he's having them computerized so as to show what Hodge looks like now. Furthermore, he's heading off for Dingle, Ireland, next week, so I'd suggest warning your big brother that a visitor is on the way. Mr. Czako is very smart and he'll leave no stone unturned."

"Ah, Ma. Come on. Who is this guy? Are you sure you can trust him? Dingle? Jimmy Hoffa? You didn't pay him in advance, did you?"

This is how bad it's gotten. Oh, God, Dingle. I didn't even know there was a Dingle. There's not a Dingle, is there? That was another of my little . . . routines. I let it drop one night at Christmas, like, making a toast: to Hodge in Dingle! Like I was letting something slip. Evil. Oh, and you've got to imagine Mom, our own Mom, the cool, collected woman who guided the PTA through every crisis, Mom who raised five kids on *choices* and *responsibility,* Mom who talked two renowned ski coaches out of kicking her son off their teams. Mom the calm, Mom the brilliant, Mom the trustworthy, panicked: "Trust Mr. Czako? He's not the one I need to worry about trusting! It's certainly not as if *you* are going to raise a finger to help me. You're just not going to *help*, are you?"

She's not herself, Hodge. She's over the top. She hangs up on me, and again the phone rings immediately. I let the machine get it, thinking I can't possibly stand anymore. I'm making these foof noises, still breathing like a bellows, staring at the machine as it talks in my voice and beeps. It's Roddy, gentle Roddy. She seems so serene. Into the machine she says, "This is a call for Mr. Henry." She's discreet. She says, "I don't know if this is a big deal or not, Mr. Henry, but Claudio Abruzzi's coming to Aspen."

I pick up. "Well, Ms. Manor. Why would Mr. Abruzzi's arrival in Aspen be a big deal?"

"Oh, Coop. Oh, Mr. Henry. He knows. I know we said we wouldn't talk till Maine, but . . . "

"Claudio?"

"Your *wife* apparently called him, three in the morning, before I was even back from the funeral and told him I don't know what. Oh, Coop, what a mess. But, really, no really, I'm so pleased you told her."

"She just knew," I say.

"You mean you didn't tell her?"

"It just kind of got . . . obvious. I guess."

"I told Claudio the whole story."

"The whole thing?"

"Oh, Coop. He said he'll punch you in the eye. He's on his way to Aspen, anyway. Or actually, he's *in* Aspen by now. Are you okay? You sound . . . out of breath."

"I just talked to my mother."

"That's what phone machines are for."

"Claudio doesn't worry me."

Long pause. Roddy says, "I'm feeling just . . . *tragic* about you."

"Why so tragic?"

"You don't want me, it turns out."

"No, I do. I really do. But it's not so easy, is it?"

"Well, it could be."

"I thought you and Claudio had . . . reconciled."

"I never said that."

"Your visit. You were so distant."

"I just didn't want to stress you out there in the hospital."

Now I'm the one who's quiet. One minute, two. Finally I say, "Really, Rod, why is Claudio coming to Aspen?"

"I thought you'd already know."

"Ah, shit." Newsflash: Claudio is going to be Rick Baldwin's Executive Associate, Hodge. That's why. An Italian skier with whom I've split my races for an entire career, and whose career I've watched go two Olympics longer. Two gold and a silver to my bronze.

"Also, he's planning to kill you."

"I'll kill him right back."

"Ah, Mr. Henry. Let's do what we talked about. Let's take the team to Maine. We'll make it the last splash. Let's spend the month and help the transition happen and just see what's next. Okay? I have lots of ideas for us. You could come to Burlington with me in January. Perfect, right? I'll finish my course work, pass my orals, write my dissertation, and you'll ski. Right? And we'll ski together. We can do that backcountry telemark thing we always talk about. In fact, it's all I've been thinking about. Let's go to the fall workout in Maine and be together, then let's both quietly quit. I'm through. You're through. We don't have to take it too seriously. We can bunk together, Coop. You'll have two black eyes from Claudio and we can just pretty much hide out. *Non ha l'ottimo artista alcun concetto . . . !*"

"You are killing me."

"All you have to do is act, Coop. And I'm going to tell you something here: I love you. That's all I can do about it. I have loved you a long time. I love you, okay? Are you listening to me? I feel like I just learned what the word means. I love you, boy."

"A month in Maine."

"That's it."

"Do I have to get a note from my wife?"

Roddy's quiet a long time. Finally she says, "That's really mean."

"I'm just trying to say it's complicated."

"I'm just trying to say it's *not* complicated. You want out? You act."

"I do love you, you know. A lot."

"Listen, I'm serious. Claudio's coming to Aspen."

We get off the phone after another fraught silence—maybe Rod's crying at the other end—and I'm just sitting there frozen in confusion, heart in my ears, tears in my eyes. The damn phone rings *again*.

It's Dad. He's pissed off, not hiding his anger. "Coop, goddamn. Your mother is in tears here, and while I'll be the first to confess that her histrionics are unproductive, I'm about sick and tired of your goddamn baiting her. No, let me finish. Coop, your brother means an awful lot to us as do all of you kids and it would seem to me to be a matter of common goddamn decency for him to send along a note and for you to facilitate the process to the very best of your abilities. But you, you take the goddamn phone off the hook!" His whole life is a board meeting.

So I hang up on him. And the phone rings immediately. I let the machine take it; I am not talking to any corporate managers tonight, not even retired corporate managers. But it's Roddy again. "Pick up," she says. "Just quick."

I pick up.

She says, "I just wanted to say I love you one more time, Coop, and farewell."

I say, "The good-bye part's not necessary." I'm thinking of her on Frank Kobil's couch, and I don't want to lose her. I say, "I don't want to lose you."

"Act," she says soberly.

We're just silent for a couple of expensive cross-Atlantic minutes until she firmly says good-bye.

And the black damn phone rings *again*. It's Madeline. "Who've you been talking to?" she says.

"Phone won't stop ringing."

"Charlie Merck is suing us."

"What?"

"Charlie Merck has instituted a civil suit, Coop. I just got the papers."

"Ah, Christ."

She's got clients, can't talk, just wanted to drop a little bomb. She'll be home by seven. Wants dinner ready at seven.

"You called Claudio," I say. I need to be angry.

"Oh, I see. You know. So it's Roddy you've been talking to."

"It's just . . . "

"I've got work," says she. Slam.

The phone rings yet *again*. It's someone tentative, a woman: "Coop Henry?"

"Mom?"

"No, no, Coop, it's Linda? Frank's daughter? Linda *Kobil* Orichibi?"

"Oh, Linda, Linda, hello."

"Coop, I just wanted to let you know that Dad has left you his car in his will? And we thought it might be best if you picked it up now while we're around and so you won't have to wait? I mean if it's convenient for you?"

"Ah, Linda, you don't have to." She's being nice, I know it. They think I wrecked my car from grief.

"He wanted it this way? And you can come get it right away if you like—Sis has gone on home? Katie? I've got to leave shortly, myself? Everything was neat and in order, as you might expect. We won't be able to transfer the title till later, in a couple of months, after probate? Katie and I thought you could make use of the car now, though? Hope it's true?"

"Linda, I don't know what to say. You're awfully nice." She's awfully nice.

"You were Dad's best friend, Coop. He always talked about you and admired you."

She's awfully, awfully nice. The things she could say. We talk a little longer, sigh a little over her dad. The car she's going to leave in the lot behind Madeline's office for me. Enormous green Mercedes, brand new last summer. Thank you Frank.

The second we're off, the phone rings again.

Rick Baldwin: "Listen Coop," he says. "Let's just be friends, what d'ya say?"

"I say pretty much fuck you, Rick." My voice breaks, my emotion pours forth, immediately I'm Dad: "I'm sorry, but that's pretty much what I got to say, at least at the moment. You can't ski, you can't coach, you're the wrong man for the job. You've been jockeying and manipulating since the day I met you. My take on this is pretty much, fuck you. Rick. That's pretty much all of it. In a nutshell."

"Well, Coop. We need you. So when you feel better . . . "

I hang up. The phone doesn't ring. The phone doesn't ring at all, and Madeline does not come home at seven (though I'm boiling spaghetti, heating sauce from a jar) and the house is quiet as trouble itself, quiet like a mad dog slipping up behind, quiet as a turd on the lawn.

I'm not sure what to do with myself, sort of pace around, stare at the spaghetti bubbling in the pot, make a salad, wait for the phone to ring again. It does not. The spaghetti's ready and I make up two big plates. I grate parmesan, dress the salad, set the table, serve up a hell of a pretty meal in a fury. I do not have a beer but just stare at the bookshelves a long, long time, dinner served.

Then there're lights in the drive and it's Madeline home, and I'm all resolution, I'm going to tell her: Coop Henry is going to Maine, to Roddy. I hear her crunching along in the leaves, then I hear her stop, and she stops a hell of a long time. Then the front door takes a terrible cracking blow, then another, then flies open behind Claudio's foot. And Claudio's bursting in shouting in Italian, and a little English, something like, *So you say you are a lover!* And Hodge, he's on me and the two of us are all over the house, wrestling, very civilized really, nice solid punches, two old friends, no hair pulling, nothing below the belt, Claudio occasionally spitting "You cocksuck-*er*," no other cursing or yelling, just very quietly rumbling around the house knocking over the heavy coffee table, then the couch, then Maddy's fish tank. We actually roll on the ground with wriggling fish in broken glass and homemade seawater, throwing fists, getting up, wrestling (almost hugging), separating, glaring (he's got deep, dark-brown eyes, hypnotic), leaping back to the fray, punching. I don't know, Hodge. I seem to have retained my talent for fist fighting. I keep saying, "Had enough?"

But Claudio is a rough customer. He keeps his feet, keeps swinging till he finally catches my chin. I reel backwards two steps, three, fall over an end table, land on the floor. I'm just too tired to stand up one more time. Claudio, he's tired too. We gaze at each other long and hard. No one has won, that's clear.

He says, "You are my friend!" This is both a statement of fact and an accusation. And then he staggers out the splintered front door trailing blood from his chin and nose and knuckles.

The spaghetti's on the floor and I'm lying among the bloody strands of it bleeding too, just looking at the ceiling, happily unvanquished, worrying, actually worrying, whether Claudio will stain the seats of his rental car with blood. He always gets the upgrade, always it's a Cadillac with white upholstery.

It's not long before Madeline pops in the front door all merry, ready to forgive, ready to be fed, sees the mess, the trail of Claudio's blood, cries, "What have you done? Cooper Henry? What's happened? What have you done!"

At length and laconically from the floor I say: "*You,* you mean. What have *you* done?"

And it doesn't take her a second: she knows. "Claudio?"

"Claudio."

Maddy appraises me. "Let's talk straight," she says.

Okay, straight. I say, "I'm in love with Roddy."

"Oh . . . *yuck,*" she says.

I try to soften the tone, but it's a harsh goddamn message, croaked from the floor where I lie amid dead fish and flung spaghetti: "I mean, I think I'm love with Roddy. I mean, to the extent I know what that means I'd say I am in love with Roddy."

"Oh Cooper. You are such an . . . immense . . . *bummer! Roddy Manor? Love?*" Madeline doesn't appear angry, only crestfallen, defeated in competition, maybe a little disgusted, crosses her arms over her chest, examines her foot tapping the floor. There's a case to construct.

But first, a dramatic pause. The prosecutor sniffs the air of the room, marches expertly to the oven, flings open its spotted door, slumps at the vision therein, snatches our longest knife out of its wooden block and spears my efforts at garlic bread (which, while Claudio and Coopio did their awful dance, was unsafely in the protection of the oven, burning up).

I have acted. But I take it back: "With you as well," says I.

Tap tap tap. She knocks the bread smoking onto our oaken

cutting board, stabs the knife into the wood (where it quivers), breathes deeply, turns to face me in a posture of infinite leaning patience against the counter, says woefully, "That's a deep consolation, Cooper Henry." She regards me lying there on the floor as long as she can stand it, then shoves her hands into her rabbit-shaped oven mitts, subdues the garlic bread, takes up the long knife, scrapes away blackened crust disconsolately, completely dresses the whole loaf, taking her time. When she's done, she cuts herself a diminutive chunk, crunches into it with her large, perfect teeth.

I take the opportunity to stand, a long process. I say, "Oh, Mad," trying in my tone to convey everything about all the complications between us. I know she understands: that we operate on different planets with different atmospheres, that we don't have enough sex to get an R rating, that we don't even sleep in the same room most nights, that we can't much speak of our work to one another, that we are mired in family histories, family constructs and competitions that we do nothing to dispel. There's the next thing, though, the final straw, and I'm not so sure she understands, and that next thing is you, bro, our stone, our glue.

I sit up, then slowly stand, go to her.

"So," Madeline says. And she means by this that there isn't any rush, really, that we shouldn't be leaping into decisions, that we shouldn't utter the word *divorce*. We stand there in the wreck of our house like survivors of a natural disaster, Jesus, a long time.

"He was awful to look at, wasn't he. . . ," I say.

"I didn't see him, Coop. But it looks like he got his licks in, too."

I'm talking about you, of course, she about Claudio, the Italian Stallion.

We stand there in our miscommunication a long time.

"Are you okay?" Madeline says finally. She steps as close to me as she's been in months and checks the cut on my eyebrow: Claudio's Olympic ring.

"Bucket," I say softly.

"You get in the shower." This sorrowfully.

I say, "First, I guess, I'll clean the house a little." And then the two of us are picking up puny dead fish and pieces of the smashed aquarium and mopping up spaghetti and stacking magazines, all businesslike and still exactly in our relationship (this friendship that is no longer a romance and that has not been a romance for years and maybe wasn't ever), righting the furniture, putting the knickknacks back on their shelves (shelves and shells and figurines need dusting anyway, Mad observes). And nothing has changed really, though it's as if a bright light has been shone upon us and a clarity has come to the house on the river.

We both jump when the phone rings. It's been a night of phone calls, all right. It would be unseemly not to pick up, so I do, dreading all possibilities.

"Anthony Henry?"

Phone sales. Kindly, relieved, I say, "Nah, Christ, do you ever leave a man alone?"

"Mr. Henry, this is Tip Czako. I'm an investigator by contract. Your mother has hired me to find your older brother."

"Oh, Christ."

"And what's happening here is that I pretty much ain't finding him."

A long, long, *very* long pause ensues. I look at Madeline. This, she's not going to like. She looks back, finds my unblinking eye, thinks what she thinks, turns on her heel into her room so as not to hear. I say, "How was Ireland?"

"Ireland? That lie? I didn't go to Ireland. Your big brother was never there. I have him in Chicago. I have him in Seattle. Summer of 1969. And then he's just gone."

"I think that's amazing. You've found out what everyone already knows. How much do you charge to read old newspapers at the library?"

"And, Tony—can I call you Tony?—I have you *with* him in Chicago. And then in Seattle. And that's not from any newspaper. But it's as much as I've got. Except that I have the idea you know some of the answers here."

This day of phone calls. "My brother is dead," says I.

"Dead," says Czako.

"Dead," says I.

"How'd he get that way?" says Czako. He sounds like a nice man, not tough at all, a sweetheart imitating a dick, genuinely concerned though professionally skeptical.

"Well. I don't know for sure that he died," says I, backing away from honesty. "That's just a guess. Just because I have this strong belief that he would have gotten in touch with me if alive." Strong belief? I threw dirt on you, brother, dirt and stones and guns, filled in the hole, mounded the earth, spread leaves around as camouflage, sticks, pinecones.

"That's all I'm going to get from you, isn't it?" says Czako.

"That's all there is," says I.

"Well, son, let me just say this. I've come to the same conclusion. He's dead. In fact, I know quite a little bit more than you're probably prepared to believe I know. But I don't need any more information. What I need is some help telling your mother this truth I've found out."

"Nice try, Mr. Czako."

"Nice try yourself, Tony."

Bang. I hang up, unplug the phone, look for a book—something to read, anything. Mad's in the bathroom, washing up.

Chapter Four

1

Well, bro, I was mistaken. Baldwin's contract starts him immediately. And immediately he's going to Maine to run fall training. My own contract is in force, it's true, but effectively I don't have a job, unless I want to go listen to Baldwin talk dietary fiber and media relations with the skiers. The new snow coach—er, Executive Associate—is Claudio Abruzzi, as everyone knows. Baldwin despite everything has been generous with me, has invited me to use sick leave, to take it easy while gathering paychecks, to *get perspective.*

Perspective I've got plenty of. Here I am in the margins of the Frying Pan Road with my garbage bags and reflective vest, my litter-prong and rake and hoe, trying to get my community service hours in before snow comes. That's perspective.

Plenty to think about as I work, patiently spearing Red Man pouches and diet soda cans, digging out tires and diaper balls and jettisoned porn mags—lovely mornings really, just me alone, doing my penance at the failed end of autumn. I've got a nice pace going, an eye for garbage. I've grown acquisitive; it's an easy lepidoptery. I have a theory that all this trash is the work of one person, a little something tossed out the car window every trip to town for a year and every trip back, and he's got the world looking like the insides of his head. *Perspective.*

And then there's Roddy. Misery, bro, right here in my jacket pocket, folded envelope. Her handwriting like a little boy's, big gnarly script, generous and uneven, everything impeccably spelled:

> *Dear Mr. Henry:* This is hard to write, hard to even bend my thoughts to. But Claudio insists I make a clear break, and I think Claudio is right. The two of us have solved our difficulties. Certainly the little casual fling with you had something to do with that. Claudio is really TALKING to me now, and I am really talking to him. We have resolved to do the COMMUNI-CATION necessary to be together.
>
> Here's the big news: this coming June, Claudio and I will be married, probably in Italy, if my parents can swing the trip. He asked me our first night here in Maine. And I said okay. I believe you have said the same to Madeline, some long years ago. What have we got without COMMITMENT, Mr. Henry?
>
> But enough of that. I know you're already thinking along the same lines, anyway. I hope we will be friends again, all of us.
>
> So let's see. The snow is TERRIBLE. They had rain and flooding and subsequent erosion, then all that froze and it's like skiing on the Grand Canyon. So it's cross training, day after day, which I HATE.
>
> Two girls have come up in downhill. Noriko Asagi is one. Have you read about her? She's faster than I'll ever be again. My knee is DREADFUL. But Maine is lovely, and I quite enjoy being with the women. Mr. Baldwin says I'll make a good coach. He's wrong about that.
>
> Claudio would like to apologize, even if indirectly, for abus-

ing you. He's an angry man and JEALOUS and he is working
on both.

I finished my Michelangelo paper. Won't you be proud
when I publish it! So now I can turn to other subjects for a
few weeks before diving back in. Poor Vittoria!

Non Vi Si Pensa Quanto Sangue Costa!

I'm finally reading a book (I bought it in Aspen years ago!)
called *The Object Stares Back,* by James Elkins. It's about seeing, about how people see or don't see. In one chapter he talks
about how there are images we can't look at, from which we
avert our eyes as if they were not in our control, or at which we
stare too long. He gives Courbet's painting THE ORIGIN OF
THE WORLD as an example. He says he either looks away
from it or looks at it too much. You know that painting? Please
look it up. There is a message in it for you! Elkins talks about
faces, too, how it's hard to bring faces to mind and hard—so
hard—to clearly keep the image of a face in mind.

What are YOU reading?

Good-bye for now.

Sincerely, Veronica M.

Over the Sincerely she's written *I love you,* blue ink over the
black. I'm going to have to find this Courbet painting—get my
message, whatever it might be. And it's *my* face she can't quite see.
I want to believe I know what happened: Claudio insisted she write
the letter, and then insisted on seeing it. Hodge, tell me I'm wrong:
she added the *I love you* after Claudio checked up on her, maybe
added it hastily. And if you read only the words she's cast in capi-
tals, there's a secret communication: TALKING COMMUNICAT-
ING COMMITMENT TERRIBLE HATE DREADFUL JEALOUS.
THE ORIGIN OF THE WORLD, YOU.

Well, maybe not. I put the letter back in my jacket and poke my
litter spear in the mouth of the fiftieth empty Rainier bottle in a

mile (it's one guy, I'm telling you—Rainier Beer's not popular in Colorado—and how many guys you know buy a magazine called *Bung Busters?* Six issues, I find, and avert my eyes for sure). I move along briskly, leave neatly stuffed and tied garbage bags on the shoulder of the road, a couple of miles of them.

Roddy's right. And now engaged, which is what I guess she wanted in the first place. So it's me and Madeline—of course it's me and Madeline—me and Mad forever. She's back in her routine, twelve- and sixteen-hour workdays. And we in ours, like nothing's different. Breakfast together daily. The late news together nightly. She wants me to think about what's next. College coaching? High school? Ski school at the Highlands or maybe Snowmass? Mountain Rescue, professional?

What I'd really like to do is return to something fairly abstract, something I left off years ago, which the more I think about it (*thirty-seven* Egg McMuffin wrappers in a half mile, *scores* of soggy Winston packs—no other brands) is maybe something to do with formal education. Two years and part of a semester more and I could have a bachelor's degree. In what, bro, I can't say. History?

Talk of school displeases Madeline, because she knows who got me started. Too, she values her position as the educated one in the family. "What's this vague unrest?" she says with her most menacing look (a kind of grin): "Why not finish your crisis right here in the house? You've done the bimbo thing. You've got your Mercedes. Now you just need a tattoo and a pierced tongue." She'll lose her Sisyphus if he starts rolling his own boulder. And Frank's green Mercedes really bugs her, if all the insults about it are any clue: "You look like an old rich turtle with your shell on your back."

I like this work. Each bag filled is a triumph, and the day is sunny and fine. I stop for lunch at noon, wash my hands happily in the river, pull out the salami sandwich I made myself this morning, sit on a rock over the water, just watch the standing waves. A

man needs a job that leaves time to think. This, I haven't had for
years.

The river passes. The day is bright and poignant. A lone elk
grazes her way through the trees on the other side of the Frying
Pan, the mountains lean in. I'm surprised not to see more deer,
not to hear gunshots. Dirk Collins up the road in Meredith says
he's seen a regular parade of black bear at night. It's that time of
year, he says; they're looking for dens.

I find I can think about you again, brother. I'm finding I can
think about you then, and not only about you as the brother I've
brought along, always a few years older than however old I am.
No, I mean, really you, the way you were, which wasn't always nice.
I can remember our summer. I can face it straight on, even if just a
little at a time. I can even smile doing it, feel affection. I sit on a
rock over the river and let it come, don't push it down. I see Tricia
clearly on the plane to Chicago. That smart wrangler: she called
the travel agent in Seattle and said she was Grandma and got my
ticket home converted—just like that—into two tickets for
Chicago. I can't remember for my life how she got to the airport,
but she did, and Grandma didn't know Tricia was there in line for
the plane or that when I got my big Grandma hug and two big
kisses I was looking at Tricia over the fragrant, ancient shoulder.

Barely. I can barely face it directly. Knowing what came. Uh.
The Frying Pan River courses by and the sun is hot and this is
heaven, really. I read Roddy's letter again and settle into my fate.
Which is Madeline. But Madeline and I must talk directly about
you bro and face what must be faced if we are to go on. And Mom
and Dad must know, bro: I'm going to tell them. Madeline first.
Then Mom and Dad. Then our siblings. Things come simply on
autumn days.

Tricia Thomas and Coop Henry on the plane: we pretended we
were Russian spies, I think, and giggled and made out, but I was

doubly quaking—Dad was going to kill me, for one, tear my hair from my head a handful at a time. For two, I thought for certain I was going to see *you*, like standing on some corner the minute we arrived. What'd the cowgirl and I do? We got in a cab to town, which anxious ride cost us every cent of our combined cash, I remember that. And then there we were in Chicago, of all places, stranded and broke and pretty well fucked. We had the name Geoff Street as a clue from your letter to Grandma, just that. And the day—my God—it was raging hot. That heat, I remember well. And the images of the Chicago cops beating hippies was in my mind, too. Not Tricia's. For her this was all but a poem. And we wandered the big town, actually asking people if they knew you, and asking for Geoff Street, which wasn't a street at all, as it turned out, but a building, and we weren't going to find it like that.

After midnight and total despair, nothing to eat but pizza from a trash can. And Tricia shoplifts some kind of can of Vienna sausages from a Mexican store and the guy's chasing us and cursing us out and catches us by the collars, calling us *mocosos* and *Anglos miserables*, like that, words I never forgot. And drags us back (we dragging our suitcases) and his wife calls the cops and the cops come and Tricia plays nice girl and I play nice boy and we pretend we're going to pay and Tricia leaps out the door of the store and runs away and I leap after her, but too late, and these two very gentle cops snag me and handcuff me and talk about their locker assignments the whole way to the station—don't even look for Tricia. Another suburban kid, so what? And I ought to have been desolate, but in a way I was relieved: I was going home.

Then in the station this sweet Black kid on the bench next to me, another minor miscreant, convinces me to flee—him they've cuffed to the bench for being Black (else why him and not me— two suburban kids?)—and I slip out behind some lawyer and I'm free on the street with my hands cuffed behind my back and Tricia nowhere in sight. My suitcase full of new clothes from Grandma is gone, everything gone. Oh shit, and I'm wandering around and this pair of *players* comes along and boom, I'm on the pavement, nasty punch to the side of my head, and *they steal my shoes.* And whatever's in my pockets, including Grandma's photo of you, pal, in its silver frame. And they kick my face a couple of times for fun. Then I'm staggering fearlessly around some neighborhood in Chicago, fifteen years old, spitting out blood and walking my socks black and pissing my pants because I'm in cuffs and can't do anything else. And scaring the shit out of everyone I encounter till I slip into a fish-stinking garbage shed behind a row of nice houses and sleep.

Oh, fuck, bro. I can't do this, I can't.

2

Coop woke and couldn't stretch, his neck stiff in painful rays from his chin. He stood awkwardly and reeled out onto the street and began to cry. Immediately a tall older girl was in front of him, tenderly saying "What's wrong, baby?" and checking out the handcuffs. She sniffed at his smell but didn't flinch. "Y'all okay?"

Coop couldn't even say it, sniffled.

"Y'all got in some kind of trouble? Got away from the pigs?"

He said, "I'm okay."

"I'm Bailey," said Bailey. She took off her jacket, a crazy long-tailed thing from another century, another world, hung it on Coop's shoulders to hide the handcuffs.

Coop was an old general, brass buttons, hot wool. "I'm sorry. I had to piss," he said.

"God help y'all when it's time to *crap!*" Bailey laughed hard at her own joke, poked Coop. He laughed, too, couldn't help it, came up out of his misery and just laughed hard. Bailey laughed right back, upped the ante: "We better get you *unhitched* so we can clean you up and *smooch!*"

Oh, Coop laughed. She was kidding and not kidding. She was pretty and tough, both. He liked her grand Texas accent, her clear eyes, her carefree hilarity, pure confidence, pink sneakers, tight-crotch bell-bottom jeans, skinny legs. She had curly, dark-dark brown hair cut neatly at her shoulders but unbrushed. Her nose was big, great-big, her eyes big, too, warmest brown, lit up at the moment with screaming excitement, joy even, sexy, noisy, alive. Suddenly the laugh left her eyes, which flooded with caring: "How'd y'all get in this ungodly *mess?*"

Coop told her his story in a tumble.

Bailey listened carefully, a finger to her lips. She softened at the mention of Tricia, loved to hear about Tricia. "We'll find her," she said. "We'll find her right *now.*"

And off she strode, Coop struggling to keep up, his arms and hands behind him, long coat falling off his shoulders. They marched into the day, Bailey waving her hands. She was eighteen and excited and seemed to know everything: "Chicago is run by *pigs,* they own these big-ass ol' companies that make it dead *impossible* for Afro-American people and *poor* people and almost *anybody* to get ahead at all! Did you see the Democratic Convention last summer? The *pigs* beat *reporters!* They beat *congressmen!* They beat up little *kids!* With their nightsticks. Right on TV. *Violence,*" she said, "that's the *primary* evil. I just had to be here! Right here! So I hitched straight up! Poor Bobby Seale! Poor Chicago Seven! Framed! Set up, y'all! And I'm supposed to just go off to college come fall, y'all? No way, José! I'm here for some *action!*"

So she'd just arrived in Chicago, too. Coop marched beside her like a prisoner, handcuffed. He got solemn, trying to impress her, then trying not to try, but said, "My brother's gone *underground.* He's here in Chicago, somewhere, at least I think he is."

"Cool, baby. *Cool! Far out!* We'll find him, too! My golly you are a pretty boy!"

Oh, he liked her—she made him feel *great*. They laughed and gabbed and marched along the hard streets, Coop sweating in the antique coat, Bailey lecturing on the grotesque injustice of the *police action* in Vietnam, on the grotesque *violence* of the SDS (y'all), on the *beauty* of peace, on *love*. "*Love*, baby! But the world is *fucked*: kids are goin' to *jail* for simple . . . pleasures! For *pot*, for *fuckin*', Coop. Kids are gettin' killed in *Vietnam*; Bobby Kennedy is *dead*," (she said it *did*), "and Martin Luther King, too, and soon everyone'll know who really done it: it's the CIA, y'all, it's the FBI; and *NASA*, fuckin' *NASA* is spendin' *billions* to put some *fuckers* on the moon; the churches, oh, Coop, fuck us-all, the *churches* go around actin' all *moral* and *superior* but they don't say one fuckin' thing about the *violence!*"

Coop was moved to argue, felt like Dad, said, "Of course the Manned Mission costs money!"

"Y'all are too *trustin*'," Bailey said. "It's just another military shot. It's just a way for the fat guys to make more money. The astronauts are *pawns*, baby. Don't y'all be one, *too*."

Coop thought of his gentle minister, of the hero astronauts. Nothing he had known up till now was true! In a hardware store with indifferent clerks Bailey yanked a bolt cutter straight off the pegboard rack and nipped the chain of the handcuffs twice, leaving Coop in loose bracelets that the cutters could barely dent. She found a pair of flip-flops in a sale bin, spent a quarter to buy them for Coop. And she wasn't embarrassed to ask for a bathroom. Coop, wow, Coop could have smooched her, all right.

After he'd used the pot and cleaned up a little, the two *intrepid trekkers* (Bailey said) made their way to Lincoln Park, stood on the huge stone blocks of the seawall in no breeze. A heavy scum with boards in it and dead seagulls surged on the water, no place to swim. Bailey said, "We will find y'all's lady friend in *this here park*.

I *declare* it! And we will find y'all's brother, too! This is the *place!* Everyone ends up right *here! Don't* y'all *feel* it?"

"I *feel* it," Coop said. He liked teasing her.

"But first rest we the *weary!*" She liked being teased.

"We *rest!*" Coop said.

They flopped on the grass under a grand old sycamore, Bailey seemingly out of talk. In minutes, Coop was asleep, his head on Bailey's folded coat. Next thing, two cops woke him by banging on the tree trunk with their night sticks. Bailey was gone. "No sleeping," one of the cops said, not gently. He had a name plate on his breast: Donalan. His partner was silent. Coop thought what they would say if he used the word on his mind: *Pigs.*

"I wasn't asleep," Coop said, gentler than he wished. "I was just thinking."

Donalan said, "Think about sitting up."

Coop sat, hiding the remains of his handcuffs, a badly dented and pinching pair of steel bracelets, hiding them in the coat as best he could, gave the cops a mannerly smile.

The cops ambled off, laughing with themselves.

Sweating and stinking all the more of piss, Coop watched the dead calm lake, found a boat to study, heard laughter, thought of Tricia. Anything might have happened to her. He kept forgetting that his hands were free. He could touch his hair, scratch his neck.

Bailey jogged back with a pair of blue jeans she'd seen a guy *sellin'* but got for *nothin',* "Just only by *kissin'* him *twice!*" and served as lookout while Coop changed into them. They fit funny, but felt just great. The pissed pants—Tricia's brother's giant blue jeans—Coop threw into the bushes.

"Pigs woke me up," Coop said.

"*Fuckin'* pigs," Bailey said. She took a tough stance on her thin legs, balled her fists. Her eyes flashed fiercely. "They think kids have no *rights!* They know we're powerless, so they *hassle* us. Y'all want to know why? Because they don't have any power themselves, baby! *None.* Their bosses *oppress* them, and they take it out on us. They're *scared shitless* because they know this trial and everything they do is *criminal.*"

Coop and Bailey covered the entire park then, bought one hot dog from a vendor, split it (Bailey liked mustard too, lots of mustard; Bailey had some money, not much), but didn't see Tricia, didn't see Hodge, didn't see any big groups of hippies hitting drums. Midafternoon they heard thunder, then more thunder, then more and saw lightning, too, and soon they were in a downpour. Coop took his T-shirt off and stood with his face up and eyes closed, like a hummingbird he'd seen once. When he got tired of that he blinked and shouted, rubbed the sweat from his chest, saw Bailey dancing shirtless toward him, laughing. Her bosoms (Mom's embarrassed word) were juggly and sort of cross-eyed, not sexy exactly, not so private as Coop would have thought. Comradely, is what they were. And Coop and Bailey leapt and danced, new friends, till the two of them were goosebumps everywhere and muddy and had to struggle back into wet shirts.

They walked through the afternoon, drying, walked into the evening. Bailey, unembarrassed by her shirt plastered over her chest, knew where to go: The Free Store. Which turned out to be several surly guys with goatees. They didn't know Hodge, scoffed at the name Geoff Street. Coop could see they'd heard of it all right.

"But where is it?"

"Skokie," one of them said, making the whole mean gang laugh, except one tall man. He shook his head: "That ain't right, don't listen to these guys."

Coop persisted: "And we're looking for a girl named Tricia."

"We ain't the *fucking lost and found,*" the meanest one said.

Bailey said, "Peace, y'all, we need a fuckin' place to *stay*."

The men looked at each other, looked at Bailey from the tits down.

"You got one night," said the sort of nice one, red hair. His name was Murph. He rummaged in a drawer, came up with a mimeographed map, pointed to a street, wrote the address and the apartment number right on the page with a dirty pencil. He said, "My shack. Key's under the outside mat."

On the street Bailey danced and sang, and she danced and sang till dusk, as she and Coop tumbled through twenty neighborhoods and twenty tempers. Halfway to Murph's, Bailey lunged into a liquor store, no thought of her age, boldly bought a quart of sloe gin. "The real *stuff*," said she. Closer to Murph's she said, "If you gots some money, you gots to *spend* it," and bought a loaf of bread and a big block of cheese and a jar of lemonade.

To Murph's!

Coop had never seen anything like the place: one smallish room, worn wooden floor, sort-of kitchen in the corner, claw-foot bathtub in the kitchen, toilet in a closet where Murph's clothes hung, mattress on the floor, snapshots of three different pretty girls on the fridge, more clothes in a basket, nothing else.

Creepy. They sat on the mattress and drank the weird sloe gin and Coop ate the bread and cheese. Bailey talked: the Universe, Fate, God, Love, Buddha, Grace Slick, Birth Control, Thomas Mann, Nature, Enlightenment. She knew a little about everything. She showed Coop how to sit lotus, cracked his ankles bending him into it, and they sat quietly, passing the gin. When it grew too dark to see, Bailey found a fat candle and lit it.

Later than midnight, Murph came home. Close up, Coop saw he was old, thirty or worse. He had a big cloud of reddish hair, seemed pissed to remember there'd be kids in his place, seemed pissed they'd lit his candle. But Bailey relentlessly talked to him till he began to soften, till he sat between them on his mattress, their six legs stretched out on the floor. Slowly the conversation (black beauties, mescaline, Quaaludes, psilocybin, junk, ope, trips good and bad, the spiritual qualities of each drug, the experiential qualities, the physical) got to be between just Bailey and Murph, which left Coop thinking disconsolately of Tricia. Soon enough Bailey lay back, and then Murphy too (Murphy with his tall legs and skinny, tiny butt), and the two of them talked with their heads propped, almost whispering. Bailey was so good at talking, always had something arresting at the tip of her tongue.

"Bath," Coop said. "Okay if I take a bath?"

Murph said, "Sure, man, right-on," and went back to telling about his part in the riots last summer, how he'd been clocked twice in the face by a guy in a suit who might have been a cop, man, or might have been FBI and how this big *soul brother* had seen it, man, and come from behind and knocked the guy out with two big punches, man, and they'd got away.

Bailey stiffened. All violence made her *sick* and she said so.

In candlelight Coop ran hot water into the tub, planning how to undress. When the tub was near full he just dropped his new pants and old shirt and stepped in quickly, tried to sit, stood. Too hot. Bailey didn't seem to be paying the least attention anyway. So, slowly Coop sank in. Oh, boy, ah. He washed his matted hair and soaped himself up and leaned back enveloped. He conked out in seconds.

When he woke the water was just cold and Bailey and Murph (his first name was Leslie, same as Coop's mother!), Bailey and Leslie were kissing on the bed, or more than that: Bailey was half on top of Murph and Murph's hand was in the back of Bailey's pants which were loose at the belt, you could see. Tricia's silver cowboy buckle floated into Coop's thoughts. Tricia was safe, he felt this. Coop sat quietly in the cooling water and watched Bailey and Murph gently tussle, watched Murph kiss Bailey's stomach and saw her spreading breasts and watched Bailey pull her own pants off. She said, "axquisite, axquisite," softly.

Guilty hard-on in the tub as Murph (this total stranger!) climbed kissing upward and kissed Bailey's face hidden in the covers and they started in fucking and Coop could see Murph's little butt at it and Bailey's knees in the air and the water getting cold. Coop closed his eyes in the cooling tub and thought he'd better be still so as not to embarrass the lovers. Quickly Murph made a grunt and Bailey said a soulful Texas *Jaysus* and they giggled and were off each other. The water seemed very cold suddenly so Coop said, "Shit," yawningly as if waking up, said, "Fell asleep."

"That sloe gin," Murph said.

"Jaysus," Bailey said, just the way she'd said it before, as if Coop weren't there at all.

"I'm getting out," Coop said. He dried facing away from them and heard them getting dressed, got back in his jeans with no underpants (he'd never wear any again ever), got back in his shirt and felt clean and empty and almost as if it were he who'd had sex.

When he turned they weren't dressed at all but naked completely and just getting under the covers.

"Fell asleep," Coop said. He wanted it clear he hadn't overheard them.

"We were *screwin'*," Bailey said.

They all laughed hard.

"And the whole damn *bottle* is gone," Bailey said.

"It's sloe gin," Murph said. "Goes fast." He pinched something under the covers and Bailey shrieked and sat up.

During the night Coop heard Bailey and Murph screwing over and over again, or maybe he just woke in and out of once.

Morning and the sun came in hot. Coop found himself on the floor and smelled sex, but the lovers were asleep. He rose and stretched in his rumpled clothes in the still air. Suddenly Murph's apartment was the most wonderful place Coop had ever been:

unsullied by real adults, unadorned but for its tenant's scant belongings. The sun hit Murph's one houseplant; a faint breeze blew up the dust on the floor; the windows streaked the sunbeams with poor cleaning; the traffic trundled below.

The door creaked. The apartment door creaked unmistakably and opened as Coop turned. A soldier stood there in green fatigues, still getting his key out of the lock. The soldier said, "Marian! Sweetheart? It's me! Forty-eight hours!" because that's what he'd planned on saying, but his face was already falling.

"Bruce?" Murphy said.

"Bruce?" Bailey said sitting up. The same word but a different question.

"Marian is at her parents' place," Murph said, clearly scared. "She's at her folks' place." Begging. He leapt up and struggled into his pants.

"I got forty-eight hours," Bruce wailed.

Murph straightened himself, puffed his thin chest pitifully, said, "Bruce, this is between Marian and you."

Coop watched, amazed, trying to figure it out: Murph had just fucked Bailey in his girl Marian's apartment, bad enough, but his girl was this Bruce's girl, too. Worse.

Bruce made a leap to get Murphy by the scrawny knees, knocking him to the bare floor. Quickly Bruce crawled atop him, turned him face to the wood in a strong man's wrestling move, got Murph by his orange hair and began to bang his face hard on the floorboards.

"Bruce, baby, back off!" Bailey said. She tried to pull him off her new lover.

But Bruce was pissed, fresh out of basic, was going for the kill.

Coop stepped over, said, "Cut it out," remembering his entirely untested fighting lessons from Hodge: hit fast, hit first, get out of there.

He kicked Bruce in the head with his heel, just hard enough to stop him hurting Murph. Bruce did let go of Murphy, all right, in fact he stood up and faced Coop—not that big, but tough looking in his uniform. Coop strode right to him and threw a fake left, a trick from Hodge—Bruce's eyes followed—then smashed cheekbone with his right, twice, hurting his own hand. Bruce sat down hard.

"Coop, no," Bailey said. She was at the door, clutching her clothes about her.

"Shit," Murphy said. He looked at Bruce, looked at Bailey, looked at Coop, took an armful of clothes from the toilet room and leapt out the door and down the stairs. Bailey got her pants on, put her shirt on backwards and ran after. Coop stayed a second to see how Bruce looked—addled, but sitting up—then bounded out the door to follow.

"See, it's his girlfriend's apartment," Murph said breathlessly on the fourth landing down.

Bruce wasn't coming.

"He's an *asshole*," Bailey said. "And, Coop, y'all are an *asshole's* asshole. Punchin' folks!"

"But . . . ," Coop said. He turned in appeal to Murphy, whom he'd saved.

"But *nothin'*, baby. No *violence*. Not even if he hit y'all *first*, if that's what y'all are fixin' to say!"

Murphy turned. He said, "Bruce is my best friend," sorrowfully. He started up the stairs, his arms full of clothing. "My main man."

"*Violence*," Bailey spat, like the word was shit in her mouth. She stomped ahead of Coop down the stairs and away from Murphy and stormed ahead of Coop holding her lower belly like it was sore all the way back to the lake, and that was miles. They'd left Bailey's cool coat behind, Coop kept thinking, gone forever.

3

The first twenty minutes on the high pond trail I'm steaming and ruminating and planning grand speeches about my feelings here: for years Madeline's been saying that I ought to express my feelings better, but the truth is—boundaries, intimacy, control—she doesn't want to hear my feelings if my feelings mean she'll have to change in any way herself. I keep rephrasing these charges, rehearsing speeches, marching up the mountain. But fury wanes as the day warms and I warm and the trail is in front of me, steep and rocky and hard. There is bear sign but the bears have gone in. There is elk sign, too, but I see no creatures till the height of the trail: on the banks of the pond (lost in its crater beneath three peaks), I see one preternaturally beautiful raven, that's all. One enormous, glistening raven, his feathers blowing in the chill wind. And he doesn't quoth a goddamn thing, but hops along the ice fringe studying its margins, looking for meals of dead fish. It's good up here and quiet. I think of the ways I am to blame.

Madeline should have been out on this hike, but she's gone into the office—there's work to be done, Thanksgiving or no—Buck

Holander called in a panic this morning: the Caltrex deposition is missing.

Crap.

And then there's the annual party at Anstedt's. My feelings, ha ha. I've expressed my feelings: I'm ashamed to show my face at the judge's and don't really want to see anybody, especially any of Madeline's colleagues in small-town law. "Full circle," says she. "Your community service is done," says she. "Time to come back to the fold." But it's her fold, not mine.

The drive into town at five o'clock is magnificent. No, really: it's beautiful. Frank's Mercedes humming, an S–600, the biggest car they make, sixteen-valve, four doors, leather everything, absurdly mine now. The familiar shapes of the peaks are like the faces of friends, the spotless shoulders of the road are like healthy human boundaries, the many hard curves and humps and hills are as familiar as the shapes of my own legs, my arms, my mind. Frank's movie-theatre music system plays his last CD: Schumann. Slow pace, and slower. I stop to pick up the one bit of litter I see along the shoulder of the road: empty pack of Winstons.

At Judge and Mrs. Anstedt's, fifteen cars already fill the grand loop of driveway. I pull in at the end of the line and wait a long time, car running, assessing the scene. This is going to be a big party, which Madeline must have known. There's Porter Austen's car. I'm not worried about seeing Porter, particularly. There's the Bennetts' car, and the Friedmans' and Nicki Frost's. There's Jane Holander's Kharmann Ghia, some kind of statement: why not take Bucky's Bimmer? There're two or three cars I don't know. And Christ, Hodge, there's Rick Baldwin's spanking-new Range Rover.

The Hennypen Diner's open in Basalt with a hot turkey sand-wich Thanksgiving special (I've seen the hand-lettered sign), and that's what I'm thinking, backing out the driveway. And it's because I'm backing out that Mad and Holander don't see me. And it's because I'm backing away that I see them pulling in the other end of the circular drive in Holander's sleek black BMW. They are leaning at each other, and she shakes her head just so, laughing, and they talk a full minute having parked. From the bend of her neck I know it, even at a hundred paces. From the way his hand smooths his hair when the laugh is laughed. From the space between them, neither great nor small.

Even before their long, soulful kiss I know what I know, and know how many years I've been blind to it.

4

Clouds coursed over Lake Michigan. Coop and Bailey roamed, quixotically asking after Hodge, arguing more and less heatedly about applications of violence. Coop just thought bad people should be punished. Bailey said that was *Judeo-Christian* bullshit. "Judgement is always *flawed!*" she said. She cadged two warm beers from a group of guys who liked her, then scored a slice of pizza from someone's picnic.

Evening found them all the way back downtown, Grant Park, where kids did go, and where in all that big city one lost kid might most likely find another. That's what everyone said. Bailey marched up to three young businessmen who had got loose from the sunny bluff of tall buildings. They didn't know Hodge, but they offered hits off a fat, smoldering joint. Bailey took the reefer, puffed it, handed it to Coop. In ten minutes Coop was giggling, in twenty minutes he was dizzy, in a half hour he staggered off to vomit, then had to lie down next to a dignified and ancient tree.

Bailey followed, touched Coop's hair. She said "*Shit y'all,*" many times, meaning how high she was. "We've been *dosed!*"

Coop lay back. Bailey squatted in a sway beside him exclaiming and, despite the bad LSD or whatever the *fuck* it was, leaped up and jogged fearlessly to talk to people who walked nearby, long gesticulating conversations with anyone who passed, fearless. After each encounter she returned to Coop and reported the jokes she'd made, or the *weirdness* she'd found. Hodge? Tricia? No luck.

Coop sprawled in the grass and sent his vision up into the tree and felt the crawling earth under him and wished so mightily for Tricia that a hole opened up in him, a void opened up. An entire person's worth of his *self* was missing.

"Those guys are *Hare Krishnas*," Bailey puffed, returning from somewhere when Coop didn't even know she'd been gone and couldn't rise to look.

Bailey said, "Are you crying?"

"*Everything* cries!" Coop told her.

And Bailey flew off again, chittering something about the *water*, going down by the *water* to see what was *happenin'*.

"I'll accompany," Coop said, digging out the word, but he lolled, face sopped with tears, blurred eyes attached despite him to the web of leaves above, maple leaves above, branches (black branches) above against tatters of blue sky, tatters of sky and four leaves dead at the end of a broken twig: in the air between all those leaves Coop lived, and the tree had strong powers.

At length (not straight time but something spherical) two cops appeared in the space between the ground and the first branches, maple leaves, air, two cops kicking lightly at Coop's ribs with blunt shoes.

"Get up," a mouth said in a mustache. Coop wobbled into the height of the tree. The cops inspected him, looked into his eyes, not entirely unkindly.

"Looking a little bleary, there, chief," a wet mouth near a pimpled cheek said.

"Let's have you empty your pockets," the mustache said, with yellow teeth.

"Wait up," the pimpled cheek said wrinkling: "You got some cuffs on there, do you? Now just where in the hell did those come from?"

"It's just jewelry, y'all," Coop said, exactly what Bailey had told him to say, including the drawl.

In his pockets (not even his own pockets, pockets soft with someone else's use), Coop had a penny left and two round stones. He held the stuff in his hands, smiling broadly, remembering to smile, remembering to show he was a good kid.

"Inside out," the pimpled cheek said, with a blue eye looking.

Coop turned pants pockets out for him.

"No I.D.?"

"Mislaid it," Coop said. They had guns in leather holsters.

The mustache said, "'Mislaid,' huh? Kind of fucked up, there, are you?"

"Your mama and poppa know you're such a fuck-up?" the acne one said, then with a hard stick lifted Coop's chin till the pimples and blue eye saw him.

"It's just adornment. It's only make-believe." That second phrase had been his own idea about the handcuffs, rejected by Bailey. When the nightstick withdrew, Coop flopped back to the ground, hard. He thought of his parents. His parents must be sick worrying about him.

"Ah, crap," one of the cop voices said. "It's that fruitfly lawyer."

The cops' two stares had left Coop and were aimed so hard that Coop sent his eyes there too, found a vision of beads, of feathered headband, of God's own stream of wavingly gray hair, God's own wavingly long gray beard—help or damnation, Coop didn't know which was coming, felt both inside him.

The bearded man didn't smile at the cops. He didn't say hello.

He knelt serenely and put a hand on Coop's shoulder, spoke to the cops as inferiors. "All right, what's the problem here, fellers?"

The cops looked at one another with a head-waggling show of not being impressed, yet even Coop felt the bearded man's huge power over them.

"No problem here, Tonto," the pimply cop said. Both cops were young as children, Coop saw, years younger than the lawyer. "We just got a runaway here with no I.D. and no brain left."

"Gentlemen, this boy's my son. He's suffering heat stroke, clearly. Now leave him alone, and watch the insults. He's every right to be here and recover."

"He's a vagrant."

"He's a citizen of the United States of America," the man said gently. "And he's my son." This added with a certain acknowledging humor: every runaway boy in this place was going to be his son and the cops knew it.

"You don't have any kids, *counselor*," the mustache said, and even Coop could hear he was kidding now, could hear that the trouble was over.

"So you'll want to arrest me for lying. And arrest my boy here, right now, or leave him in peace."

"Have you found Hodge?" Coop said. The men stood over him, frozen in a triangle above him, an impasse framed by the leaves of the tree above. The cop heads looked at each other, looked down at Coop. The cop shoulders shrugged then, as if Coop had only been a joke they were playing. The cop bodies left the triangle, leaving God above.

And God shook his head after them. "Stupid," he thundered, crouching. He took Coop's head in both his hands, looked into Coop's eyes so deeply that Coop felt actual warmth. And God rubbed the dirt off Coop's forehead, inspected his clothes, speak-

ing softly all the while: "Those two ought to be arrested themselves." He got Coop to stand, assessed his tottering posture,
escorted him to the tree trunk, helped him sit propped against it.
"Got high, huh? Got hold of something bad? Do you know what
you took?

Suddenly, deeply, Coop grew suspicious. "She's lost," he said,
picturing Tricia.

"She. Okay. Did she get high with you? Do you know what you
took?"

Coop said, "And Bailey."

"Okay, my friend. Okay. You're coming down now. You're going
to be all right. It's just the drug, whatever you feel. It's only the
drug. Okay?"

The man wasn't even a man. Coop was in the hands of an angel
or a gentle older brother and on the roots of the tree. The vision
nodded his head peacefully. "You'll be fine," he said. "Listen, my
man, I'm going to make a circuit here. I'll keep my eyes open for a
little chicken high as you. I'll be back around. Don't get up. Don't
lie down. If the pigs hassle you—you hear me?—if the pigs hassle
you, don't forget that they've got to *bust* you before they can *search*
you. And don't be afraid. They know the law." He winked, to show
that he didn't believe this. "I'm Jefferson Freedom. I'm from the
Geoff Street Collective. I'm an attorney, and they know it. Use my
name."

"Geoff Street?" Coop said.

The angel nodded his head seriously, pulled a nicely printed
brochure out of a pocket in his vest, stuffed it in Coop's shirt. "In
the event you get lost again: that's our address. Hear me? We're
way back west on Ontario Street—just keep walking—it's a yellow
brick building, nothing special, little sign out front. We could
spring those cuffs off you, for one thing. And you've puked your-

self. We've got clothes; you can get a shower if you like, and a meal. So stick right here, all right? I'll be back." Sweetly, as if he were talking to a baby. "We're there for people just like you."

The tree was solid behind Coop, and Freedom stood up before him like ascending, said, "Take this." He pulled a big square paperback book out of his knapsack. "If the pigs come by, just make like you're reading. Everyone respects a man who's reading."

Now words failed Coop; none would come to keep Jefferson talking; Jefferson only patted him on the shoulder and left him, walked off after Baker and Hardesty. The book was *Be Here Now,* by one Baba Ram Dass. Coop held it purple in his lap, stroked it, watched it, and the tree was behind him solid as the world. He opened the book and saw shouting words and odd drawings and spirals of calligraphy. The lack of sense there became sense slowly.

Coop turned to say something important to Tricia. Tricia not there. But the book told him not to worry. Starving empty stomach. Geoff Street! But the book said not to worry. Bailey gloomy with him for his violence, his knuckles sore and cut on his right hand, his badness. But the book said it over and over again: *be here now; now be here; be nowhere.*

In curving time, Coop grew calm. He sat himself up straight and looked out over the lawns to the important waves of the lake and watched and waited and hummed to himself till Bailey came rushing through the trees, staggering and panting, muddy and shoeless, grinning broadly—pulling some reluctant girl along behind, pulling Tricia Thomas by the hand.

5

The choice to drive there is irrational, come to think of it, but the decision is not. I don't even blink. I don't risk calling Roddy, just load half my clothes in the huge trunk of Frank's S–600, angle four pair of skis across the endless back seat, let an enormous box of books ride shotgun. I'm moving stuff fast, ten trips back and forth to the car, trying to guess what I'll need for my years to come, alone. My two jammed toolboxes fit in the trunk. Several pair of ski boots on the floor in back. Three fishing rods broken down fit between the seats. A stack of CDs, carefully my own alone, and then—oh!—my climbing ropes and crampons, not that I've been on any steeprock since my knees. The barrel cactus I've raised from a seed I put on the dashboard in its clay pot on a tiny porcelain dish I know to be Mad's, the only bit of her I'll steal. The little painting Roddy helped me buy, wrapped in shopping bags. My checkbook. My passport. Somewhat weirdly a shovel I'm fond of, into the trunk. My toothbrush, my hairbrush. Aspirin, hand cream, one bottle of shampoo, Tums, floss, razor and gone.

Basalt to Glenwood Springs to the great highway east, energized, untired, grateful on Thanksgiving night to Buck Holander and even to Madeline, going like hell, I-70 East through the canyon of the Colorado, then up and up the sweeping curves of Loveland Pass in the dark, then over the top and on to Denver. Then I'm falling off the mountains the whole way to the Mississippi River, listening to *Turandot* and *La Bohème* loud as hell, all night, Frank's opera, melodramatic enough to fit my mood, pure passionate bellowing, explosions of brass. I think of Roddy and Claudio COMMUNICATING. I think of Madeline and Buck Holander draped over the leather-top desk in her office, the fancy panties she wears only to work down around her ankles. I think of Michelangelo and Vittoria, the love that couldn't be. According to Roddy, the showoff.

Through Kansas I'm energized, elated: I'll not stop till Roddy's in my arms. But I have to stop: for gas twice, then (after a strong battle to stay awake) for three wretched hours of sleep in a rest area among rumbling trucks.

Gray of morning and nothing seems simple anymore. Roddy's made it clear whose arms she wants to rest in. But onward: Missouri, Illinois, Indiana. Biggest shopping day of the year, the highway packed with families on Thanksgiving missions, license plates from across the land. In Elkhart on Route I-80, night again, I stop at a decent motel and stare at the old dial phone on the nightstand. A man could call ahead. A man could call behind. But I don't even touch the phone, just climb between stiff, starched sheets and sleep like a hammer. Next day Ohio, Pennsylvania, Upstate New York. Under a thin surface of resolve I'm growing weary, desperate, remembering all the things I've left in Colorado (my house, my river, my life), thinking of all the trouble I have caused (Charlie Merck's civil suit—what about that!), thinking yet again and in an endlessly replaying tumble—words and visions—of Mad with Holander, of Roddy with Claudio Abruzzi.

I grow delirious with weariness, almost hysterical, the new states coming slowly. Massachusetts. New Hampshire. Maine at last! Maine, where no one wants me. Snow everywhere. According to the pump kid where I stop for gas in Augusta, they've had three storms in a week. A foot before Thanksgiving, half a foot Thanksgiving day, another half foot just yesterday. And a real storm expected right now, says the kid, See the sky? He's charged up, I'm charged up.

The New England boy is home! I drive in sifting snow, singing with Frank's super radio: "Touch of Gray," "Deal," "Sugaree." It must be poor Jerry Garcia's birthday.

In Farmington, a sweet little town maybe thirty miles from Sugarloaf, I stop at a place I've stayed twice before, once with Frank, years back, once alone when I stormed off the mountain after trouble with Baldwin. The County Seat Inn, it's called, a decent small place like staying at your aunt's house, and there I let goodly Rose Carter take care of me (she never forgets a guest). She's got flour on her apron and hugs me and asks after Frank Kobil and Julie Tinker and Roddy, too, and asks after my health. She cries when she hears Frank's dead, and keeps crying—I can hear her in her room. He called her Hurricane Carter, I recall.

I barely sleep. All night the plows are going by. Sunday morning, the church bells of Farmington ring gaily, sun shines on powdery-beautiful and deep new cover, and Coop Henry wakes in horror at what he has done.

The second waking is better, almost ten o'clock. Good Rose cooks me breakfast, sits with me as I eat it, says lightly she's read of my hardware-store escapade. She's not someone who needs to know more. She says nimbly she's read of my ouster from the team, too. She's a reader, that Rose, a subscriber to magazines. You must be shaken, says she, meaning Frank's death.

I tell her sprightly it's worse than that, that I've left my wife. I smile saying it, pleased with how consistently the truth is at my lips these days. But still Rose's frown is with me all the way to the mountain as I speed along the steaming rapids of the Carrabassett River. Perfect new snow lies everywhere, deep. At Kingfield I book a room at the Herbert Hotel, which reminds me maybe a little of the Jerome in Aspen, which in turn, of course, reminds me of Madeline. I'm the only guest so early in the season. I unload the car for half an hour, box by box to my room. Shovel, too. And I'm thinking of you Hodge. It was a miracle I found you in Chicago, wasn't it? Wasn't everything a fucking miracle then? The way Bailey found Tricia—Bailey just *expected* miracles. The way Jefferson Freedom found me. All of it felt preordained, but it was not, it was all dumb, hippie luck.

Tricia got us to the Geoff Street Collective—this I recall in vaguest terms. And the drug trip had turned a little sweet—everything *bent* still, but everything amusing now that Tricia was there to interpret. At the collective—an old mansion in a bombed-out neighborhood—the collectivists were grumpy saints, didn't like our giggling, but gave us a room with three cots in the attic and showed us to a roomful of free used clothes. I recall a desk covered with pamphlets and FREE HUEY buttons, a paper bucket of condoms. Bailey and I were so tripped out on horse tranks or whatever we'd smoked that Tricia had to practically force us down the dark attic hallway to the bathroom up there, maybe one of the first indoor bathrooms in the world, built for many rich children to share. Weirdly, it's this windowless attic bathroom that I remember perfectly of all memories from that time—I remember it every time I smell Ivory Soap or mildew. Tricia pushed Bailey and me in there and went to pick us out clothes from the piles of donations. And *zowee* the tiles in there, the tiny checkerboard tiles swinging in zany moiré patterns in front of our addled eyes and Bailey just flinging off her clothes and I too, leaping out of my clothes and the two of us climbing into the huge marble *sinks* and splashing under the faucets of these pedestal *sinks* like crazy children screaming with laughter. Everything was particular, pure detail, almost molecular. No way to get the whole picture at once. Tricia appeared in the opening door. Sure she was jealous, that cowgirl.

"Who *are* you?" she said to Bailey.

"It's *karma*," Bailey replied.

Tricia herself, it turned out, had been smoking pot all day alone in this professor's house till her walk in the park. "Hated him," she said.

That's a lucky fifteen-year-old boy in the shower there with those two high girls—we soaked and huddled and hugged—it wasn't hump and thrust and squirt, none of that, but it was sex, all right, loving and memorable in living, electrified skin—sex till a whole old mansion's worth of hot water ran out, then we dressed in used clothes. The collective people were calling upstairs— dinnertime in the faded ballroom—folding tables, old church pews, fifty or more people getting ready to eat, we the only run- aways, the rest the sort of people that Dad would call the Great Unwashed: exhausted people, quiet and beaten, old men and women, crazy people missing teeth, ten dirty children too tired to make noise.

And we got chores. I did dishes, bro. With your colleague Able Steven. I told him I was looking for you and he pretended he knew nothing of any kind about you. I said something like, "My brother's wanted by the police." And he just looked at me for the longest time with his Afro and his welted Afro-American skin (how fiercely and with what innocence I noticed his skin!) and laid into me: "To you, man, that's news. *My* brothers are why the motherfucking police *exist*." So I said, "I got beat up by some cops in Idaho." And he said, "I been *killed* by the pigs." So I said, "Well, I got sick today from some kind of dope." And he said, "White boy, let me tell you something: I am *dead* from drugs, you hear me? I been dead for fifty motherfucking years!"

He called me *Lord Fauntler-honkey,* this much I recall, started to crack a grin.

Later the girls and I hung out in the common room, just amazed by all the people. Tricia sat beside me with hickeys on her neck: the professor. And the whole night people slunk in or crashed in or waltzed in, Jefferson Freedom himself turning up and speaking to me warmly but briefly: everyone had to talk to him. That was a good person, Jefferson Freedom (his real name Alan Greenbaum, Able Steven told me, snorting, dismissive, insinuating exactly what I wasn't sure), a good person despite all you said about him, bro—he helped people without judgement. He knew the law. He worked inside the system and hurt no one while he helped. He was the true perfect hippie, with all the graces that made that designation seem almost holy to me then, and make me proud of it still.

People cleared away the plates and folded up tables and the big community room dimmed and grew noisier and smoky. I remember looking into each face and having my first profound thought, a string of druggy utterances I couldn't hang on to, like, I was not separate, I was part of some pattern, a pattern suddenly visible. The girls were with me; Able Steven had decided to accept me (or then again maybe he just liked the *chicks*), sat near. Across the room a pair of older women soulfully *kissed*—I was on a hell of a learning curve that night. An ancient man coughed uncontrollably; a faint, hot breeze made spirals in all the cigarette smoke; a frail old couple played chess beside a bookcase. These images are among my clearest memories. Why?

I watched everyone, trying to catch my thoughts. A group of Afro-American kids bobbed in through those big double doors at the top of the main stairs, argued amongst themselves loudly. Pot smoke—I remember pot smoke layered in the air. And similar layers of bad stuff floating inside me, layers that linger: some lecherous professor and Able Steven's anger and Bailey's knees up in the air under Murphy and my own violence and Hodge lost and Tricia's neck bruised and probably Mom and Dad dying with worry.

Able Steven said he could get the handcuffs off me, a gesture of friendship. He picked at the locks with a paperclip a very long time while I watched those stair doors, high as a cloud—watched those stair doors flying open squealing again and again. Those stair doors had all my interest. Why?

Jefferson Freedom sat down with the angry teens, I recall, listened to them closely, calming them. Those doors squealed open, two women. Those doors again, and a boy with a guitar in no case. Those doors squealed open again, and it was you.

No, it really was. It was you, Hodge. The tension in that place just clicked up ten notches. Freedom was scared of you, even I could see that. And you busted right over to him and dressed him down, and I was slow to really believe it was you. And I told the girls: *Shit, this is Hodge.* Something like that. And Bailey said "*Karma,*" again, meaning what exactly I didn't know and don't know now.

Hodge, you were *pissed,* furious. You pulled Able Steven up by his shirt and just growled in his face. No matter how scary he was to me, you *dominated* that guy. You were *Dad.* I'm sorry, but you were *Dad.* Freedom tried to talk to you, and Able Steven cowered, and the muscles stood out of your shirt and your neck was taut and every inch of you just grew harder as Jefferson Freedom murmured, the whole big room full of people straining to hear.

The cops had come looking for you, was the news. Able Steven had done some indiscreet thing buying parts for pipe bombs and *got your ass caught.* And there I was, ten feet away, heart pounding furiously, room in a spin, and I rose and marched right up and pushed my way in front of you. "You'll have to leave tonight," Freedom was saying to you.

I said something incredibly lame, like, "Hi it's me!"

The look on your face, bro, that was the worst thing that had ever happened to me up to that moment.

And you are involved in every worse thing that followed, all the way to the moment I find myself alone at the Herbert Hotel, Kingfield of-all-places Maine. I just stop my thoughts right there, that look on your face, bury my thoughts, stuff them down inside, and get busy putting my bachelor's room in order: clothes, books, push a chair over by the light, and really, I'm feeling better. Calm.

At the mountain, I pull my dirt skis out of Frank's back seat, clack into my heaviest, sweetest boots—the slowest, least radical equipment I own—march to the booth under the lodge where I buy an all-lifts, all-day ticket, something I've never had to buy in thirty years. I ride two fast lifts to the top of the snow, which is not quite yet the top of this honest and agreeable and blowy mountain. The day is not particularly cold, the sky is white, the snow is fresh and deep. I ski easily, carve wide turns. I am not trying for speed, I am only skiing the mountain. I am not thinking of Detmar Brink, who beat me at Sapporo for the silver. I am not thinking of that .016 seconds. I am not thinking of Detmar's fellow Austrian, the famous Klaus Klineschmidt, who beat us for the gold. I am not thinking of that .024 seconds. I'm not thinking of the World Cups in 1974, the crash and brief coma that were the end of my knees and the beginning of coaching, that crash in the second half of a suicide run for which my split time was two seconds up on the guy who got gold, Franz Klammer, that year, those fucking Austrians. I am not attempting particular grace or economy, I am only skiing the mountain, falling into gravity. I am not looking for the practice course, I am only skiing. I am not looking for the team. I am not looking for Roddy Manor. I am skiing, only that.

On the lift—two runs, then three, then four—I talk to strangers volubly. I tell them I'm a ski bum. I tell them I'm in love. I tell them I lost my brother when I was young. How about that? They tell me their jobs and their theories and two of them their sadnesses (oh Lord, to lose your child to illness!, to watch your business collapse!). I think of you skiing when we were young, your all-out attack on the mountain, no slope too steep, none too icy, no lift line you wouldn't cut. You crashed through drifts and leapt off ridges, you smoked hash on the ride up, skied closed trails on the way down, found girls in the lodge, girls on the lifts, girls on the bunny trails. You outran the ski patrol, got in fistfights with irate boyfriends. You jumped from the lift if it stalled, no matter how high, argued with lift guys, broke skis in grand crashes, swooped through the trees. I had to keep up, that's all: good training. You liked it when I got fast and started beating you. I remember your smile those times, you swooping up and stopping yourself all sloppy behind me, proud.

I sweep all over Sugarloaf in the perfect new snow, zero crowds, my slow skis humming. I'm furious for twenty minutes, then nothing, no emotion at all. I just work the whole mountain, not searching for Roddy, not thinking about you, just skiing till I get to the eastern trails. And there in the wide glade is the U.S. Women's Team, working out. I can see them from the headwall: Spiderwoman spandex, musculature and expertise, fear and confidence, equipment lying all over, half the mountain roped off.

I ski right up to the barrier. What am I going to do, hide? And in a large knot of local fans I stand and watch practice. I know everybody, except for a handful of new prospects. This Noriko kid Roddy has spoken of comes down like an artillery shell, straight and tight, scorching the pine trees, I mean it bro, melting snow. Top time. Then Mary Frawley, who has retired but coaches now, now likes to ski with the team. Then Picabo Street, struggling badly. Then Julie Tinker, who's only stretching out, slow as the freestyler she is, skating at the end, the only skier having any fun in this crowd. People clap to see her. Then Roddy, too slow for a bomber, her hair caught under her headband, snow still in her ear and across her eyebrows from what must have been a terrible fall, her helmet broken under her arm, a deep frown on her face as she skis past the women waiting, skis straight to Claudio, whose arms are folded unacceptingly across his chest. You can see he's talking to her as coach to skier, you can see how she's resisting this. Prince Claudio saying (no doubt), *You've had a bad a-run, that's all, quiet now, focus and a-ski.* But, let's face it, she's an intense person and competitive, listens only slowly. I've coached her so I know. I can almost supply her speech. Her face gets red. I hear fragments of her words, some of it Italian. Claudio speaks reasonably. She slams her helmet to the snow at his feet (it's cracked, all right, breaks in half), stomps her skis, pushes off and away from him, skate-skate and down the mountain, ditching the team. I push off, too, follow her all the way to the lodge, faster than I want to go, unable to catch her up. At the hay bales above the ski racks she fairly leaps out of her bindings as I ski up and stop softly beside her. She gives me a chill look, a look for a creepy stranger, then breaks into recognition: "Coop!"

I say, "I've run away."

She doesn't say a word, just stares at me aghast. Her eyes are brown and deep and hurt and I know I've done the right thing coming here. Inanely I say, "I'm at the Herbert."

And, Hodge, she belts me. Makes a fist and knocks me right on the chin, then hits me again on the forehead, nothing girly, sharp punches—she's strong. I fall over the hay bales, tangled in my poles and skis. Roddy pops back into her race-day bindings and flies away without another word, down the bunny slope to the lower lodges, speed of light.

6

Hodge drove pissed, fists crushing the steering wheel, not speaking and brooking no speech. His hair was cut down to a new crew-cut closer than Dad's, his beard shaved and gone, his chin nicked, neck taut, jaw working. Coop, Tricia, Bailey, Hodge—they'd left in a hurry, middle of the night, as the astronauts landed on the moon. Instead of outer space Coop had the back of the Geoff Street Collective's VW bus to contemplate, the whole back to himself, while the girls rode up front with Hodge.

In Minnesota, midafternoon, the dark mood of the night and morning began to float and stratify and slowly to dissipate out the windows of the bus. Hodge's head got looser on his neck. They'd made their escape. Coop struggled up on his knees, put his chin on the back of the seat between Bailey and Tricia, watched the road come at them. In some dead-still town a man in a wheelchair waved to them. A father hugged his teenage son. And mile after mile, Bailey sang Motown songs, sang them well.

The gang pulled up at a little grocery for bread and famous local cheese (the sign said) and what was called *pop* by the clerk; they got the gas tank filled by a genuine muscle man at an Esso station. Back on the road, Tricia said, *"Plunder,"* and passed around packs of Camels and candy bars.

Coop said, "Haven't you fucking *learned?*" He did sound like Hodge, like Dad. What was left of the handcuffs from Tricia's last adventure in shoplifting had come off Coop's wrists painfully in the night, cut by Able Steven with some special kind of hacksaw. Hodge tapped a cigarette on his wide palm, only half steering, looking over Bailey to Tricia, look back at Coop a long time, chilly.

He said, "Don't give your chick a hard time."

And Bailey, too—Bailey rode closer and closer to Hodge's side, practically under his arm now as he tirelessly drove.

Coop dropped back down on the tatty mattress, the only seat in back. Grandma would be in Japan by now. The new gang had a whole month in her empty house if they wanted it. He thought of his two girls in the shower like otters, all skin. Hodge drove the roaring bus. Hodge meant to see Boyd Friendly, old chum in Seattle. Hodge had some kind of plan with Boyd, wouldn't say what. Bailey leaned her head on Hodge's shoulder, hummed. Tricia watched out her window, silent—corn in long rows and distant farmsteads—watched and watched, building a poem. Coop knew not to bother her, thought of her hand on him, thought of lying in the moss and twigs with her at the DuPonts' Cascade cabin, all that kissing and nuzzling and slick-slidy fun. More of that, is what Coop wanted.

At great length Tricia said, "We'll be going through Montana."

"Someone else is going to have to drive soon," Hodge said. He ran a hand over his Marine Corps haircut.

"Me," Coop said. He'd get through Montana so fast Tricia'd not even think of getting out.

Hodge said, "Someone with a license, jerkwad."

Coop lay back down, played with two packs of cigarettes for many flat miles.

At last, Bailey spoke, apropos nothing, unless it was the reunion of brothers. Her voice was uncharacteristically soft: "One time I was with my sister Petie at some hot-damn *function* in Houston, some government thing of my Daddy's and I just looked at Petie and stared at her, and I could not figure out who she *was*, all of a sudden, just like that, just could not get it. I mean, I looked at her and I said, baby, *who are y'all?*"

"Quiet," Hodge said.

Next tank of gas, South Dakota, Bailey drove. That put Tricia in the middle, Hodge shotgun, Coop still in the back like a little kid—some squirt of a kid—but at least a kid with cigarettes. A cop doing maybe a *hundred* passed them, not so much as a sideways look. Coop had to be in back because his hair was long. *Cop bait,* Hodge had called him. The sun dropped, the night came on. Tricia took over the wheel. She drove fast as hell, didn't slow down for towns, even with Hodge mad at her. Hodge had no power over her, none at all. When he said to slow down, the bus gave a leap.

In the dark Bailey crawled over the seat, got in back with Coop. She lay on the thin twin mattress close beside him, one leg crossed over the other same as his.

"He is *gorgeous,*" Bailey whispered.

"You think everyone's *gorgeous.*"

"He's *scared.*"

Hidden back there in the dark of night Bailey let her hand fall so it touched Coop's hip, then his belly. Then skillfully she opened his pants—Jesus—and with giggles for the secret of it, started to jerk him off.

Tricia suddenly said, "Okay, Hodge Henry: tell us what happened!"

Hodge didn't answer for a long mile.

Bailey paused in her ministrations at the question. Coop put a beseeching hand on her hip, wow.

Hodge spoke. Like a bomb was nothing, he said, "I put a little pipe bomb in the file room at the Detroit draft board."

"Y'all did *what?*" Bailey said. "I don't think we can *hear* back here." She sat up fast, abandoned Coop just like that, Coop who was pent to pop.

Hodge said, "Bombed the draft board on Belson Street in Detroit."

Tricia closed her window to hear better. Hodge closed his.

Bailey said, "Y'all *bombed* something?"

"Just enough powder in a pipe to blow the files all over the room. And out the windows, too. Like a snowstorm. Just beautiful."

"Y'all did *violence?*"

Hodge said, "Deliberate Destruction of Government Property, I believe is the charge. And endangerment."

"You hurt someone?" Tricia said.

"No, little girl. Just blew paper all over the fucking place. By the time they sort all that shit back out, Nixon'll be Nehru."

Bailey said, "Violence is bad karma, baby. And now you got *caught.*"

"Not exactly caught," Hodge said.

"Then exactly *what?*" Bailey said. She got up on her knees, leaned over the seat, ready to fight. Coop and his anxious boner she'd forgotten completely. He packed himself away, zipped up, disconsolate.

"Someone got hurt?" Tricia said.

Hodge looked at her a long, long time. His chin was hard, his arm over the seat taut and tense, all muscles. He said, "No, little girl. Small bombs. Careful drops. I've just done too many. I had a puffer in Madison, and then another in Cincinnati. Misfires. And that means, you know, they got the poppers. They got the poppers, they got my fingerprints, they got my materials, they got to Jackson's Industrial and Educational, and Jackson's had the Geoff Street phone number because that little nigger Able Steven is a *moron,* and then the pigs turned up." He stared ahead, seemed to study the thousand bugs on the windshield.

"You're calling Steven a *nigger?*" Tricia said.

Bailey: "Y'all's violence isn't *justified* by their violence. I'm sorry."

"That's what he is, little girl, a nigger fuckup."

"*Violence,*" Bailey said.

"Turns out you're the one who's a pig," Tricia said.

"Everyone calm down?" Coop said.

Hodge: "The revolution has to proceed by any means."

"Oh, Jaysus," Bailey said.

"How about osmosis?" Tricia said, hard at the wheel, the bus in her hands careening through the night. "How about by sedimentation? How about the simple passage of time?"

Hodge, finally joking: "You really are a dumb cunt, aren't you?"

He looked at Tricia and shrugged to show he was kidding, looked at her a long time again as she drove, and that shrug and that long, proprietary gaze after violent insult would make its way into Tricia's next poem, and that poem would make its way in ten years into Tricia's posthumous book of poems and the shrug would be specifically mentioned in a review by a writer for *The New York Times,* and Coop, incredibly, would see the critic's words one morning as he aimlessly read the *Book Review* (Frank Kobil always perused the *Sunday Times Book Review,* though he never read a book that Coop saw) at the team breakfast table, Sun Valley,

Utah. And he would remember the shrug absolutely and the gaze always, and both three ways: in memory, in the poem, in the kitchen of a ski-team condo.

Bailey was steamed. She flopped back on the mattress beside Coop, arms folded over her chest, legs crossed, foot waggling fiercely. Coop had no faint idea of what to do with himself. He hated that Hodge was hateful; he hurt badly in his balls.

The bus was about out of gas—all seemed desperate—as lights came in view, some townless town before Murdo, just twenty houses. Not even a church. But fortunately a gas station, unfortunately closed up. Hodge and Coop jumped quick to check the pumps—not a drop left to fill a coffee can.

"Fuckers drained the hoses," Hodge said. From his shirt pocket he retrieved his signature box of kitchen matches, and while Coop held the pump gun, Hodge delicately stuffed the nozzle with wooden flares, heads out. "Works about half the time," he said. "First thing tomorrow these cheap fuckers pull the nozzle out, the matches click, and pretty soon the whole fucking town's in flames." Hodge grinned. Coop thought how seldom he'd seen Hodge grin, watched him swagger off, quickly pulled the matches out of the nozzle, afraid to his feet that they'd ignite, afraid worse that Hodge would turn and catch him.

They successfully siphoned a tank of gas from a parked church van, carried on. Now Coop got to ride shotgun, guiltily dropping to sleep suffering fucking *blue balls*. Permanent damage? He didn't know, just didn't know anything except that he was sleepy, very sleepy. Hodge and Bailey lay on the mattress in back. Coop didn't dare to turn and look. Who knew what might be going on back there? He felt he loved Bailey now. He loved Tricia too. He was full of love and was maybe a hippie after all. He slept.

All night Tricia drove, waking the others only when it was time to siphon gas or time to piss. Heroically long she drove, the dawn behind them, bright sun high as she crashed over the tall curb into Grandma's short driveway waking the rest of the gang. Coop vaulted out of the bus, found the extra house key on its hook behind a porch stanchion.

The beloved musty-floral smell of the place greeted him, Grandma so strongly present that Coop got the sudden spooked feeling she was *home*, maybe still asleep in her great bed. He listened, slunk into the living room. On her grand desk was her itinerary: Japan, South Korea, Ceylon, home a month hence. The thick curtains checked the assault of the summer sun, and the place was darkly Coop's, all his.

Once they were fed there wasn't much to say.

So up the back stairs Hodge and Bailey went and before long Coop heard them unmistakably fucking *("Jaysus, oh Jaysus!")* in the little girls' room. So into the living room, where he sat at Tricia's knees and watched her sleep. She was very crazy. That's all. Her flannel shirt was open at the neck showing her yellowing professorial hickey and flushed skin over clavicles rising, falling. He lay beside her, balanced just at the edge of the couch, put his lips to her ear, said, "I know you're tired because you've been awake two days and I'm glad you're asleep and I'm not worried for you at all and I love you." He threw his leg over both of hers protectively, threw an arm over her chest, tucked his hand in her far armpit keeping her safe. Soon he slept, smelling her, feeling like an altogether different person than the daydreaming boy who'd come to Grandma's not three weeks before, a boy who'd had real sex, who'd traveled the hard way, who'd been dosed and kicked and harassed by the pigs, a boy in love with two women at once.

Bailey woke him in the house's dusk, which came much earlier than the dusk of the day. He'd slept all afternoon, balanced on the edge of the couch. Tricia hadn't moved at all. To her name repeated sweetly in her ear she grunted a little, seemed to try to open her eyes, an improvement.

"Tired girl," Bailey said. She was in some shirt of Grandma's, shiny silk, monogrammed pocket, tails that didn't quite cover her up. Her legs were olive dark and smooth, a little downy at the thighs, nice to see. Her hair hung in strings, wet from a shower that had made her pink. She seemed concerned with something, held her lips taut, looked at Coop without seeing him exactly, like she was looking just in front of him.

Coop struggled upright, moved Tricia's long legs to make room to sit, put his hand familiarly high inside Tricia's thigh, showing off that he could touch her where he would. He said, "Did you sleep?"

Bailey made a joke of coming out of her reverie, shook her head, blinked her eyes. She said, "I think so, baby. Some serious *humping* went on up there. At least I got *laid!*" Then she wasn't joking: "Oh, baby, I'm in *love.*" She shrugged her shoulders up comically, turned her hands in the air in front of her like the Southern belle she was not, said, "Who would *think?* I'm in *love* with a violent *man!*" Then serious again: "He's got more of that shit in mind! He wants to blow up the whole country, baby! I told him what he's really tryin' to do is to kill y'all's *daddy,* or maybe his self. Coop, baby, I need y'all to talk him out of these crazy *ideas.*"

Coop said, "Right."

"He respects y'all a lot, Coop."

If that were true!

Coop and Bailey looked into each other a long time, as if it were they who were in love. Coop fought his jealousy—only fighting it made sense. Then Hodge appeared, wearing just his cheap Geoff Street pants. His broad chest and deep stomach were like armor. The tendons stood out in his neck. His arms were thewed and muscled, big as clubs, swung a little stiffly from his wide shoulders. His eyes were tired and he steered himself slowly and tensely into the room.

Bailey contrived to put her foot up on the couch by Coop. She brushed at her toenails, showed him her bare self under the silken shirttails. A boy looks at what a girl chooses to show him. She turned just so, supposedly to look at her roughened heel but Coop saw, saw her sweet curled pubic hair and the pink of what showed through the hair, certainly swollen from the screwing. Bailey dropped her foot after a long, *long* interval, yawned, elaborately stretched in front of Coop, said, "I'm fixin' to create us a little *meal.*"

"Starving," Hodge said, oblivious.

"The two of you-all just lounge here and have a little *chat,* okay? Coop's been tellin' me some *things* he aims to tell y'all." She sashayed into the kitchen, paused just to look back at Coop, lifted her shirttail, showed him her little butt, wise-guy grin on her face—it was all just a joke, everything a joke to her.

"I want you to know I like her," Coop said.

"What about this one?" Hodge said. He sat at the edge of the couch, touched Tricia's shoulder.

"Her too," Coop said. "She's my girl."

Hodge leaned to Grandma's myopic TV, clicked it on, got the news with Huntley and Brinkley. "Look at this crap," he said. Chet Huntley talked seriously about the moon, Brinkley interviewed a NASA guy. The astronauts would be back on earth tomorrow. Coop remembered what Bailey had said and suddenly didn't trust the scientist who spoke, this white coat talking bullshit just the way Dad did and teachers did and all adults. The scientist was only making a paycheck for himself, spending billions while people went hungry, while people had to live at Geoff Street and worse, while people got shot in the head in Vietnam.

"Moon walk," Coop said derisively. Only a month past he had loved NASA with pure poignant passion.

Hodge said, "Listen, Tony. The pigs are going to be looking for me. They're going to find me, okay? That's what I want you to know. We have a couple days at most. Then I'm going to have to split."

Coop said, "Please don't call me Tony, okay?"

"Oh, that's right."

They watched the television.

Coop said, "I'm sticking with you."

Hodge didn't answer. He rubbed his face. At length he said, "I got one more project, okay? Boyd Friendly's thing. All right? Then I'm going to split, and you can't tag along. You're hearing me, right?"

"No, I'm sticking," Coop said. "You'll let me stick, right? What about Bailey? Bailey likes you, Hodge." He didn't want to say what she'd said about being in love. "She'll come with us, too."

"Not after Boyd and I get through, she won't. She's got a little . . . sensitivity problem."

Coop thought of her face laughing and welled with a great surge of love for her and her sensitivity.

Hodge said, "She ain't going to like Boyd Friendly."

Coop remembered Boyd Friendly, all right. Even smelled him— pine boards just cut. Mom and Dad hated Boyd Friendly because he was phony polite and shifty-eyed. He'd done something bad to his parents, burned their house down or something. Boyd in front of a movie theater on First Avenue with Hodge and two girls in dresses had said: *Fuck you, birthday boy,* because Coop at ten years old had said it was curfew.

Chet Huntley showed film from Vietnam, then announced the body count. Two American boys, seventeen South Vietnamese, forty-one North Vietnamese. "Shit," Hodge said. "You add 'em up we've killed the whole country seven fucking times."

"Well you and Boyd wrecking stuff won't help," Coop said reasonably, plunging. He'd promised Bailey. "Two wrongs don't make a right."

"Okay, Chief."

Tricia woke grumpy. "You guys quiet," she said.

Hodge looked at her coldly: "Quiet yourself, little girl."

After their dinner—Bailey had made good spaghetti somehow just from the junk in the pantry—Hodge gave Coop a job: call Boyd Friendly from a pay phone far from the house. He gave a code to use, too.

"Cute," Bailey said. "What's *my* mission, General Doom?"

Hodge just got colder yet: "Why don't you go with Tony, flower girl? There's a revolution in progress—we all have to chip in."

Bailey stood up fast, marched outside, furious. Hodge had that effect on her.

"I'm going to go up and sleep some more," Tricia said. She'd finished her plate, then Coop's, was now eating what pasta was left in the bowl, eyes half closed.

So Coop followed Bailey, caught her up a block away, Bailey *cruising* down the hill toward the city.

He said, "I tried to talk to him." They walked all the way downtown, all the way to the waterfront, a full hour's hard march, Bailey calming, in fact slowly growing cheerful, even to the point of singing loud songs, getting silly. They got to the piers in time to watch the Alaska ferry come in, the day go dark over Puget Sound. For another hour they played pinball in a movie lobby on just three dimes, then went into a fancy bar and got kicked out. Next try, some kind of sailor bar, they got served beers, sat in a wooden booth side by side. Coop thought to kiss Bailey, but there wasn't an opening: even drunk they were the wrong kind of friends. Even after the dark-bus half-a-*hand-job* last night. Damaged-looking men in the bar stared.

"We better call Friendly," Coop said at last.

"We are not callin' anyone," Bailey said, her brown eyes clear. "We are not callin' Boyd Friendly."

That was that. Coop felt himself firmly on Bailey's side. They laughed at foiling Hodge and Friendly, drank another beer in the smoke, held hands, no kisses.

Back in the air, they walked up and down First Avenue among street hippies, got a hit of a joint from a Black man—an Afro-American (right, right)—who'd greeted Bailey charmingly, lurked with him a while, walked on. Coop eyed each pay phone, clicked the lone dime in his pocket with his fingernail.

At last Bailey had to piss. She ducked into a diner full of truckers and drunks who noticed her flagrantly as she flounced to the back. When she was out of sight, they turned their heads to stare at Coop. He fumbled to make a fast telephone call, dialed the number he'd got by heart. A girl answered, jolting Coop from his planned speech.

"Uh, who's this?" he said, lamely.

Brightly: "Madeline. Who's this?"

"I'm Marco's brother," Coop said, just as he'd been told. In years to come he'd have reason to remember the girl's voice at the other end of the line. In years to come he'd think often that this betrayal of Bailey brought him Madeline. He gave in to Hodge, and got Maddy on the line. In years to come and always Coop would think about the ways one meets the elements of one's fate: one at a time, all unawares. Jesus, hurry Madeline, Bailey won't piss long.

"Groove! You want Boyd," Madeline said. In years to come Coop would not forget this first sound of her voice, the snappy confidence of her hippie vocabulary: "I'll get him. You hang!"

Coop waited, watching the ladies' room, blind to the future—how could he not be?

Friendly got on: "Yeah." No doubt it was he, all boom and thunder, no mistaking that low voice.

"I'm Marco's little brother," Coop said again.

Friendly rumbled, "Well, fuck you." This was supposed to be funny.

"We are in town. Please stop by." That was what he was supposed to say exactly.

"Done," Friendly rumbled.

Coop hung up fast and slipped outside, breathing hard. He looked up the street and down and jumped when Bailey tapped his shoulder.

She said, "Howdy, gorgeous."

And Coop said hi, like he hadn't just completely violated her trust and violated everything that was peaceful and good in the world.

The whole long walk home Bailey talked about wondrous things: college was *useless,* God was *various,* bathtubs were the *best* place to fuck or masturbate, sex should be free, jealousy was all about ownership and *both* those things were wrong, football was stupid and Texas the *capital* of football so bad she'd had to go to private school, oral sex regardless of gender harked back to *breast feeding* and so satisfied both recipient and giver. She talked about Hodge a long time, too, said finally, "I know what y'all are thinkin', Coop, baby. Y'all're thinkin' it's *bad news* not doin' what he said. But get it straight: y'all did the right *thing,* and the right *thing,* baby, is the only thing to do. Let's tell him this: Friendly says the plan is *off.*"

"I can't lie to my brother," Coop said. The beer sloshed in his stomach, swirled in his brain.

In the attic Hodge was stretched out on the bunk beside Tricia, under a sheet. He didn't jump up, didn't seem caught at anything, and Tricia was heavily asleep, but their clothes and shoes were piled at the side of the bed, her white underpants topmost, and both big brother and sweetheart were plainly naked.

Bailey said, "What's this?"

Hodge slithered out of bed, stood, slipped into his revolutionary's khaki boxers, covered Tricia, who was out cold. He said, "What'd Friendly have to say?"

And Bailey said it again, not like someone who'd conquered jealousy: "What's this?"

"Don't ask," Hodge said, frosty.

"Friendly says the plan's off," Coop lied. "He says, tell your brother get out of town."

7

At the Herbert Hotel you walk in the doors and the heat settles on you like caring and these huge Canadian work dogs greet you, these huge and impassive old Labradors, totally accepting. They walk you to the couches in front of the fire in the enormous parlor and there is no one there, not a soul. No one at the desk, no one in the dining room. Just the dogs. Just me, Hodge, and to a certain extent, you, grown older than in life, forgiven. I watch the fire, think of the days Kobil and I used to spend drinking whiskey right here. I think of you lying with Tricia, and how strained those next days among us really were, as we headed into the inferno.

I'm not drinking, so it's up to my room with a box of books transported from home. I haven't yet called Madeline, not quite sure what to say. My jaw is okay, but Roddy has put a nice lump on my forehead.

Bailey Shapiro's dream of free love was as preposterous as yours of a violent revolution. And if it were free, why did she only grab me in secret, in Grandma's larder, in the thorns behind the house? I did everything to keep you and Tricia apart (you both utterly silent about the scope of your liaison), and succeeded, did everything to turn Bailey from her infatuation—gigantic—with you. Boyd Friendly's visits, you two planning and scheming, sure helped my cause. Boyd Friendly was a beast, he really was, with that deep voice, dead eyes, leather necklace, blue enamel beads. Bailey didn't *get* what Madeline saw in him, willowy Madeline with her airs and long skirts.

"Greetings," says a voice, the only human sound I've heard. It's the owner of the hotel, an affable fellow with excellent boundaries, who has somehow appeared behind the desk. He doesn't exactly look at me.

"Greetings yourself," I say.

"How's your room?"

"Very quiet," I say.

"How's skiing?"

"Knocked my head," I say, and point to the bruise Roddy's fist made.

He looks at my noggin, like, what'd you expect?, says, "Maybe next time she'll kill you." He means the mountain.

In my room I pull out my books from their banana carton, maybe thirty of them, stuff I've meant to read for years, some of it. My idea has been to start back among the ancients and to read my way up to the present, a pretty hackneyed ideal, I know, but start way back and fill in the huge holes in my reading, read what's past with the idea that I'll give myself what's next. The Herbert is as good as anyplace to start the project.

My room is off in some lost corner of an upper floor, freshly painted, hundreds of square feet, with a couch and two easy chairs, an armoire and coffee table, braided rug. A brass light fixture hangs down just to where the hair of my head brushes it when I pass under. The bathroom is as big as an entire Holiday Inn room, with a tub you could wash a VW bus in. Wainscoting. $155.00 a night, which I figure I can afford till Madeline gets the MasterCard bill. And I can't think where else to go. I'm confused, terribly confused: which woman is breaking my heart?

5:30 P.M. and it's already been dark an hour. I settle into one of the easy chairs in my room, put my feet on the coffee table, get to work reading Homer's *Odyssey*. This, I know, I read at Colgate in my beleaguered freshman year, my only full year of college. The cover design is a memory in itself. On the title page there are my doodles, squares within squares that form flowers, drawn by my hand all those years past. And I've written the name Gail Stetson over and over in the first twenty pages. And underlined passages. And dog-eared pages from front to back. And I don't remember a word. Don't remember any face of a professor. Don't quite remember the face attached to this Gail Stetson, though I remember a striped skirt she wore and her mouth and some great emotion: loss.

I read till seven o'clock, transported, amazed at how fast the verses spin past, amazed too that most of the first part of the book is Telemachus looking for his dad. It's just great stuff and I take notes and am filled with hope after a day of skiing and a week of rejection. One's new life starts like this, rising from desperation in a wainscoted hotel room somewhere in Maine with Odysseus.

I would like a beer. But I have vowed not to drink. I would like dinner. Dinner is certainly allowed. I will bring Robert Fitzgerald's translation of Homer to the table, and the two of them, translator and poet, both long dead, will be my company for the night. I will abandon Hodge, forget the story of Tricia and Bailey for this older one. So down the stairs.

In the lobby there is no one. None of the skiers who will come in a month's time, none of the local drunks, none of the new coaching staff (teetotalers to a man and to a woman). Nor Madeline. Nor Mom. Nor speedy Noriko. Nor Prick Baldwin. Nor Frank Kobil. Nor Tricia's shade, nor even yours, pal. Just Coop himself and the big Canadian work dogs and the fire in the wide fireplace. There I stand. And in a minute I hear the great door open. This is profoundly irritating: I want to be the only guest, the between-season exception. The dogs stir mildly to see who's coming in, the fire jumps as the door closes. I'm going to ignore this person. And my ignoring works; whoever it is goes away and there's just silence, and Coop Henry standing in an Odyssean fog, reading:

> What more can this hulk suffer? What comes now?
> In vigil through the night here by the river
> how can I not succumb, being weak and sick,
> to the night's damp and hoarfrost of the morning?

Then someone's laying a hand on my shoulder. Roddy, of course. And the Universe shifts just that much. I turn to her and we're both sheepish smiles. What I like about her is she doesn't apologize for the knot on my head. She just inspects it with a certain pride. I look at her eyes and she looks in me and the fire is hot on my legs and the air of the room is close around us.

"Sit," she says.

We fall back into one of the grand sofas.

"We're always on couches," she says.

"I've been reading the *Odyssey*," I say.

And then we just look at the fire. There's a lot to get straight in our heads. We hold hands and watch the fire and I'm the first one who tries: "Urgh."

At great length an ancient waitress totters out of the kitchen, gasps to see us, to have been derelict in her simple duty; but how was she to know that people had appeared? She pats through the dining room in a doddering rush, enters the parlor with a deep breath, clears her throat, looks down upon us with pure benevolence.

"Do you two want drinks or to be alone?"

The dogs slump to the floor, the waitress waits. Roddy says "Cognac," and you can see how much the older gal admires her, how Roddy accepts the waitress as her equal, as a complete person. The comparison to Madeline's snobbery drifts across the room, settles on the faded floral wallpaper, blends in but will not entirely disappear.

"I will bring you two Remys," says the old waitress, and totters away.

"I'm not drinking," I say.

"You're not quitting now," says Roddy. She leans into me and the energy is like we've been kissing for hours, like we're swollen with kissing, though we've been in each other's company but a minute and haven't kissed for weeks and are not going to kiss now. She leans into my intimate space, but comes no closer, she on the edge of the old couch, I sinking further in. It's a big old feather sofa, instantly warm and enveloping.

"One kiss?" I say.

"I don't see how that's going to work," she says. Her face, her skin, her cheeks, the line of her nose, her lips, they are like the truth revealed. I need to study that face; that face satisfies hunger, curiosity, appetite. I look at her carefully from chin to hairline very slowly, pausing at her eyes. She's looking at my legs, she's looking at my lap. She's got the very slightest down on her upper lip, and her lips don't meet exactly at the center. One lock of her whitely bleached hair strands under her nose. I want to look in her dark nostrils. I see her ears, I see her eyelashes, I see the sclera of her eyeball glistening, the little line of eye pencil she's put on, the sweet laugh lines at the edges of her eyes. She's windburned from the day's work. She's not a girl anymore. That's long changed. She looks at me and I see back there behind her eyes her intelligence, her wisdom, her irritability, her vision, her insecurity, her childlike openness, her stormy defensiveness, her cheer, her intensity, her sensuousness, her history, her love of painting and paintings, her speed on skis, her humor, her wish to impress, her capacity for love, and, unfortunately, her resolve: she is going to marry Claudio.

The waitress comes back with our drinks on a tray and puts them on the coffee table without looking at us, pure discretion, just delicately places the snifters (humming all the while) and is gone, disappeared into the oaken woodwork of the place. It's a Monday night, early season, dead quiet.

"You may have one kiss," says Roddy, her deep eyes clear as Homer's Athena, if brown. "Just one. And later. Just before I get back in the cute little car I've rented and drive away from here. One last kiss and we say good-bye."

We settle into what passes for a companionable silence, drinking the cognac, hearing the beatific breathing of the big dogs, feeling the expansile glow of the fire. I can live with the one-last-kiss idea, but I've no idea where I'll go in the morning.

"Noriko's really good," Roddy says at length.

"She's a kid," I say, glad to be talking.

"She's fearless," says Roddy. "That's the advantage of being seventeen. You didn't see her on the head wall, Mr. Henry. She hits the ice completely closed. Completely closed! She doesn't so much as twitch her little nose."

"Roddy, you always look good coming over that wall, too. You always look better than anyone else."

"I wiped out, Mr. Henry."

"People wipe out. Probably you were pressing it, that's all. Probably you were completely closed, too, and two seconds up, and that's why you fell."

"I was a second down, and completely closed, then I completely crashed. I'm not going to make the cut."

Roddy sips her cognac breath by breath till it's gone. She's looking across me and into the flames of the fire, this exchange of logs for smoke, her face composed. She's someone who's made a decision.

I say, "You're going to do fine."

Roddy says, "Coop, I'm quitting. That's the news. I just see what a hell of a time I'm going to have staying pumped this year. I'm retiring, Mr. Henry. I'll be coming in eleventh and twelfth in the big meets, then next year it will be the Europe Cup circuit, and good-bye."

"Rick and Claudio will get you on top again. You've got enough years in you for, hell, two more World Cups and an Olympics."

"Yeah, I'm sure. And I'll come in thirty-ninth and eight-hundredth and one-millionth. Noriko's going to be peaking. Lots of fun, the commentators saying, Poor Roddy, she used to be a contender!"

Not much to say to this. She's got it right. Already last year the sportscasters started in. They loved to show Roddy's famous fall over and over again, slo-mo through the part where her boot spins nearly a full revolution while the bones in her ankle and foot pop and break and chip and the tendons stretch and let go.

I say, "With the media, Julie Tinker's got it worse."

"I just don't want that, Mr. Henry. I just don't think I want that kind of spiraling slow demise." She looks at me plainly, speaks her calm proposition: "Don't you think it's more elegant to get out while you're ahead, while you're well thought of?"

"Sure, definitely. Right after the Olympics."

"No, Coop. I'm thinking more like right now. Before I fall even one more time. I'll volunteer coach the downhill ladies for the next couple of weeks the way Mary Frawley used to do. I'll help Claudio. But I'm not skiing anymore, unless it's for fun."

"What's Claudio say about all this?"

"I haven't quite told him yet."

"Communication . . . "

The biggest dog sibilantly farts, sighs hard, stretches. Roddy looks around the empty place. "Nice paintings in here," she says. "Someone's got the eye." She puts a hand on my leg, talks to my ear, getting closer and softer. This is just friendliness. She's said she doesn't want to kiss but once and good-bye, and Roddy's good as her word. She's a woman about to get married, even looks like a woman about to get married: distant, forlorn, her thoughts abstract.

"Did I tell you officially, Mr. Henry? I'm going to close my leave of absence at the University of Vermont and I'm starting back in January. And here's the official announcement: Roddy Manor, injury-plagued Olympian, is going to retire December tenth. You know what December tenth means, right?"

"It's my parents' fiftieth anniversary."

"No way."

"Yes."

"Well it's also your last official day with the team. And now mine. How about that?"

Another long silence. I'm trying to formulate the right question here, want to put the conversation on the tack we're avoiding. Instead, and inanely, I say, "Doesn't Greg Gumbel already call you 'Scholar of the Slopes'?"

Roddy is not amused. She says, "Oh, Coop, I miss Frank. Everything's changed absolutely. *'Sì presso a morte, e sì lontan da Dio.'*"

"Translate this time!"

She frowns—what kind of knucklehead doesn't know Italian? "It's Michelangelo again: 'With death so near and God so far away.'"

More silence. Full silence, a day of hard life behind us, we sinking flank by flank into the couch, Roddy flushed with the heat of the fire and the day's windburn, the vision of her plan still in the air all around us. If she goes to Vermont, I want to know, where's Claudio? But I can't find a way to ask. Roddy stretches her legs, kicks her snow boots off one at a time, wriggles her toes in her thermal racing socks, made in Italy, a hundred bucks a pair.

Dreamily she says, "Skiing is not my life. I want to think about civilization again." On that famous bus trip some months long past she wiggled her toes under my thigh and confided to me: *half of Claudio's charm is his being Roman.* Dreamily, she shakes her head, looks at the ceiling a long time, and when she speaks it's as if she's saying how much she loves me: "It's time to think about life."

The silent waitress pads out and I realize she's in slippers. Quilted silk slippers, pink and worn. "More Remy Martin for you two?" She has a faint accent, perhaps Swedish. "Did I inform you that the dining room's open just until eight? Just for another hour? Would you like to order now? See a menu? We'll be cooking for just the two of you, it looks as if."

Roddy says, "Maybe we better eat. Coop. If I drink and don't eat anything I'll have to stay here."

"Ha-ha," says I.

The waitress says, "We've plenty of room." She looks at me only briefly, studies Roddy, likes her, wants to talk. People *like* Roddy when they see her. Strangers want to talk to her. Another comparison between Roddy and Madeline breaks away, escapes, flutters up to the wall, sticks: Madeline bugs most people, some of them on sight. It's the hippie dresses, maybe. The quick judgement always in her face. Though then again they may only be jealous of her, or find her comeliness chilling. I think of Buck Holander and Claudio and you, Hodge, in quick succession. The cognac burns my face.

"We'll eat," Roddy says.

The waitress, clearly pleased, shuffles off to warn the kitchen.

Now Roddy wants me to talk: "What's next for *you?*" she says.

"I don't know," I say. "Uh. What's it like in Burlington?" I'm breathless saying this. I love this woman like I have not loved since I was . . . fifteen. Immaturely, that is (let me admit it), but something else is growing, too. I love her and my fear has flown away. She's on the couch with me and has her hand casually on my knee, and I know there's no move I can make to win her. But I picture a successful result the way I picture the downhill course before a race: close my eyes, remember each gate, each bump, each patch of ice, actually sway and dip and think my way through a record run. I think of kissing her neck. That's what comes to mind. If I could only kiss her neck.

At dinner, just as our food arrives, Roddy says, "You and Frank were pretty close."

"I guess so. Yes, we were."

"You're feeling better?"

"I did my community service. I'll have to tell you my theory of litter."

"I love imagining you with garbage bag and poker."

"But Frank and all was only a spark. Like you are a spark. Sometime, Roddy, I have to tell you about my awful brother."

She knows not to press. We eat and drink and look at each other and no one watching would know how painful.

"Why'd you come here?"

"You told me to act."

"No, but why?"

"Madeline. She's been . . . fucking her partner on their two desks for years. I just figured it out."

"So you ran off?"

Softly: "I acted."

"Well, no. You *re*-acted."

"Not good enough?"

"You'll get your kiss, don't worry."

It's all elegy, as far as I can see. The chef comes out, a portly, bearded boy-man with a checked apron and clean hands, glass of heavy red wine balanced on his palm. He's all smiles, half smashed, his first customers of the season, new menu: "You like the sea bass?"

"I love the sea bass," Roddy says.

The chef beams. He's made a meal just for us, for two lovers strange to him, or more precisely, for Roddy, whom he plainly finds appealing.

"I'm about to try my first bite," says I.

The waitress pads back out with one more cognac each. "On the house," she says and pads away with a smile, pulling the chef behind her.

Roddy stretches her hand out across the table, touches my elbow, looks at me unhappily. She says, "Don't forget to eat." She's got a big fat ring flashing on her left hand, a ring I've managed not to notice until now.

I pick up my glass. Roddy hers. At length I get the right words, say, "Here's to retirement."

"Retirement," she says hotly.

"To whatever comes next."

"Whatever comes," Roddy says.

"To your wedding," I say, valiantly.

Roddy sips her cognac and tries to laugh but instead and abruptly she's a great font of tears, looking through tears, gasping. "Do you have a room here?" she says. "You better have a room."

The old waitress pads out the kitchen door, pauses a moment, not watching us but seeing nonetheless. Satisfied, she slips back away.

Roddy says, "I want to give you that kiss."

Chapter Five

1

When I finally come awake it's noon and there isn't one sign that Roddy has been here except the smell of her hair in the pillows. She's neatly made the side of the bed she ended up on, righted the ottoman we knocked over, mopped up the many gallons of water we splashed out of the tub, hung the seven sumptuous towels we used. She's even folded my blue jeans and my shirt. She's gone.

At first as I lie there the question is what's next? I mean, I'm in Peanut Falls, Maine, and listen, you dead piece of shit, in my own way I'm extinct, too. I'm flipping through all the old friends I can think of, all the towns I've been fond of, all the long white beaches, nothing very helpful. Then the question simply goes away. I'm thinking of Roddy, steeped in Roddy, and today I'm going skiing, and that's it: I'm out of bed, I'm in the shower, I'm in a hurry, the best I've felt since I was ten with my red bike under me and school out for summer, my brother Hodge somewhere near.

A half-day ticket from the desk at the lodge, a hamburger at the Bag, which is one of those boot-beaten ski-resort restaurants with windows looking up the skirts of its mountain, thoroughly empty by the time I get there. I feel pummeled by some monumental boxer, proud to have survived. I'm trying to eat lunch in a blizzard of glimpses and brushes and flavors of Roddy. Oh, Roddy. That was some last kiss!

Another customer walks in, this out-of-place shambly fellow with a big head like Ted Kennedy's. He's in slacks and a sports jacket, crisp white shirt, striped tie, clothes you just don't see at Sugarloaf, a snacks salesman on the punishment route out of Boston. The bartender has disappeared back into the kitchen someplace, and our man just patiently waits, hands folded on the bar, kindly eyes. He's got all the time in the world. He's not a guy who's going to have a drink. Maybe a glass of milk before he gets back in the company Taurus and heads home to put his head in the oven.

When he finally decides to have a look around he sees me and brightens. I can tell he knows me. A fan. He's got that look fans have: sweet open face. He already likes me, nothing I can do will stop that. He looks apologetic, shambles over with his hands a mile in his pockets, shambles right up to my table, looks at my food.

I say, "Sir?"

And he says, "Always works out this way, doesn't it? I could look for you weeks on end, and then, here we go, we meet up just like this. Let me say what a pleasure it is, after all I've heard." He sticks out his hand and I go ahead and reluctantly shake it. He's got deep lines around his eyes, a worried brow. He says, "Tip Czako. You won't like this, but I'm the guy your mother hired to dig up your brother. We've talked on the phone."

"Oh, Christ."

"Your wife said you'd left home."

"Oh, Jesus H. Christ."

"Madeline, correct? She says give her a call. She says she understands."

"Right. And now you've got two clients."

"Also, she says tell you a certain lawsuit has been dropped."

"Charlie Merck? She sent you to tell me about Charlie Merck?"

"Anthony, I like you. I was told I would like you and I do. Do you have a minute?"

The strange thing is, I like him, too. He's followed me to Maine and knows things about me, and the truly curious thing is that I find his knowledge intimate. He seems the friend I need.

But what I let him see is anger. I say, "How the fuck did you get here?"

And Czako says, "A little help from your wife. From Madeline. Just a phone call, that's all. She wouldn't say much, except she's worried about you. She goes, 'First the explosion at Merck's True Value Hardware, now this.'" Czako does a fair imitation of Madeline's high courtroom style, holding his hands in the air and waving them as he's correctly guessed Madeline would: "'A friend's death, a reversal at work, mid-life crunch.' She's worried, Tony, she's emotional. I got her to put me on hold and call your, uh, let's see, Chase Manhattan MasterCard, and ask what the latest charges to the old family account were. And here we are: gasoline at eight stations west to east—poor mileage, Anthony, these Mercedes are big cars, but don't get me wrong, you're lucky to have it and I'm jealous—three nights lodging, a fairly hefty cash advance at the First Clarion Bank, Clarion, P.A. Lots to eat at nice restaurants. What's the deal? You don't like Burger King? Then we've got lift tickets at Sugarloaf here. I didn't want to bother you at your hotel this A.M. Stayed down with Rose Carter in Farmington last night. She says hello. And here we are."

"Thanks for your deep concern, Mr. Czako."

Czako sees he's got me, looks amused. That furrowed brow relaxes. He says, "I don't want to keep you. I'm thinking I'll earn my money right here. Can I call you Tony?"

I shake my head no, finish the first neat half of my burger, start looking for the mysterious bartender.

Czako says, "Tony, I have a theory about your brother, and I'd like to try it out on you."

Here we are in this big empty restaurant. In a few weeks it's going to be packed to the rafters with children and parents and ski bums and college kids. Right now there's no one but Czako and me, he with his beseeching, warm eyes, I still glowering. It's so quiet in the place you can hear the radio in the kitchen, a faint rendition of "Get Together," which is a song of our summer, dead boy: 1969. And which despite knowing how absurd I am for doing so I take as a sign that Czako's come to save me.

I say, "Call me Coop."

"Oh, hell, yes, that's right, of course, Jesus, I'm sorry about that, Coop. This ain't easy. Okay. I'm glad you're ready to hear me out. Here goes—correct me if I get it wrong: your brother is dead. Just like you told me. I thought you were jazzing me on the phone that night, but by now I've talked to a few people. First this Bailey Miller, Bailey Shapiro, as you knew her. Now, I get her on the phone down there in Texas, and she's sweet as can be, calm and cheerful, open like a book. Oh, yes, she knew you well. Oh, he's terrific, he's a skier, he's bad at keeping in touch, he's the hero of his town. Y'all, and by golly. You've seen her exactly twice since your big summer together. Once in 1976—you took a long trip to Texas. Once in '77 she came up to Aspen—too sad, too sad, that's what she says—though I must say she appears damn fond of you, sad or no. Two kids, pottery wheel, couple pounds overweight, great big house, husband works aerospace in Houston, it's an American story.

"But then we get to Hodge. Oh, now it's all past tense. She goes: He was chilly, he was careless, he was cocky, opinionated, mean. She goes: He was gorgeous, he was complicated, he was the first man she loved. She's getting gloomy. She says she's got to go, and just sort of offhand and obviously fibbing says Hodge is in Boston or someplace. But the way she says it, Tony. Cooper. It's an admission. The guy's fucking dead. This, even I can see."

I'm not going to be finishing lunch. I push back in my seat, fold my arms across my chest, look again for the bartender. I just need another face. I say, "I told you that plainly a month ago." Bailey and I had a nice few weeks down there in Texas, a great trip to Big Bend country, a near romance weighted fatally by that stone I keep talking about: you, bro.

Czako shakes his big head, continues his monologue: "Your brother, your brother. From your mother I gather he had a, let's say, *stormy* childhood. His whole record at Johnson Elementary— right?—his whole record in their files is fistfights and tantrums and assaults on other kids. At Memorial Junior High he's got truancy problems, a pregnant girlfriend—he's twelve years old for the love of Christ—broken windows in the gym, detentions, suspensions, a broken arm for one Dick Sheffield. You smile.

"High school and his grades are falling down to C's and D's, he's in guidance for threatening the French teacher, suspended again and again for fights—no kidding, your parents are down there twice a week talking to the principal—but he's a football star, am I right? Terrorizing halfback, so everyone protects him. He gets arrested just once, in Stamford, charges dropped, no record of the crime itself. You smile again. I won't ask. Plenty pranks on record. He comes up through the hatch door in the middle of the class play stark naked—this is before any streaking craze—he's pushing a math teacher's car off the rocks into the Norwalk River. Finally, he's punching the football coach in the throat and putting him in the hospital three weeks, end of the protection. He turns eighteen and leaves home, highjacked van, diploma left behind. All this from school records. Next thing he's in trouble in Chicago, gets himself named in some minor bombing schemes, arson, draft boards all around the Midwest, the Chicago office of Dow Chemical, couple of other biggies. Then we have him in Seattle. See? I know a few things.

"But there the record stops. So I go down the list of defendants in the Boeing indictment. Boyd Friendly? No one can find Boyd Friendly. How many bombings stick to that creep? Thirty-seven, I believe. And four counts murder. That dirtball. The Weather Underground was nothing compared to him all by himself. Outstanding charges: four murders, conspiracy, destruction of government property, harassment, sedition, illegal arsenal, drug charges (his apartment, my God, a storehouse), racketeering, the works for this guy. He's not a friend of yours, I pray. He best not. Probably he's an investment banker in Hong Kong by now. So no help there, though he's left traces. Florida, quite possibly. Key West. This clue, that one. Which your brother hasn't left at all, not a damn thing. Your brother: murder, sedition, conspiracy, racketeering—heavy rap, Tony. Coop. A very heavy rap.

"Patricia Thomas? Jesus, my friend, I'm sorry about Patricia Thomas. Her dad didn't want to hear from me, tell you what. Wish I'd never phoned him. He said those were sorry times and he'd rather not ever be reminded. He's one of the folks who said what a good kid you were back then. He wishes you well, by the way. Patricia Thomas—state's evidence, like you and Bailey—you children. What a legal team you had! Who was bankrolling that? No, no—don't bother—I know who. *Okay,* I ask myself. Who's next? And the answer is . . . Madeline."

"Let's not talk about Madeline."

"She's a hell of a practiced dissembler, Tony. Talking to her I didn't know what hit me. These fucking lawyers, right? But something else Bailey accidentally let on to: Madeline was there. One and the same. Madeline, it turns out, is one of the missing girls that fool policeman kept talking about. Madeline, Bailey lets slip, was Boyd Friendly's girlfriend. The same Madeline you're married to, am I right? What can account for this? Bailey tells me that Madeline took off walking through the woods with Boyd Friendly after your gang's little—altercation. Bailey's got it right?"

"Different Madeline," says I, lying despite myself.

"We're all different people, aren't we, youth to age? Madeline would probably have a little trouble with the Colorado Bar Association if all this came out, no?"

My mouth must fall open at this—Jesus, not that. But the truth is, Madeline is accomplice to nothing, managed never to be directly involved in anything, no matter what, cautiously hip even then, right bro?

Czako thinks he's scared me. He says, "No, no, I have no intention. That's not my job. So. None of you will talk about Hodge, but the original story—that he took off with Friendly—no one's saying that, either. Now I've got Madeline with Boyd, Hodge in past tense, and I'm thinking.

"So I call your wife, as I said. And, Cooper, she's running circles around me. She wants to talk about finding you, that's all she'll entertain. About Hodge she goes, Hodge Henry is very much alive. And she says probably that's where you are. With your big brother. But Hodge is dead, I go. 'Oh, no, he and Boyd Friendly took off together. Maybe to Ireland.' I go, Boyd Friendly your old boyfriend? She's sputtering now. And I go, I've got good dope here, don't I? She goes, 'My husband told you that?'

"Me, I'm just quiet. And then I get the speech: 'Cooper Henry has been under a lot of pressure. Cooper Henry has spent a little time under observation lately. Cooper Henry has these fantasies about his youth.' She gets so oratorical poetic I can just see the courtroom. You know her—I guess I don't have to tell you. Flights of passion she gives me, she's got the story worked out end to end.

I keep interrupting, asking her about Boyd Friendly, about why her name's on the phone bill and the gas bill and the electric bill from the apartment he lived in back in Seattle. And she goes, what do you want? And now she's not in court, she's negotiating—love these lawyers. I go, What happened to Hodge, that's all? And she goes, 'Hodge is dead.' I go, this I already know. She goes, 'Ask Coop.' I go, Ask Coop what? She goes, 'Ask Coop how Hodge died.' I know, I know, I'm pissing you off. Sorry Cooper—Jesus, pissing you off—but that's what she said. I felt she was assigning some blame to you in this matter."

He sits there waiting for an answer, eats my potato chips one by one, gazing at me. He reminds me of Frank Kobil, that's who. I just shake my head slowly at his skill. He cracked Madeline! Me, I'm not going to say anything no matter what he does or says.

He comes to realize this, says, "Hell, I'm in a nest of snakes here! Don't want to get between you two. Let me just continue my saga:

"I get my ass off the phone with Madeline—nice woman really, you should go back with her—anyway, I'm off the phone and I'm thinking about all this, and the truth is, I cannot get it straight. You kids do your little fireworks show at Boeing. Well, certainly not you. It's Boyd Friendly and your brother. 'Friendly'—nice name for a rat. Things go bad and the FBI is on you so fast you barely get time to get out of town to that cabin up there. This, I've had no trouble detecting.

"Now here's where it gets dicey: the local-yokel police officer takes it upon himself to go get you. Question one: how did he know you kids were there? Question two: why the fuck would he go out there by himself? I'd ask him, but he's dead ten years. Question three: he says in his deposition and in front of the grand jury and every time they ask that he didn't hit anyone with his six shots out of his revolver, which was a nice old Colt. He was scared, he freely admits, he fired wild. So the $64,000 question is: If Hodge

Henry is really dead, how'd it happen? Are these people all just trying to fuck with me? Is Hodge Henry out there alive somewhere?"

I say, "Maybe the cop was a better shot than he says. Maybe
Hodge was shot in the heart."

And that stops the conversation again. I want to talk to this
man, but my lips close after the one short sentence.

Piece by piece my potato chips have disappeared from my plate.
Czako leans and without permission or embarrassment picks up
the half of my burger I haven't touched, takes a big bite, chews
thoughtfully. Somehow the plate has gotten closer to his side of
the table. He wipes his mouth, moves the plate closer yet, takes
another bite of the burger, as if he's genuinely forgotten that it's
my food. Chewing, he says: "Shot in the heart. Killed. Then what?
What did you do with the guy's remains? And why? I see this is
painful for you. But we're almost done here."

"Thanks for your sympathy, Mr. Czako."

"Okay. Of course. And thanks for yours. Next thing anyone
knows, we have Anthony Cooper Henry and Bailey Shapiro and
Patricia Thomas coming in under your Grandmother's—
Congressman Vanderhoop's—wing as state's evidence. No Boyd
Friendly. No you-know-who. No trace of Madeline and not one
word about her in the grand jury proceedings. You and Bailey and
Patricia Thomas tell the court that the big boys planned and did
everything. Undoubtedly true. You were just kids following along,
didn't know a thing. Undoubtedly, undoubtedly. You tell the court
Hodge is run off with Boyd. Not a mention of Madeline. And that's
it, you're off the hook. Boyd and Hodge are fugitives, indicted on
umpteen counts. You'll testify against them when they turn up.
You go home, you ski your way to fame and fortune. And that's
the story."

"Have a potato chip, Tip. Have a bite of my hamburger."

"The food in this place is surprisingly good, Cooper."

"Where are we headed here?"

"Well, nowhere, really. It's just that your mother and probably your father can't finish this up till they know for sure what happened. They aren't dummies, those two. But they've got *hope*. And hope makes a person miserable. You hear me? Miserable. I'm just looking for the facts."

"You've got the facts, detective. My brother is dead. He's shot in the heart and dead."

"You put him in the earth?"

"We took good care of him."

"Your mother will want to know all this."

"You tell her."

"*Me?*" Czako grows indignant, and his passion tells me that he's not doing this for the money, not only for the money. He's a friend come to help. He must see my face soften: "Tony. *Tony.* How can I be the one who tells? You've held onto this thing for thirty years almost. Thirty years, that's a long time. You look at a car that's thirty years old you think, Look at that frigging bomb. Right? Thirty years of this ghost following you every goddamn place you go. Tell you what: you drive yourself down to Connecticut. That's your next stop. You go to your folks. You pick a good moment before your brothers and sister are there for this anniversary business of your mom's . . ." He goes silent, watching me. "Hey," he says. "Hey, boy. Here. Here's a handkerchief, fresh."

And we just sit there in the beer-soaked Bag like priest and penitent. He lets me weep awhile. Then he gets hold of his tie, straightens the knot, rebuttons his suit jacket, brushes off crumbs from the chips. Softly he says, "I don't want to tell her, Anthony. It's not going to fix me to tell her."

I just nod and sniff, head down.

Czako says, "But I'll get a few bucks off your wife for finding you." It's a joke.

I manage to laugh.

Czako says, "Go see that mother of yours. She's an awfully good soul. No one in the world as big hearted as her. And funny, too. No phone calls, now. You go down there and you see them. You be generous with them. Be a grown son. You're not a kid anymore. Your folks are *elderly*. The civil war's *over*. Come out of your *cave*, soldier. And what I'll do, with your permission, is call her and tell her you're coming."

"Jesus," I say. Then I say it again. And I'm up and storming out of the Bag, leaving my check there for Czako to pay. Screw him: I'm going to ski.

2

Coop Henry crept down the steel stairway from the double chain-link perimeter fence above the vast field of hangars at the Boeing plant. Boyd Friendly had simply unlocked the gates at the backlot employee entrance: he had all the right keys by way of his father's dresser drawers over the course of years, and he knew his way around Boeing brilliantly from an entire childhood of tours his dad had given him in lieu of any other companionship at all. Boyd and Hodge and Coop had huddled and watched the last flight come in at Boeing Field, miles away. *"Los Angeles, TWA flight 457,"* Boyd recited as the plane went over. He knew the proceedings here intimately and hated the place. He touched his necklace, rolled the blue beads in his fingers.

The stair railing burned Coop's hand as if it had been in the sun, but there was no sun, only yard lights bright as moons illuminating cyclonic cones of mist in the Boeing plant's vast yards. The breeze remained steady and strong and provided cover noise, small blasts of fear: newspaper blowing, flagpole lanyard tapping metal, sheet tin banging intermittently on a shed wall. Coop had stood nearly forever in the shadow at the top of the stairs as Friendly had told him to do, stood shielding his eyes, doing his job, which was to watch.

Coop was on his way down the stairs because he'd seen a man hunching along far from the guard route Boyd had drawn, hunching slowly in the direction of the mammoth hangar into which Hodge and Friendly had five eon-minutes ago disappeared. Or Coop thought he'd seen a man. Was at least fairly sure he'd seen a man. Though the shape was so far away it could have been mist blowing. Mist hunching along just as Friendly had described the guard Lumpy's walk. Lumpy loved pie. Lumpy was a clown. Lumpy loved to bowl. Lumpy was married with two teenage kids, nerds. Lumpy loved a drink of schnapps. Lumpy had babysat Boyd Friendly through many a long day after Boyd's folks split up and his Dad got summer custody and summer meant the Boeing plant, all day, every day. Lumpy was more a substitute father than any kind of pig. Coop tried hard to think of how only one guard would be there and that in the end this guard was just a *babysitter* anyway, just a big, simple guy who would know Boyd's face.

Coop was supposed to watch and he had been watching so hard his eyes went watery and now maybe he'd seen Lumpy or maybe he'd not. Nothing moving. Just the wind and that gonging flagstaff, the startling sheet of tin banging in no rhythm. Okay. If Lumpy hadn't been there, way over there, it would make no difference if Coop warned Hodge and Boyd falsely; in fact if he warned Hodge and Boyd falsely, maybe they'd stop and Coop could talk to Bailey again, Bailey who was furious at him and had shouted at him and called him a liar and a coward and a pig, though to Hodge she'd said nothing, just built an unassailable castle of angry silence.

But if that was Lumpy Coop had seen, if Lumpy was coming, there'd be a horrifying difference if Coop did not make the warning: Hodge and Friendly caught. Though by whom? By Lumpy. An old pal. A miscreant himself. Boyd had said how he'd talk his way out of anything bad that came up, that even if Lumpy really had to radio for the real pigs and couldn't be dissuaded and the gang got actually popped (and if they didn't just knock the Lump over the head, ha ha): the bust would be for trespassing or mischief and nothing worse.

Shit. Down the stairs, fast, two stories down into the yard. Then run. The distance boggling, unclear, otherworldly. Coop had to back off his sprint; the buildings were so gargantuan that he'd thought them closer. On the tarmac, huge mixed aircraft seemed to nod. The slouching man, if he was really there, was way on the other side, very far away, maybe a mile, even, or a hundred miles.

Coop jogged from light to shadow quickly, berating himself, huffing harder than the running alone could explain, the breathing in his ears. At the corner of the mammoth hangar, Coop found the loose panel Friendly had described ten times up in Grandma's attic the last two nights in the smoke of reefers and home-rolled cigarettes and the sweet scent of gun oil (Friendly cleaning Grandpa's old guns lovingly with his girlfriend hard at his side, ignored: willowy young Madeline). The secret entrance was just a half sheet of tin unbolted so Lumpy and the day guards could get smoke breaks unobserved.

Inside in blackness Coop put the panel back in place so no one walking outside would see. He took a few steps into the vast hangar. Exit lights across the expanse made pinkish weak light like the light of dawn.

Coop crept into the deepness of the place, just stood till he heard a sound and saw the thin beam of Friendly's flashlight. He thought of Tricia back up past the fence with the car, hoped no one had happened upon her, hoped she hadn't had to move it for some couple wanting to neck, hoped she hadn't had to talk to any cop. He got a picture in his head of Tricia, Tricia that very morning, all awake and back to normal velocity and sheepish about her stealing and her manic blather lately and about something else she was less clear about—her moment with Hodge.

Coop tripped on something, fell onto his hands hard on cold smooth cement. Some thick cable. His pupils had opened full and he could see the whole place now, a row of great bombers that he couldn't help but love instantly and want to touch and fly. He'd built so many models and bombed so many sandbox Krauts and Japs and Commies. He trotted now, leaping cables, soundless in his Geoff Street sneakers, right to the flashlight beams under the nose of one of the bombers.

Hodge was handing something up to Boyd Friendly hidden in the enormous landing gear.

Coop said, "I saw Lumpy."

"Shit!" said Hodge, startled by him.

Coop said it again: "I saw Lumpy."

"We're almost done, chickenshit," Hodge snarled.

Silence in the hangar.

Friendly scaled down the struts and stanchions, trailing wires, nodded at Coop.

Coop said it another time: "I saw Lumpy."

"Fuck the Lump," Friendly rumbled. "One more ship. Move it."

Now Coop saw the wires that led from this bomber's nosegear to the nosegear on the next, then on down the line.

"Boom," Friendly said.

Hodge said a kind of laugh, nothing amused in it.

Boyd glowered at Coop, rumbled, "Check the caps and leads." He didn't want to hear any warnings, especially Coop's false warnings. "Nothing loose, or we've got nothing. And don't touch." He picked up his knapsack, the spool of expensive wire, never took his eyes off Coop. And Hodge too, both of them looking at Coop like if there was a fuck-up in the world Coop was it and this because Coop had lied about Boyd's plan, for one, had argued on Bailey's side against this mission, for another, a long night in the attic. But still they needed him. And it was he who'd dug Grandpa's guns out (but only when Bailey left the attic to read downstairs in *peace*). It was he who'd known exactly where to look. It was he who'd dug out the gun oil and the barrel brush and the cloths and stock cream—he knew exactly which of the old Allied Van Lines boxes to look in. He wanted Hodge's respect, was it. But he wanted Bailey's too. And Boyd's too, and Tricia's. Madeline, maybe a little. He felt oxen tied to his arms and legs all pulling different ways.

Boyd Friendly and Hodge trotted with their two khaki knapsacks to the last huge plane on line, and Boyd climbed up inside expertly, his sixth set.

Coop followed the wires back in the dim pink fire-exit glow, one imposing plane to the next, smell of fuel and a little of fire and some smell like plain hugeness, the smell of a room big enough to have weather. He walked quickly, thought he heard other steps, stopped, sweated, smelled everything, heard Bailey saying how if he had a chance to thwart this plan he should thwart it and fast, like a *Bodhisattva,* she said, and he heard Hodge saying to Bailey in a heated voice in the hot attic how these planes were only metal and money and evil all bolted together, that no harm would come to anyone unless the planes were allowed to fly again, and he heard Tricia saying how she'd begun to see the point: if something was evil you acted. Her argument was opposite from a mere half-week back. Hodge's argument had become hers.

Coop followed the wires to the last plane and then to the steel I-beam that supported the peak of the distant roof and there in the poor light examined the great blob of what Boyd called *C-4* sometimes and *plastique* sometimes and *plastic explosives* the rest of the time, a substance like putty or Play-doh pressed onto the beam. Boyd had *twenty pounds* of it from his bad-news cousin who was a demolition expert with the Seabees and a triumphant pilferer as well. *Twenty pounds* of like *Play-doh,* a few ounces of which was supposed to take down bridges. You could just pull this wire free and that would be the end of it. A puffer, as Hodge called it. Not even a puffer. They'd hook the battery on and nothing would happen. Coop gripped the wire, studied how it entered the fuse-cap, thought, Pull! But he didn't pull. He didn't know if pulling the wire would detonate the many bombs, if pulling (say) this wire and not the other would blow the whole thing up and Coop with it. He didn't know if he pulled the wire and nothing blew that Boyd Friendly wouldn't catch him. And if Friendly caught him that would be much worse than blowing up; it would be the end of Hodge's stern regard.

Coop held the wire but didn't pull. Instead he gingerly dropped it and jogged back to the far end of the hangar, where Hodge shone the flashlight on Boyd's fingers pressing dough into the I-beam there, pressing all that was left of the C-4 into the trough of the beam, a huge thick beam, so thick Coop knew the Play-doh couldn't harm it; Jesus, look, nothing could dent that beam. They'd get six flat tires on six great warships and a big dent each on two thirty-inch I-beams and that would be the end of that.

Nothing for Bailey to get worked up about. Hodge puffed and Coop puffed, but Boyd Friendly worked methodically, nervelessly, just pressing the dough with steady hands, then plugging the cap into it, then wiring the cap. "Got it," he rumbled. "Let's go."

He spooled two wires along the clean cement floor and out the trap door and Hodge and Coop followed him dragging backpacks across the endless lot far too long in the blazing lights of the yard, then up the steep flight of hot steel steps, followed by wires, twenty-one minutes in and out, faster by four minutes than planned.

They trailed wires out the two gates, locking them behind. They trailed the wires into a great knot of weeds, and there Boyd Friendly stripped insulation off the wire ends while Hodge got the battery ready, just a box battery from what would be the world's biggest flashlight, nothing fancier than that, except that it was stenciled with the words U.S. NAVY and rows of numbers and symbols. Coop stared, breathing. The thing wouldn't blow up a Tonka Toy. This game was at its grandest nothing but great silliness and nothing as horrible as Bailey said. Boyd screwed one of the wires to one of the terminals.

"One last look," he rumbled, grinning smally. And he and Hodge and Coop looked at the hangar a long time together, just this big hulk far away that they knew what was inside of exactly. And Boyd picked up the loose wire, easy as that, held it poised above the second terminal of the navy battery. They watched the hangar another few seconds. "Here goes."

And as Boyd's hand moved, the hangar lights went on. Small square windows blinked twice and lit fluorescent, as if that were the explosion, but it was not.

Coop said, "Wait" sharply, but Boyd's hand moved and the little plain wire touched the battery terminal with no particular drama, only the tiniest click of a spark.

Jesus! Starflash at the hangar. The great roof slumped. The lights blinked off, then darkness. Then pure thick sound, the bombs in a great single thud, metal squealing and tearing, debris flapping and clattering inside a great space. Then an astonishing, hard thump that blew Coop's hair back and punched into his chest and gut. Then silence.

"Shit!" Hodge said.

"Beautiful," Boyd rumbled.

"Lumpy was in there," Coop said.

The great hangar sagged again, settled, then fell in on itself.

"Let us split," Friendly rumbled wryly.

"Lumpy was *in* there," Coop said again.

But Friendly was already gathering his backpack, pulling in the detonator wires fast, hand over hand. To the VW bus, where Tricia waited. "I *felt* it," she said grinning broadly at Hodge.

3

I ski the west mountain because the idea isn't to see Roddy or even glimpse her but to ski, just to put my feet on the boards and the boards on the snow and go. I ski hard on my longest and heaviest pair of comps, which means I ski fast, and I think about the man we killed, Hodge, until the skiing takes over, takes out the thinking and I'm only skiing and riding up on the lift, the attendant grinning at how fast my runs are, how often he sees me, and it's all good. Mom and her hungry detective slip from my mind and the wet snow takes over and my speed on skis takes over, still speed enough to startle the few folks who are on the west mountain with me, maybe half the old speed but still scary, with good air in the best tuck I can manage, fists together in front of my face. At the start of every run I remember Frank, how he said, Watch the ice, and stared into me, knowing I wouldn't watch it but would hit it with everything, everything. We skiers and coaches and officials had lingered around the Patrol shed two hours through the freak rain and then freak cold front coming through, line of clearest blue sky, lowering afternoon, everything turning to ice. These days, they'd close the course, they'd disallow the early times (Kline-schmidt and Brink? They weren't even contenders!), but back then, no way, one toughed it out and we did, only seven out of eighteen skiers making the bottom of the run, dismal times for superstars, all the falls and slow finishes because of the ice, the ice, the ice.

And I crouch as if in the gate, the old mechanical gates we used, and feel my heart beating like that, and stand into my poles and skate skate skate down the steep opening play, and around the first gate, remembering every gate and the anticipation of that field of ice coming and my determination to take the fucking ice no mat-ter what, gaining speed like I never had, skiing after my crazy brother, at least thinking of you every scrape of the way past every gate, falling faster and faster, air, bad snow, ice and all.

And I do get air and my heart does pound, and I'm two seconds up on everyone and I do hit the ice the fastest I've ever skied and I yell, I yell, I yell every run remembering the original yell and how my edges bit because I had the muscles and I had the skis and I was ripped and young and just didn't care. I was ready to win or break myself into a million pieces trying, yet the thing was, I knew I couldn't ski it. The edge of the trail was right there at the worst of the ice field, no nets off-course like they have now to catch a per-son, no nothing, just Japanese boulders off the brink of the moun-tain, blowing trees. But I made it, everyone knows I made it, that somehow I made it. Maybe it was the yell, maybe that was it, or maybe you made it happen, maybe you, was how I thought about it then.

And I'm skiing and remembering all this, remembering every gate after the ice, every turn, the finish coming rage fast, and then the crushing hugs, the jubilation: I had come in third. I had been ranked seventeen. And suddenly third wasn't good enough. The two weeks then of obliterating parties.

Now I'm back on the lift and remembering again, trying to let it go: .016, .024. Those fucking Austrians. Also the ice. Also the dark urge. I ski like a kid.

At 3:45 the grinning boy attending the lift says, "Last run," so it's one long, slow traverse on an access trail across the mountain to come out on Skidway, high above the lodge. There I pause to catch the late winter light on Bigelow Mountain beyond the valley of the Carrabassett River. Exhausted, I stare and don't think, don't think, don't think, but can't shake Roddy, who is not only in my thoughts but in my cells. And who—I have to accept this—is gone.

In the lodge I know what to do. I head straight downstairs, what's really the basement, home of the ski school, home of the rental shop, home of the long ticket counter, the bowels of skiing commerce where none of the team folks are going to turn up ever. And down there I punch out numbers on a big pay phone, get Madeline in one ring.

"Well," she says. Long pause.

"Hello," I say. An even longer pause.

"You're still angry?" she says. Longer pause yet.

"I believe we were coming to this," I say.

"Bucky wants to apologize to you."

"He's forgiven."

"You're in Maine?"

"Yes, Ma'am, certainly," I say. An old joke between us, an imitation of a happy mailman we once had in Aspen.

Generously, Madeline laughs. She says, "You're with Roddy?"

"No, ma'am, that didn't work out."

"Coop. I just want to say."

"No, no, no. You don't have to say anything."

Silence until she breathes and says, "So we're on the same wavelength."

Calmly and without rancor: "I'm not sure, Madeline." *Act.* "Not to be difficult, but I'm not actually sure what wavelength you're on. But there is something I've got to say: I'm not planning to come back." My strong heart begins to pound: "And it's not about Holander. Don't get me wrong. And not about Roddy. Roddy's marrying Claudio, as planned." Adrenaline as before a race in bad weather. I push through the gate, hit the ice flying: "It's not about others at all, not even about fidelity. It's just about what's needed between you and me. We don't have a marriage, if we're going to be honest. We're already separated, really, we're going to have to admit." Trying to control the speed of the flow of my words: "The trial separation we've done, really, these last few years, no? That, I guess, is the wavelength I'm on. It's time to act."

And then I just listen to the phone line. My ears are hot, my face. Across the expanse of the chilly room a cocky assistant-manager type is counting money with one of the ticket clerks, who looks nervous. A couple of college kids come clomping down the stairs, laughing and shoving, fight their way into the men's bathroom, boot buckles rattling. Cheerful voices—end of the workday—boom out of the rental shop.

I say, "We don't have to get it all said right now."

More silence.

Evenly Madeline says, "I understand if you're furious, Cooper. But I want to point out the balancing effect here. You've expressed your needs via Veronica Manor. I've expressed mine via Buck Holander. What is it you hope to accomplish with a formal separation?"

"I'm not all that furious."

"How furious are you, exactly?"

"You asked what I hope to accomplish. I hope to accomplish the end of our unhappy marriage." I'd like to say more, bro, something about you, but I can't get the words right.

Mad and I hold an extraordinarily long silence, a silence the likes of which (and not long ago) would have presaged the joining of battle, a sorry escalation of words. But nothing. Just further silence. The students come back out of the bathroom, still tussling and hilarious with themselves. Sounds in the air of the bar upstairs coming slightly to life.

Tone shift: "Coop, take a week or two. Then we can have this talk. I see you need more time to . . . to *calm your jets*."

"My jets are calm, Mad. I'm just calmly not coming back."

"Well, we'll decide that in a week or two."

"Let me give you an itinerary. Later today I'll be driving down to my folks'. Their anniversary is next week, remember? All the kids are going, grandchildren, the works. Except Hodge, of course."

She says, "You talked to that Tip Czako character, didn't you?"

"From what he told me, you made sure he found me."

"You told him about me, didn't you?"

"I believe *you* told him about you. That's an old trick he pulled on you. And I believe you told him more than that."

Madeline clears her throat. Curtly she says, "Well."

I say it too: "Well."

"Well. And now you tell your parents."

"It's time to get it out, isn't it?"

In the next silence I hear her breathing, and then hear her court-room manner slipping behind the speed of her speech: "Don't you think it's a little odd that you decide to dump me and then imme-diately you're making this other decision?"

I can't help my own emotion: "I'm not dumping you. Only acknowledging something we both know."

Madeline's not going to let our marriage be the subject. That motion she's already tabled. Instead, brother, and heatedly, the subject is you. Her cool has crumbled, she hisses, "We had a pact, Cooper Henry, a lifelong pact."

"He's dead, Mad."

"So you'll torture your mom with that? You'd ruin their anniversary like that? You'd betray us all?"

"They're not going to call CNN."

"Don't forget I know something about you, too, Coop Henry."

"Is that what this is about?"

We hold yet another silence, this one so long I can actually hear the long distance meter clicking. Finally, I manage to restrain all the words vying to get said and say this, calmly: "So, yes, counselor, I'll be down in Connecticut there a little while. After that, I don't know. What I'm thinking is, I'll go ski. And then establish myself someplace with a mountain, get a job with a ski school or a ski team."

Another silence. Mad says, "You deserve some time to yourself."

Despite the ambiguity of which I tell her, "Well, thanks."

4

Coop woke in his bunk in Grandma's attic and was a little kid again, eyes popped open, plans for the day rushing over him like puppies. But Tricia was beside him and soon all he could see was the hangar slumping, and all he could feel was the fat concussion to his chest.

In bed, Coop thought how if he'd just pulled one of the stripped wire ends out of the Play-doh stuff the blast wouldn't have happened. How the lights would have gone on, how the wire in Boyd's hand would have touched the terminal, and how nothing would have happened at all, just Lumpy shuffling to his bottle of Irish whiskey or schnapps or whatever it was he was up to, no building slumping, no great bombers falling on their chins, no roof crushing them.

Hodge had been stony riding home. Tricia drove the VW bus incautiously, and Coop could see she was buzzed, on fire. In fact, she would want to talk all night, wouldn't be able to sleep at all, but Coop would keep thinking of Lumpy's slouching walk in the shadows, how that was maybe Lumpy's last walk, and wouldn't be able to stay concentrated on Tricia's monologue or even her long hands, her half-expert overtures. After the blast the night was all panicked fragments.

They'd left the bus in the Vo-Tech High School lot in a line of seven battered VW buses the school used for shop projects (Boyd Friendly had every angle figured). Then it was a five-minute walk up the long slope to Grandma's on Capitol Hill in silence.

Home, Coop rushed to close the big front door behind the gang. Bailey looked up from the TV. You could actually see her heart sink when she saw from their faces what the gang had done, see her slump a little inside (two stages to it, like the hangar settling). Madeline, though, sleek Madeline was excited and rushed to Boyd: "It worked?"

Boyd rumbled, "That shit was like, *boom.*"

Bailey sank further into the couch. She said, "And y'all are like, *boom,* going to prison."

Coop studied the floor. He could have just plucked that detonator wire goddamn it he could have just.

Friendly broke the stretching silence, eager as he got, which was barely: "Anything on TV?"

"Oh, *jaysus,*" Bailey said. Her voice mounted from disgust to fury word by word, her eyes went black: "That's what y'all want, in't! Y'all won't be happy till there's a *television* picture of y'all's heads three fenceposts from y'all's *necks* and some pig sayin' how fuckin' stupid y'all were!"

Pugnacious Madeline said, "Bailey, you don't know *Boyd Friendly. Boyd Friendly* leaves no evidence. *Boyd Friendly* doesn't get caught."

Boyd tilted his head back, superior. "We won," he rumbled. He took Madeline by her elbow and the air of the room was all affronted glowering till they turned and climbed stately up the curving stairs in the dark to get where they might celebrate success without Bailey's bad conscience harping.

Hodge tried to go to Bailey. But that look on her face stopped even him ten feet from the couch. She held his eye furiously as she stood to turn off whatever ancient movie was on the TV. She fell back into the deep cushions, waited. But there was nothing for Hodge to say. He just looked serious and haughty and after a minute turned to follow Boyd and Madeline.

"Soap opera," Tricia said contemptuously. She went in the kitchen, banged the cabinet doors.

Now Bailey's stare fixed Coop, who alone among the gang members was contrite in its glare. He said, "The lights came on." He didn't want her to find out some other way.

"Lights?" Bailey said.

"Some lights in the hangar. A guard might have been in there."

Bailey thought about that a long time, said, "Oh, jaysus, baby, now what? Someone *in* there?"

"Maybe not," Coop said. He could hear Tricia clomping up the back stairway in her cowboy boots, then clomping to the attic. That meant she and Hodge were going to be up there alone.

Coop had better get up there, quick. He said, "Maybe I didn't see this guy I thought I saw and Boyd says the lights are on a timer in there, so . . . "

But in the radiance of morning the truth seemed plain. Coop lay and held Tricia (she'd been *electrified* by the blast, as if it had gone off in her head; she'd talked all night, poems and ideas and admiration of Hodge and Boyd, none of the love talk Coop liked so well though she lay beside him in underpants only and cuddled him and though they'd eventually made love), and couldn't sleep. The gang was a gang of killers now. Boyd Friendly was what Bailey said: stupid. And Hodge was like Friendly, really: stupid as hell and heartless.

In the other room Hodge's bunk creaked and creaked again. So Hodge wasn't sleeping either. Of course in the night he would have heard Tricia, who seemed to be making a point of her passion with a kind of loud growling she'd not made before, making a point of it for whom else but Hodge?

Coop nuzzled Tricia, who slept in her dead-woman way, so barely moving you had to concentrate for minutes to feel her breathing. So, probably Hodge had just lain down beside her the other night, that's all—the two of them half exhausted, and with Bailey and Coop downtown and all—just lain down and you really couldn't think about it if you were going to stay pleasant and happy in the bosom of the gang and face the real problem here, which was a murder—a plain murder—and not just some glorified statement about war and governments, the stuff Boyd Friendly rumbled about.

Bailey had said the best thing was to turn themselves in. Just say, Yup, we did it. Just say that the whole thing was more of a prank than anything, that the guard's death—if he really was in there—was a horrible, tragic accident. If they went in on their own, less trouble for all of them. Coop held Tricia tighter, kissed her ear, needing her to talk. But Tricia didn't wake. After a long time Coop got out of the bunk carefully, got into his clothes quietly, crept downstairs. Bailey was on the couch asleep right where she'd been, still sitting sunken in the cushions, but with used tissues and Grandma's magazines piled around her. And a long letter written on Grandma's good paper: *Dear Hodge.* Coop looked away from it, saw just the one line in his head as he slunk to the kitchen: *You know I love you but . . .*

In the refrigerator he found nothing. So water and two handfuls of Cheerios. He got soft thoughts of Grandma. He put her kitchen radio on barely. The bombing was the news. Stern radio voices, men trying to subdue their excitement. They'd determined that the *horrific* explosion was not an accident, and kept saying that the dead man very likely was involved. The physical evidence showed that at least several accomplices had taken part and successfully fled. The explosives used were state of the art, restricted to military use. Evidence of international sophistication.

Then they talked about the dead man. That's all Coop could really hear. The FBI was checking the background of the *dead man* for links to international groups.

Hodge creaked down the back steps, stood there disheveled in his pants. He listened to the radio awhile—speculation about the *dead man*'s connections to foreign powers—then sighed mightily, clicked the old thing off. He said, "We got their attention, I guess."

"Bailey says we should turn ourselves in."

"Tony. Don't be an asshole. This is big. If you can't take it, you best head home. And keep your fucking chicken beak sealed along the way." Hodge looked as if he hadn't slept at all, glared at Coop, a challenge. He said, "You're almost a man. Act like one, all right?"

Coop watched him minutely. Hodge was someone who'd get in bed with your girl and he was someone who had used violence his whole life.

Coop said, "Bailey says turn ourselves in."

"Right, bro. We're going to walk into FBI headquarters and ask to use the soda machine."

A whole life of violence, really, just as Bailey said. "Grandma will help us," Coop said. If you could just go back one single day you could look at those wires again, put your hand on a wire again, think hard about the consequences once again, and this time pull the fucking thing.

"Tony, listen up: Boyd and I have got years of work to do. You hear me? Boyd and I are just getting *started*."

Before long the rest of the gang was up. They all stood in the kitchen, chomping handfuls of Cheerios and fancy rye crackers with peanut butter. Bailey put water in Grandma's monolithic percolator, measured out Grandma's exotic coffee. Boyd smoked one Lucky Strike after the next. The radio played other news: the astronauts were back from the moon, quarantined on the U.S.S. *Enterprise.* A group of scientist-aquanauts were floating 600 meters deep in the Gulf Stream. Bailey stared and thought so hard Coop hardly knew her face. Tricia bumped petulantly past in her white cowgirl pants, which she'd washed clean and bright in Grandma's washer.

Madeline was cheerful, the victorious revolutionary, though it was she who'd decided at the last minute Tricia should drive the bus in her place—she'd had just horrible cramps—she who'd sat home with Bailey and watched TV. "Right on," she said, after each news item. "Right *on.* Outta*sight.* Right *on.*" Coop felt himself pulled to her good cheer and away from Bailey's gloom. They *had* done something big.

Friendly was like some smoking block of dry ice taking up the whole kitchen. The radio report when it finally came made him nod his head. A correspondent phoned in with the carefully unexcited news that the FBI had identified the dead guard, and had a make from clear tire marks on his accomplices' escape vehicle: foreign, probably Mercedes.

Boyd laughed at the inept cops. But he said, "We'd better clear out of here. Soon as it's dark."

"Right," Bailey said. "Clear out. Y'all make a poor fuckin' James Bond, Boyd Friendly. Like, where the *fuck* are we supposed to go? Like, where are they not gonna find us, babydoll? Y'all did *murder,* fellas. Y'all killed some . . . some *bowlin' champ.* This is gonna be the real pigs, *cowboys.*"

"I know a place we can go," Coop said, but he was ignored.

Friendly shook his head at Bailey, raised his eyebrows, looked at the ceiling, puffed his cigarette. "Warships," he rumbled, meaning how they'd taken out six bombers just like that, gone. "People are going to die."

Madeline imitated her lover's coolness, shook her hair out. She curled her lip at Bailey, said, "Don't impose your trip." Coop saw how loyal she was to Boyd and liked her for that. But Bailey was right. It was murder and for murder they probably *hung* you in the great state of Washington.

The coffee finished perking. That gave Bailey something to do and occupied the tense silence. She poured coffee and passed cups around before another word was said.

Friendly downed his coffee fast, hot as it was, poured himself more. Hodge didn't drink, just held his cup in two hands as if it were a beating heart. He looked at Bailey, looked at Boyd Friendly a long time. At length he said: "Death is a necessary by-product of the revolution." He was quoting someone.

"Lumpy a martyr," Boyd rumbled wryly.

"Oh, now it's a joke," Bailey said.

Coop urgently said, "I know a cabin we can go to. Just an hour away. When Grandma gets back she can make sure we're all treated fair. We didn't mean to *hurt* anybody. You didn't mean to *hurt* anybody, Hodge."

Quickly, Friendly rumbled, "What cabin?"

"It's a friend of Grandma's. Up in the Cascades. Tricia and I were there."

"I know the way," Tricia said, excited at the prospect. "It's near a town called Silverton."

"We're better off goin' in," Bailey said disconsolately.

Madeline drew herself up, affronted, though she and Bailey were the ones who'd stayed home: "What, Bailey? We're supposed to go down to the pig palace with Hodge's *grandmother* and rap with them? 'We're the mad *bombers?*' Won't they want to kind of *keep* us?"

Coop saw himself in court, then in jail, then dead. He knew just the thing to do: call Dad. And quickly he knew how stupid that would be. Tad Thomas? No way. Grandma in Japan. So Friendly was it; Friendly was in charge.

Boyd Friendly rumbled, "Cabin is good. We split at dark." He kept drinking coffee, finished off the pot himself.

"After that, Tony, you go home," said Hodge.

The unhappy gang stood in the kitchen a long time then, just staring, till Hodge turned and disappeared up the back stairs slowly. Bailey waited awhile but followed Hodge, having softened to him in some way that Coop could not understand.

Then Boyd and Madeline went up to Grandma's room tussling and tickling like nothing was amiss. Tricia, she wandered into the paneled dining room with her notebooks, sat and wrote fast and hard at Grandma's table. Coop didn't know what to do. He poked around the house, feeling blown up like a balloon. He tried reading, tried drawing Tricia, tried watching TV, tried a game of one-man Scrabble, tried cleaning up the kitchen, tried calisthenics. He couldn't stay with anything. He stood out on the porch and watched the rain. He thought longingly of Grandma sweeping her walk, as if with the broom she'd get the lawn mown and the hedges trimmed. He sat in her porch swing and gave himself to thought.

Late in the afternoon a gray car pulled up and parked three houses down and across the street. The two guys in it just sat there, unmoving. Coop felt invisible in the twilight of the porch eaves. At dinnertime, another gray car arrived and parked two houses the other way. Coop stood and stretched and yawned and nonchalantly went inside. He rushed to the back porch for a look: gray car in the alley below the house. He pictured himself surrendering, saw himself just walking out there and giving himself up.

No way.

Coop shot up the back stairs to wake Boyd. And Boyd was on his feet and in his pants like a fireman at the sound of the bell. Madeline got out of bed too, deeply flushed and, except for her dangling earrings and the many brass bracelets above her biceps and a long silver chain low around her waist, plain naked, her body long in the torso like a dancer's. She hummed excitedly, like a big door-smashing raid of a bust was just what she'd always dreamed. Her hippie frankness under Coop's gaze seemed forced as she bent for her clothes. This bending Coop would always see— even through their courting, even married to her, even after that.

Boyd and Coop crept down the hall and into the little girls' room and the two of them peered up and down Boylston Street in the growing dusk. Now another car pulled up, four men inside.

"Fuck," Friendly rumbled. "Get your brother. We got to move."

Coop came up with the plan in an inspired burst on the way to Hodge in the attic. They could escape out the basement bulkhead doors, one by one down the path to the fortress, which was a kind of cavern in the blackberries against the frowzy hedge. From there an ancient and eternal dogs' and kids' path took you all the way down along the alley to behind the Meriweathers' garage at the far end, then through their hedge and out onto Tuck Street. Then it would get dangerous: a long trot down the hill to the Vo-Tech and the car.

Hodge and Bailey were asleep in their clothes, faces still holding onto their argument. All Coop needed to say was "Hurry," and Hodge was up and putting shoes on. Not a word from Bailey about surrendering, not now. She got up and dressed too, afraid.

Quickly, the disharmonious gang gathered in Grandma's room, lights out. Boyd whispered strategy and no one argued: they'd send one of the girls out to make it seem they weren't aware of anything. Then escape. Quickly again, they took positions. Calm Madeline stepped out into the night according to plan, singing to herself. She was a good actress, ambled to the end of the walk, made an elaborate stretch, yawned, walked a few steps south, seemed to change her mind, turned north, ambled up the street, just perfect. The men in the cars tried to seem not to watch, turned their heads subtly.

Hodge and Bailey hit the basement. Tricia said she was afraid of spiders, but managed to follow. Boyd led Coop upstairs, pulled the guns he'd been oiling for two days out of the moving boxes: Grandpa's 30.06 rifle, Grandpa's old .45, and finally, the polite-looking .32, Grandpa's *Little Pal*. This last—stainless steel, almost dainty—Boyd handed to Coop. "That's a one shot," Boyd rumbled. "It's loaded, no safety, watch it." And then he handed over a familiar, near-empty box of shells, playthings of Coop's childhood.

"These are so old," Coop said, excited despite himself.

Friendly just said, "What's the worst that could happen?" He hefted the 30.06 rifle with its heavy, old-fashioned scope in his left hand, hefted the .45 in his right, and used both to point Coop down the stairs, to point Coop into the dark of the little girls' room, no compunction about the black barrels aimed at Coop's neck.

Coop took position by a dark window. His little gun gave him no courage. He'd never shot it or any handgun (he'd shot only rifles and those only at summer camp) and knew he'd never be able to aim it at a real person. He was only *more* scared to have the little warming thing in his hand. How often he'd played with it! Not a move in the gray cars. Night coming. The only car to worry over was the one in the alley. Coop felt a wash of self-importance. It was he and he alone who'd seen the cops pull up, now it was he who would show the gang through the blackberry brambles to safety. He held the little living handgun and watched out the window, feeling his bravery like strange clothing.

Boyd was in Grandma's room. In the quiet Coop could hear him loading Grandpa's hunting rifle and checking the action, hear him loading the .45, spinning the barrel, muttering. Boyd gave Madeline fifteen excruciating minutes for her saunter to the Vo-Tech. Nothing on the street in Coop's sight changed. Suddenly from the doorway—startling—Boyd said, "Here we go." Coop put the little gun in his shirt pocket, at his breast.

In the basement, Hodge said, "Right," when he saw the rifle in Boyd's hands. He said, "Give me the banger."

Friendly didn't argue, handed over the .45, handed over the thick old box of bullets in their brass cartridges. Tricia looked on with interest.

"Y'all aren't fixin' to use those anyhow," Bailey said. "Let's us just leave 'em here. They'll just add to the *mess* we're in."

Hodge looked at her evenly—Coop could all but read his thoughts.

Boyd rumbled, "Quiet, little girl." He had his leather jacket on.

Coop carefully avoided Bailey's eye. If he looked at her she'd know just what was in his shirt pocket.

Hodge opened the squeaky and scraping bulkhead door slowly. The gang crouched and waited, the cool evening falling into the basement around them, a misty rain. No response from the night. Nothing at all. Coop first. Around the dead swimming pool, into the brambles at the familiar old entrance to his childhood forts and tunnels, the gun in his pocket patting at his chest like an outside heart. Bailey came next, then Tricia, last Hodge. Coop went ahead and into what was once the main citadel of his fortress, an opening under a yew tree surrounded by brambles. He waited till everyone crowded in, huffing and panting. "Go," Friendly said.

And they went, taking scratches silently. Coop popped out of a well-kept hedge at the far end of the alley. The cop car seemed close. No way to say where the pigs inside were looking. On all fours Coop crossed the pavement fast, a game he'd played a million times, World War II. The gang followed, one by one. Safely on Tuck Avenue, Hodge stripped out of his jacket and swore: Friendly held Grandpa's rifle in plain sight. Boyd wrapped the rifle fast in the jacket. Hodge scared Boyd, too, Coop was glad to see. He took Tricia's hand and skipping, as planned, they started for the Vo-Tech.

Bailey and Hodge came next, holding hands and mewling at each other like a couple of lovers, which was the idea.

Then Friendly, walking like a sailor with a wooden leg, the rifle wrapped at his side.

Sixteen, Coop thought from nowhere, I am sixteen in two days.

The Vo-Tech in misty streetlights reminded Coop of Boeing and his heart raced as he and Tricia casually walked across the pavement of the large parking lot to the line of buses, where Madeline stood, gaping and panting. They tumbled into the Geoff Street collective's fateful VW bus, Tricia in the driver's seat. She started it—heartstopping roar—and backed it up quick. At Westlake Avenue they picked up Hodge and Bailey, then Boyd with his rifle, all of them piled in back sitting down on the floor jittering.

Quietly Bailey said, "Jaysus."

Friendly said, "Left at the light, then get on the highway."

"How far is it?" Tricia said.

"A long fucking way in this vehicle," Hodge said.

Coop remembered a different life: the kitchen at home, Mom's hair in a towel after shampoo.

Tricia hit the gas, got on the freeway north. They passed a cop who'd stopped some rusty old heap, but Tricia drove steadily by.

Hodge said, "Bailey, get up there. Coop, back here."

And then it was a couple of pretty girls bopping along in their VW bus. No one said anything, except Boyd, repeating the number of the exit they were to take until Tricia was irritated. The bus was loud, louder than on the trip west, louder even than on the endless trip back from Boeing. It bounced and dove, but Tricia grappled confidently with the wheel. They made their exit in a half hour, turned on to the dark road into the Cascades.

Relax. Bailey began to sing. Tricia pushed that bus hard up the grades, let it fly downhill. Madeline cuddled to Boyd, and Boyd actually kissed her lips, the first Coop had seen of their affection.

Even Hodge let his big shoulders fall a little, laughed at some crack Tricia made.

Just before the tiny town of Silverton, Tricia hurtled past a cop in his cruiser. He pulled right out. Friendly rumbled, "Shit," pushed Madeline away from him.

"Oh, boy," Tricia said, craning to see in the mirror.

"He doesn't know who we are," Bailey said.

Hodge pulled Grandpa's .45 out of his shirt. "Doesn't matter either way," he said.

Friendly clicked the safety off Grandpa's 30.06, lay the rifle hidden along the side of the mattress.

Coop put his hair in his collar. The only thing he imagined doing with his *Little Pal* was giving it to the policeman, handle first.

"Busted," Madeline said, panicked.

"Nice kids," Bailey said. "We're just a nice bunch of kids."

Tricia slowed down, then slowed down some more, slower and slower, twenty miles an hour, then ten, then five.

"Faster," Hodge said.

But the cop's lights began to flash.

Tricia drove slower yet, just crawling, didn't stop. "Shit, boys," she said.

"Pull on over," Hodge said. He held Grandpa's old handgun along his leg.

"Busted, my ass," Friendly rumbled.

"Remember we're just nice kids," Bailey said. "We're just goin' up to our folks's place in the mountains."

"Kill him," Boyd said.

"My shot," said Hodge.

"Don't y'all be *morons*," Bailey said.

At the edge of town after laboring the poor bus up a hill, Tricia finally pulled over. The cop took his time, eventually ambled to

Tricia's window. He said nothing at first, just put his flashlight beam in her face. He relaxed visibly at sight of her.

He said, "You drunk, young lady?"

Tricia said, "It's the car that's drunk."

Bailey laughed, but the cop didn't. He shined his beam on Bailey a long time, then shined it in the back. He stiffened when he caught Hodge's cold face.

"Where you kids going?"

"Up to his folks' place," Tricia said, flinging a vague thumb back into the bus. "They're up here in the mountains."

"No beer in the vehicle?"

Tricia, much used to inner pain, was good in an emergency: "*Beer?*"

"You're from Illinois?"

"She is." Tricia nodded her head at Bailey. "Me, I'm from Montana."

Coop sat up. This wasn't going to work. And that idiot Boyd was raising Grandpa's rifle. Coop put his hand on the barrel, pushed it down.

The pig said, "Young lady, what would your folks say seeing you drive like that?"

Long years later, Madeline would analyze this cop for Coop, point out how he was an old man, not used to much action—how clearly you could see that. How in his face you could see that this stop might be all he got for the night and how that made him both glad and unsatisfied and afraid. You could also see he hadn't heard about any bombing yet and you knew that when he did he'd once more feel the weight of his miserable failed life, a cop who'd never shot his gun except to kill a deer or raccoon hit by a car or a dog with rabies, a cop who'd skipped weapons practice routinely and hated his shortwave radio.

The older man looked at each of the faces in the car, kids' faces, nervous well-meaning faces, not the dark criminals he feared (Madeline later would say), this not the fatal night he'd dreamed of and worried over so many years holding his babies then children or lying awake before dawn.

Tricia said, "Sir, I have to go to the bathroom."

"I won't keep you, Miss. Just let me see your Montana license."

Amazingly, Tricia produced just that: a current, valid, neatly typed Montana license. Then Bailey dug breathlessly in the glove compartment (stolen packs of Camels and many books of matches falling at her feet), found a brown envelope with the Geoff Street registration. Coop lost hope and regained it with every gesture. At the edge of his eye he saw Hodge's hand, ready on the .45.

The pig studied the license, read the registration, handed them back. He said, "No beer, huh?"

And Tricia said, "No beer. I'm just a bad driver."

"Well, these old buses are hard to handle. And where did you say you were heading?"

"Up here a little farther."

"Up where?"

Friendly rumbled, "The gorge. Just past the gorge."

Tricia repeated it.

"By Trempers?" the gentle cop said.

"Not quite that far," Friendly rumbled.

Tricia repeated it.

The cop smiled. He wasn't investigating anything anymore. He was just fond of the territory and proud of his knowledge. "Well good night," he said. He even tipped his hat a little, relieved, went back to his car, pulled a fast U-turn before Tricia could get the old bus moving.

5

Even whipped as I am from the day's hard skiing, I follow my plan.
It takes no great prescience to know where the team's going to be
on a Saturday night. I drive down the long hill from the main
lodge, pull into the frozen parking lot of the all-new Sugarloaf
Brew Pub, park next to a white-on-white-in-white Cadillac that I
definitely know who rented, climb out of Frank's Mercedes without the least hesitation.

   In the huge trunk I've got several suitcases—all my clothes. I
stand in the cold and dig out a dress shirt. I unfold it—straight
from the cleaners two years past. I hold it up, contemplate it.
Quickly, then, I strip out of my parka and sweater and undershirt
and put the good shirt on. In my suit bag I find my one suit and
do it: quick finish dressing, shivering in a sky full of flurries. I step
out of my ski bib, step into my suit pants, get out of my ski socks,
into black wool. Last I tie my blue tie (Frank's gift, I note as I knot
it). Quick check in the Mercedes's bright side mirror (I'm closer to
myself than I appear), pat down mussed hair, button one button
of the good jacket.

I act. I steam across the parking lot. I hurl open the great wooden doors—Bear's Lair indeed. Claudio is leaning back on the bar, surrounded by his skiers. Every least one wants his attention. A rap song beats out of the jukebox, too quietly for such angry stuff, some faint voice stalking *bitches.*

Roddy's lucky: Claudio is striking, certifiably gorgeous, to use my old pal Bailey's word. He's a great skier, a good friend. The remnants of the black eye I gave him do not diminish his looks, not at all. His mother was a princess; his father some unpunished fascist general. He's a little taller than I. His voice is loud and cheerful, his laugh is a barking joy to hear. The young women around him laugh with him. The young men shout out jokes, trying to beat his.

The outside doors swing open behind me at the hands of exuberant junior skiers who—miracle of miracles—rush Rick Baldwin past me, oblivious of my presence, rush reluctant Rick into the bar. He's wearing his Alpine Director's suit and tie. He has had to okay this celebration, but he doesn't have to like it. Is the look on his face. He's weary, stressed-out. The job is tougher than anyone would think, having watched Frank Kobil handle it so smoothly for so many years. I feel nothing but compassion for old Rick Baldwin in this moment, this exact moment as the explosion dies, as the last flecks of dust from the hangar hit the tarmac, leaving a new structure—who's to say it's a bad one?—a new structure less intentional but more permanent than what got blasted.

Rick is windburned, been skiing. I watch the bartender respectfully nod and grin and pour him a beer. Rick Baldwin has ordered *beer.* This, I wish Frank could see. Rick takes the pint glass and slugs it down in great gulps.

Now Julie Tinker comes barreling in with six skiers younger than she, young men and women, all of them shouting in excitement, rushing to the bar, greeting friends. They are the freestyle

gang, every one of them as loud as Claudio. Julie looks *great*. The
bartender can't keep his cool around these stars—he's in awe, a
skier himself. He hikes the volume on the jukebox. He pours a few
beers and many soda pops. The kids shout and leap and drag stools
from the fireside. Julie rushes to Rick and hugs him. I hear her say,
"No meeting tonight?"

Roddy will marry Claudio. Rick Baldwin will know fame. He
gets Julie, too. I, I'll coach the local team in some welcoming town,
fall from the sky into paradise, the last bit of detritus from the
Boeing Bombers' blast.

The jukebox comes up louder yet, driving industrial dance
music for which I have no ear. The freestylers gang around the
pool table. Everyone, dance!

How fast can I do this? Say my good-byes? I don't want to be
here when Roddy comes, can't do that to her. We two have said our
good-bye, that's for certain.

I glide straight to Rick Baldwin, who's still at the bar.

It takes him a moment to recognize me in my suit. His business
smile fades. "Jesus," he says, then says it again, shocked: "Jesus!"

"*Coop Henry!*" Julie Tinker shouts, and hugs me, won't let go. I
shake Rick's hand, grinning, as skiers I know gather around with
smiles and great laughs and blessings. My heart, I swear it, my
heart literally swells with all the friendship.

Julie says, "I *heard* you were here!"

"Congratulations," I say straight to Rick's face. Then I go the
next step, hug Richard P. Baldwin, jacket to jacket and tie to tie.
"Rick, congratulations on the job. It's a great-looking team!"

Julie hugs us both, kisses my cheek. It's like the old days for that
moment; we're all beaming.

To both of them I say, "And hey! Congratulations on your
engagement!"

Julie laughs and shows her ring to me dramatically and to the skiers gathered around. We laugh and bubble; someone hands me an orange soda. Claudio approaches.

Claudio's a different problem, of course. Roddy got home somewhat late last night. I have no idea what argument may have transpired between them or whether he has any suspicion at all. I haven't seen him since our epic fistfight. As it is, he only steps up, chin forward, conciliatory victor, laughing, shouting: "Mr. Broken Knees!" Which is his affectionate nickname for me. "Is it skiing you are here for?"

And I hug him, too, the big lug. I'm in the middle of a sloshing, grinning crowd, happy in my heart for the first time in years. I say hello to skiers, take kisses, give hugs, work my way toward the doors, drinking orange soda. I kiss and hug (freestylers, downhillers, GS stars, snowboarders, coaches, technicians, forerunners, equipment kids) and back myself toward the door. I holler, "I'm on my way!" festively, and trot outside, already pulling my tie loose. "Good-bye, good-bye!" I shout. And I trot triumphantly to Frank's Mercedes, and suddenly it's a farewell scene, everyone pouring out into the snow and waving and shouting and wishing me luck and Godspeed, as if their party had been planned for me.

Bon voyage!

I'm off, trunk and back seat loaded with everything I need: books, clothes, ski gear, ropes, soaps and powders and lotions, shovel. And it's down the hill to Kingfield. I have acted. I will not go back to Madeline. I'm no longer a spectator. For now there's just the drive to Connecticut and the house of our parents, brother, and when I'm through there I'll never have to talk to you again.

Passing the Hotel Herbert, I actually wave. Good-bye to all that! I drive on. Five full miles down the road—ten minutes—the presence of a red new car enters my mind, a kind of material vision. A red new car parked in the one parking spot on the street in front of the Herbert. I pull a U-turn fast and speed back, five minutes. That car's there. I park in the fire lane and leap out, scope the little rental long enough to know: it's Roddy, all right. Four pair of skis jammed over the passenger seat and into the back. Paper trash and two duffel bags and an open suitcase on the back seat. Odd ski boots and three pairs of running shoes and loose socks and a hair brush. Forty or fifty books and notebooks and slide sheets slid all over everyplace, pens and pencils. It's Roddy's rental.

I don't exactly leap through the doors of the Hotel Herbert, but I'm moving fast. There are the great dogs, whom I greet each in turn before turning my eyes to our couch by the fire. Roddy's eyes are dark, her hair bright. She looks too warm in her fleece vest and warm-ups. "Hi," she says, like we'd planned to rendezvous, like I'm late. She says "Hi," and stands to greet me and gives me a peck like an understanding old wife. She says, "Let's move fast," and won't look me square in the eye. The air around her vibrates.

The desk man looks at me quizzically: *didn't you check out?*

Roddy picks herself up and businesslike carries her shoulders over to him and says, "Could you do me an enormous favor and hold some car keys for a friend?"

The desk man smiles, thoroughly smitten by her, says, *"Oui,"* thinking we're Canucks.

"Could I have an envelope to place them in?" Roddy says.

He finds her a stout little envelope. "Just put the name on it," he says and hands her a marker.

"Claudio Abruzzi," she says, writing it in big letters, really pronouncing the Italian. "He'll be by maybe tomorrow or the next day, once I call him. I'll lock the car up and bring this back to you." The envelope goes in a parka pocket.

Out in front and solemnly as a church girl, Rod unlocks her spanky red rental car, starts loading her stuff in Frank's Mercedes, piece by piece, finding room. We don't say a thing, just rearrange

and tidy and take a long half hour in the cold growing dusk loading everything she's brought into that car, which is already full of
everything I've brought. Barely a look between us.

When the red rental is empty, Roddy locks it up, tests both
doors, pulls the stout envelope from her pocket, drops the keys in.
She makes no ceremony of tugging her stony, glowing engagement
ring off—it's gorgeous—and dropping that in there, too. She
delivers the portentous envelope, sealed, to the desk man, then
she's back at my side.

"Burlington," she says.

"Aren't we going to laugh or anything?" I say.

"This is not a joke, Mr. Henry."

We climb in Frank's car and buckle our seatbelts and just sit
there awhile, both of us quite consciously leaving room for any
second thoughts Roddy might have. She looks at me like she wants
to kill me. I don't even dream of a kiss. Then we're off, bro, Roddy
and Coop are off to Vermont in the biggest Mercedes you've ever
seen.

6

Coop read a book about daily life in ancient Rome off one of the shelves in the cabin. At first it was hard to read, but before long he got the mood of it and felt the ancient world collapse in on the present. He absorbed the whole book quickly. When he looked up some of the supposed glory of Rome was in his head still and it was if the cabin were a columned Roman courtyard. Beside him on the porch Bailey read too, some thick book she'd found with *Texas* in the title. Madeline had a thin book she'd brought along in her beaded handbag called *In Watermelon Sugar*. She read nearly nonsensical passages aloud, laughed easily, went back to reading, smiled with her book and with herself. Coop could still see her long, naked torso and the silver chain around her middle just by closing his eyes.

Friendly spent the afternoon in a hammock he'd found and set on its hooks between aspens. He dozed and woke and drank from a can of beer, dozed and woke and smoked another joint. He claimed not to have slept at all since the night of the bomb. He kept Grandpa's fearsome rifle across his lap. He dozed and woke and seemed to take no interest whatever in Madeline or anyone else.

Hodge and Tricia together had taken the path that went out along the ridge. From the porch Coop could just see them, small figures in blue way up there huddling on the majestic rocks.

"See them?" is all Coop said.

Bailey wouldn't even look up.

Madeline said, "Those two have an *energy.*"

Coop turned his book on his lap, looked out on the ridge. Even from a mile away you could see what energy she meant. "They're only talking," he said.

Bailey didn't turn any pages. She just stared at the air between the book and her face. When she looked up it was to gaze out over the ridge. Coop looked too. Tricia and Hodge had walked off.

Bailey said, "Let's us-all take our own hike, baby."

"Nah," Coop said. But he put his book down, stood when Bailey did. They both stretched and feigned ease a minute before alighting from porch to mossy yard down the big stone steps trying (both of them) not to look out over the ridge.

"This way," Bailey said. They ambled past the parked VW bus and down the jeep trail till they were far enough along for Bailey to take Coop's hand. She said hotly, "Don't you worry about them."

And they walked. In the trees ahead five chickadees crossed from branch to branch. In the patch of sky above them a high hawk wheeled. Sunlight fell through the treetops in rags and shifting shadows. One deep-blue Stellar's jay landed on a square rock, cocked its head. Breeze in the high pines. All of it sitting hard on Coop so he couldn't breathe. All heavy and dark and sitting on Coop. And now he was fiercely jealous, too, one more misery.

But Bailey seemed unconcerned about sharing Hodge. Her great worry was the murder. She said softly, "The pigs, baby, the police'll be up here *tonight.*"

"Nah," Coop said. But he knew she was right. If not tonight, soon. The great house came in sight, the colossal pine tree columns of the circled drive. Bailey dropped Coop's hand.

"They'll be in here *tonight,* baby, mark my words, I can see it plain as *bread.* And they're going to be *pissed,* baby. Hundreds of 'em, like *bees.* And y'all's fool brother is gonna pull out his *pea-shooter* and Boyd is gonna fire that *deer* rifle, and y'all don't want to *visualize* what's next."

But Coop did: all of them dead, and maybe some cops dead, too. In his shirt he felt the silly weight of Grandpa's old pocket-gun. He strained not to pull it out and show Bailey, not to just fling it into the woods.

"We need to *save* ourselves," Bailey said.

"What're we supposed to do?"

"Maybe this. There's a phone in this plantation-house here, right? Maybe we just call that *sweetie* who stopped us last night. Just a hypothetical idea. Let's say we call, maybe get him up here. Y'all see what I mean? He's a *trained* man. We can give ourselves *in* to him. Let him bring us *in,* just quietly. Lumpy was a *mistake.* A person comes in voluntarily, it's better in the *courts,* baby. Coop, jaysus, are y'all listenin'? We give ourselves *up.*"

Coop felt the trees leaning in on him. Her logic wasn't great, but still somehow it was compelling like nothing had ever been compelling before. Yes, he wanted to show Bailey the *Little Pal* in his pocket, throw it down. He wanted to be home in time for school in September. Even a haircut sounded good.

Bailey grabbed him by the biceps. "If we don't do this now, baby, it's just going to happen *later.* Those big dopes are carryin' *weapons.* Hear? They killed *Lumpy.* How long before they get themselves shot? Or us? Hear me? What does *violence* breed? Let's us make a *phone call* in here."

Violence bred violence, Coop knew, because Bailey had said so,

many times. He remembered where the key to the cottage was, all
right. Tricia nuzzling Hodge on the big rocks, in plain sight like
that. What did that mean? With Bailey he stood in the pine needles
and breathed and heard the birds in the forest and the faint breezes
in the tops of the big pines and a squirrel chittering and a stick
falling on the great slate roof of the DuPont cottage, which was a
mansion by any name. Bailey was right. But what about the cop?
That nice cop? Wouldn't Hodge or Boyd just shoot him?

"What about the cop?" Coop said.

"He's handled worse than Boyd *Friendly.*"

It didn't take a minute and they were inside. The kitchen phone
had a dial tone. The phone book was in the stuffed junk drawer
beneath it. Bailey found the nonemergency number for the Police
Department, Town of Silverton. And Coop dialed the phone. He
talked to the lady dispatcher. Coop was worse than Judas; he felt
this profoundly in his heart. He put on an older voice, said what
Bailey had suggested: "This is Theophilus DuPont. Looks like
we've had some trespassers up here." He said, "Could you send one
policeman up?" It was stupid to say *one* but Coop didn't want more
than that.

7

Well, bones and skull, dust and shade, vile but beloved older brother, here I am in Burlington, great state of Vermont, on the lake of Champlain, New York State not far across the waters, Canada even closer, Green Mountains south, Adirondacks west. Good-bye to you.

The moment Roddy and I are ensconced in Professor Coxbury's tidy house (the old boy's on sabbatical), she goes out and gets hold of the university's job listings and like destiny there's a ski team position: seasonal, of course, but full time for now: snow coach. *C'est moi!* So every afternoon from our second week in Vermont I'm standing with college skiers, and most evenings a beer with the head coach, Pete "Pierre" Castonguay, an old Québecois who's mightily threatened by my every gesture, but has enough sense to know it and joke about it and be my friend. He likes to grab me and hug me and kiss my cheeks. I'm the best coach these kids will ever have, says he. He's full of praise, and finally I'm old enough to take it. And we've got at least two real skiers, one each on the men's team and the women's. And I praise the skiers to their faces—my new style—praise the lesser skiers too. If this job's a comedown, it's a gentle one.

I needn't have worried about Madeline all alone in Basalt. In response to my cowardly phone message leaving my new phone number and address on what was our machine (new recording, my voice erased), I get a cordial letter typed on her office stationery. Our mutually held credit cards have been canceled, our joint bank and mutual fund accounts frozen. Divorce papers are on their way. She will propose, she says, a fifty-fifty split of everything but her business. The house on the Frying Pan is up for sale. Which ought to ruin my day, but does not. Because Roddy's climbing up the porch steps, carrying new books, flushed and stressed-out from her meetings today with her dissertation advisor and the ferocious woman who makes the teaching assignments and a long list of others I'll hear all about.

She kisses me at the door and shrugs out of her coat, and brother it doesn't much matter that she's crabby with me, that she's sure I'm the one who should do the grocery shopping. We're on some kind of meta-honeymoon here, and her irritated kiss hello ascends gradually into passion even as she tells me about her day, which sounds rough.

"I never had this," Roddy says smooching me. She kneads my shoulders. Her hands are strong. She says, "We're like kids together in college."

"We're lucky people," says I.

"I never had what normal kids had," Roddy says. She means because she was skiing so much and so hard.

"I never did either," says I. I mean what I mean, too.

She's bought a huge bottle of old cognac and from it we drink and we're up late in Coxbury's warren of rooms. We're a new couple, true, but we're old friends, too. It's a great combination: we fight easily (she catches me coaching her and hates it, I find her defensive when no offense is in sight; I'm too neat, she's a slob; she corrects my English, I get irritable with all her untranslated Italian and French and German; I'm old, she's young; there are chores to divide and each division is a trial; her taste in music is from the boyfriend before Claudio (medieval madrigals?), mine tends toward the loud; she's anxious to go back to Aspen and get her truck, I want a little longer before we make *that* trip); but we can't wait to make love. We crack each other up, too, call each other flustering names. She loves my cooking, always loved that I cook at all. I hate her cooking: burritos every time, usually my leftovers rolled up cold. She wants a kid in the next couple of years—and until she says it, I don't know that I want a kid, too. But I do. I want a kid. A girl would be nice.

And I want peace. I want what Madeline and I could never have. Roddy and I eat and talk and make elaborate love (or simply screw) and we work and quarrel and peer into the future, and brother, that's life as God made it. A great weight, a massive boulder, has been lifted from my chest. I can hear it rumbling down the mountainside, soon to be gone forever.

Roddy hasn't told her mother over in Pennsylvania anything about us. Not yet. She says, "That woman gives the worst advice in the world. She once told me to *try to understand* when my stepdad borrowed my car and wrecked it! And she thought I should quit skiing and go into *engineering*. Art history! Don't even mention it! If I tell her about you she'll advise me to have you *fixed*."

And I've said nothing to Mom and Dad—with them, there's other business to attend to first.

Roddy reads two or three hours a morning and clacks her slides in their boxes, putting lectures together for these smart kids. She wears reading glasses for this operation, and when I come in the room looks up looking smart and pretty and bollixed: "Tell me if you think this is weird. That student I told you about? Dora

Pringle? Dora raises her hand and says, *The image of Christ has been replaced by the image of the self, would you say?* And I say, Dora, you're getting ahead of us! Like she's a troublemaker. But she's not a troublemaker—I actually think she really respects me— I just got insecure. Then I fumble around trying to give a real answer, okay? I told her I thought maybe so, maybe the image of Christ has been replaced in just that way, and she starts talking about *Lacan*. This is an undergrad? The other kids are all half asleep in the dark."

"She's trying to impress you. She wants you to like her. So, go ahead and like her, is my advice."

In my turn, I try to be equally frank about my day. If Caston-guay is bugging me, I tell her. If a kid skier is getting under my skin, I say so. She likes to listen to me.

Roddy and Coop, we're in love. Roddy and Coop, we're not skiers on the road anymore. Roddy and Coop, maybe we're going to make it, and maybe it'll always be like this, and neither of us lies there with doubts at night but sleeps for the first time in years: eight hours, nine hours, ten.

Good-bye to you, Hodge Henry.

8

Coop heard the Silverton cruiser first—squeaking frame, pine-cones popping under tires. He tapped Bailey's ankle with his sneaker, and she listened too, just the two of them perked up on the cabin's porch, where the whole gang less Boyd had pretended to go back to reading. Tricia with her shirt buttoned wrong and Hodge with leaves stuck to the back of his head lounged in rockers pointedly separated. Madeline sitting lotus right on the painted floorboards with her Richard Brautigan, a book Tricia knew about and made much of in thrilled tones to hide whatever needed hiding. That cowgirl thought Coop couldn't see. Free love was just another of Bailey's stupid, stupid ideas. Boyd was in the hammock still, Grandpa's rifle across his chest.

Coop said, "I hear a car," and the poor logic of Bailey's newest plan hit him in the gut like the hangar shock wave, worse even than the sight of Tricia and Hodge coming out of the woods.

Hodge stood up fast, listened. His face changed from skeptical to alarmed when he heard, too. "Get up here," he shouted.

"What?" Boyd called.

"Inside," Hodge said. He pulled Madeline's arm (she yelped, having missed the news), practically dragged her into the cabin, pushed Bailey ahead of them.

Boyd fell out of the hammock in his hurry, stumbled to his feet, gathered the rifle almost comically, came running.

Tricia just stood lazily, unperturbed—definitely a car was coming—calmly stepped inside the cabin. Coop waited for Boyd, let Boyd push him brusquely inside.

Bailey so gently said, "Y'all, it's time to surrender."

But Hodge pulled Grandpa's .45 out of the firewood where he'd hidden it and leaned ominously beside one of the bright windows.

Bailey went to him, stood right behind him. She said, "Listen to me, baby. Y'all don't need to fight."

Tricia made a contemptuous noise. Coop's heart plunged. What possible way would there be to get Hodge and Boyd to give in? Bailey was crazy. Panicked plan one: Coop would go out in the yard first, throw the little gun from his shirt pocket onto the ground, show the older boys what had to be done. He looked to Bailey, but she was scared, too, whispering to Hodge, who focused on the jeep trail plainly not hearing a syllable she uttered.

"We're in trouble," Madeline said, panic rising. She ducked into the smaller bedroom, rustled in there, hiding. Boyd followed her, carrying Grandpa's rifle.

Bailey implored: "It's just our guy, y'all." Then louder: "Boyd, baby, it's just our guy. Hodge, doll, it's the policeman from the other night. Y'all don't need to shoot."

"*Quiet*," Hodge said. He felt the air behind him, found Bailey, pushed her roughly away. Because between the dark trunks of a hundred trees the black-and-white car had come visible.

Bailey said, "It's just that sweet old man, Hodge Henry. Let's us-all just peacefully give in."

"I told you *shut up*," Hodge said fiercely.

"I'll talk to him," Tricia said.

"Grandma will be back," Coop implored. He and Bailey hadn't thought this thing *through*. "Hodge, Grandma will help us."

"Shut up," Hodge hissed. *"Just please shut the fuck up."*

The old car proceeded slowly into the clearing, rocked to a stop on its bad shocks.

"No violence," Bailey said. Her plan was getting away from her.

Hodge called in to Boyd: "First clear shot gets him."

Madeline yelped again, muffled. She was in the closet among old coats.

Coop felt a wave of passion rise in him: "You're not going to *shoot* him," he said, despite himself.

"Turn ourselves *in,*" Bailey cried.

"Let's just see what he does," Boyd called calmly.

One car, red bubble on top, older model, late 'fifties. TOWN OF SILVERTON written along the side, police shield painted on the driver's door. One man in there, their man, kindly old bird.

Hodge clicked the safety on Grandpa's .45. That's how quiet the cabin was now, you heard each click, each breath, each shift of weight on floorboards. And now Madeline's muffled voice, asking what was happening. And Boyd telling her *Shut up.*

The cop stepped onto the carpet of moss, climbed unhurriedly out of his car.

"It's nothing," Tricia said. "There'd be swarms if they knew."

"It's the same old man who *stopped* us," Bailey said still imploring. "Let's just go to him and give ourselves in."

Hodge muttered, "We'll make him famous."

The cop climbed out of his car, looked around, appeared to be enjoying the weather. "Halloo!" he shouted. He started toward the cabin.

And Coop could see the exact moment, after five or six long strides, the exact moment that caution took hold. The officer stopped and cocked his head and listened, then turned and listened more and looked back up the trail he'd just negotiated, thinking . . . what? How pretty it was, or how maybe he was supposed to be at the main house, or maybe already thinking, *Something's fishy*, or as Madeline would say years later, maybe thinking whatever cops about to retire think when they feel that old feeling: something wrong. He just stood there a long minute and the gang in the house stood there watching him through the windows, except Madeline, rustling and bumping in the bedroom closet, hiding herself further.

Just silence outside. For the cop it must have turned eerie, the VW bus parked there, the memory of those garrulous girls, the beer cans piled by the hammock, the strong feeling of eyes on him, no answer to his halloo. He bolted back to the car, no other way to describe it. He bolted and stood plainly spooked in the wing of his car door, thinking what to do, Coop could see, no longer any vestige of toughness apparent.

Tricia drew a big breath, stood tall, went to the door. She stepped out on the porch, all casual. Not even she—crazy girl —wanted Hodge firing off that ridiculous handgun, bullets ten years old.

"Hello yourself," Tricia said. That's all, sweet as a little girl.

"Oh, for heaven's sake," the cop said, apologizing even as he jumped, startled. A pretty cowgirl in a stone doorway. Heavens, heavens, these late fears were overtaking him: maybe that's what he was thinking. He called, "You're a guest here?"

"Yessir," Tricia said.

The rifle blast made Coop shout and dive to the floor. Bailey grabbed Hodge, maybe kept him from firing. He angrily flung her arm away. She spun to the floor, held her face in her hands. Tricia threw herself to the porch deck, crawled back inside, Coop pulling her by the arm to help. "Boyd!" Tricia shouted: "You *idiot*." Coop crawled half on top of the girl in a panic to protect her, found himself with a clear view straight out the door, line of fire.

The front tire of the cruiser hissed, went flat fast. The cop leapt in the driver's door, slid across the front seat, got out the other side, drew his Wild-West revolver, aimed it over the car roof at the cabin. He quaked, scared shitless, that's what Coop could see. The gun looked small as a toy. Tricia squirmed under Coop.

"Everyone come out of that house!" the cop shouted. "Everyone in there come out! Throw that gun out! Everyone in there come out! How many in there? Come out!" What was he supposed to do? He must have been thinking to speed away in the car, must have been thinking he'd be shot if he tried to get behind the wheel.

Coop put his hand on the oily metal in his pocket. He could throw it out the door. Show the cop all was safe.

Hodge said, "Boyd, goddamn it, bring that rifle in here, now. Throw it out the door. I'll follow it, then you girls."

"We'll give in," Bailey said.

"The fuck we will," Hodge muttered.

"Come out of that house!" the cop shouted, quavering voice. He'd have a hard time covering himself if any more shooting was coming, he must know that. Coop thought for him: *Get in the car and go!* He thought of Dad now, if the cop were Dad. *Get in that car!*

Boyd strode in from the bedroom, steady as a stump, held the rifle out to Hodge, who stuck the .45 in the back of his jeans. And Hodge without further thought just took the rifle and held it out in front of him like some harmless stick of wood, stepped boldly out on the porch, already yelling: "I'm putting this down. Putting this down. It's all we got."

"Down!" the cop said. "You get down, too."

"Oh please," Bailey said.

Hodge lay the rifle down on the porch, kicked it with his foot till it fell on the stone stairs with a wooden and metal clatter. Tricia stood and bravely stepped out after him, into this perfect sunny day. The roar of the 30.06 was still in Coop's ears, and he couldn't move easily, but rose. Bailey stepped out after Tricia, put her hands in the air.

"Stop!" the cop said. Poor old guy, Coop could see he was beside himself with fright. "One by one," the cop said. "How many are you!"

"Six," Hodge said gently. He put up his hands, though no one had said to, put them in the air, six fingers, breathed a breath so big and long that it calmed everyone. Hodge said, "Nothing to worry about now, officer," loudly, clearly.

So Bailey had prevailed. Coop touched his pocket. He'd have to step outside, get the gun out of his shirt daintily with thumb and forefinger—no threat to the cop—throw it down.

Hodge put his hands higher in the air, waved them, stepped slowly off the porch, kicked the rifle off to one side in the yard, walked out into the day, into a bright cloud of white insects in the sun.

The cop puffed his own breaths. He was old, over sixty, maybe even over *seventy* now that Coop looked at him. He shouted, "Let's get the rest of them out here, too."

Hodge said, "We're coming. It's over now."

The cop's eyes closed like his heart had skipped a beat, said, "The rest of them *out here.*"

Hodge said, "Yes, yes, we'll all come out." He motioned, meaning it for Boyd Friendly. Tricia made another step. Then Bailey. She motioned in turn and Coop stepped out, too. Madeline hadn't emerged from her closet.

"You said six," the cop shouted.

Boyd stepped out hard on the porch boards. He would run, Coop felt it. The cop would have his hands full and Boyd would run. Boyd raised his hands in the air, big man, called, "Congratu-lations, Captain, you got the Boeing Bombers!"

Coop could see the change come over the poor old cop, you could see every thought cross his face, even from across the yard—he had the bombers—or was that a joke? How was he going to handle so many at once? His eyes got big.

He said, "One at a time," too softly. He repeated it more force-fully: "*One-at-a-time.*" He was a dope to come out here alone, that's probably what he was thinking. How he didn't care to be a hero. He crouched lower behind the car. "You two, you little girls, three of you, sit down. Sit down!" Thinking Coop a girl. But how was the cop going to do this? Coop thought for him: handcuff the girls to a porch pillar, bring the men in, and Coop. If he had four pair of handcuffs he could do it, wrist to wrist.

Bailey and Tricia sank slowly down to sitting on the porch stoop. Hodge took a slow step, said, "It's all right, officer. We're ready to go." Another step.

"Stop!" the pig said to Hodge, then, "You in the blue shirt, you come down first and lie on the moss there."

Boyd didn't move.

The old cop tried a tougher voice: "*You. You come down off there and lie face down!*" He knew who the bad boys were.

Hodge took another step. The cop leveled his six-shooter, said, "*Stop!*" Then angrily to Boyd: "*You, lie down.*" He looked suddenly as simple as a substitute teacher who'd just realized the kids were much meaner than he'd thought. Just powerless, brandishing this absurd Dodge City gun. Hodge took another step.

"*Son, I said stop,*" the cop said. He pointed his gun at Hodge, watched Boyd.

Bailey said, "Cool it, y'all. Just quiet now. Listen to the officer. Boyd, y'all lie down. Do it, y'all."

Boyd seemed to listen, took a step off the porch, very slowly, arms in the air, but Coop saw and the policeman saw it was a step toward the discarded rifle. Hodge took a step at the same time, lowered his hands, took another step, faster.

Coop stepped, too—he had to stop Hodge—stepped quickly to no notice from the cop who had Boyd and Hodge to watch. Coop knew what was coming. Evenly, quietly, from behind his brother's back, he said, "Hodge don't," and took another long step. And Boyd moved, and Hodge stepped. Coop followed him, to be close enough to . . . what? Maybe tackle him. Maybe talk him down from violence.

The cop shot, a small bang in the vast, bright forest landscape. The bullet made no noise in passing but smashed a front window in the cabin, must have rocketed just over Tricia and Bailey sitting there. Inside, a muffled shriek from Madeline. Hodge was all motion at the bang, leapt forward as the cop ducked behind the car, leapt and reached behind him to pull Grandpa's heavy handgun out of his belt. Boyd Friendly leapt, too, leapt and rolled and retrieved the rifle as the cop shot again, this time at Boyd, missing again, all this motion in half a breath, all this explosion of movement in a blink, Tricia and Bailey diving back inside the cabin. The cop ducked behind his car as Hodge shot, and shot again. Then boom—the explosion of the 30.06—and a pop as the policeman shot toward Boyd once more. The women in the house began screaming, and Coop heard himself yell too at the next loud blast of the rifle and simultaneous inward shattering and splashing of the old cruiser's windshield. The cop fired, and Boyd advanced. Hodge fired, too, pop-pop, taking three steps forward. Coop followed, hastening—he could tackle Hodge, save him, save the cop, save them all. The cop stood, stupidly, aimed at Hodge. Boyd loaded, fired again though Bailey shrieked "No!", hitting the side of the cruiser, his aim getting truer. Another blast and the driver's window crumbled. Hodge took several more measured steps toward the cruiser, close as hell. Coop followed, just a few steps behind.

Boyd's next shot would have had the cop. But something audibly snapped in Grandpa's old rifle. Coop heard the jam, and looked to see Boyd frantically picking at the mechanism then plain panicking, an unlikely vision, Boyd freaking and tossing the 30.06 as far toward the pig as he could, not that far, the rifle clattering on the ground near the cop car, then crouching and fast scuttling back to the house, huffing behind Coop in plain surprising panic.

Hodge didn't so much as flinch, only faced the perplexed cop, Coop saw, leveled the handgun for a clear, close shot across the hood of the cruiser, the cop frozen in some kind of shock, foolishly watching Boyd's flight. Hodge's hand was deeply steady. The nice old cop, Coop saw, was about to be murdered, had only begun to turn his eyes and weapon to Hodge. And all in a motion, no thinking in it (no intention in it that he could detect ever, even in all the years to come obsessing on this exact moment), Coop reached in his pocket, pulled out Grandpa's *Little Pal*, pointed it. He cried *"Hodge!"* just as his big brother squeezed the heavy trigger of the .45, saw Hodge flinch, cried his brother's name and fired the *Little Pal* as Hodge turned, rageful at Coop's distraction. One shot, tiny handgun, tiny bang all but simultaneous with the bigger blast of the .45, catching Hodge in the breast pocket of his shirt, leaving a dainty hole.

Hodge dropped his head, leaned forward, put his hands on his knees. That's what Coop saw. Coop yelled—just a loud noise from his throat—yelled and flung his gun down and dove after it onto the moss, crawled fast toward his brother. All this in seconds.

The cop must have felt bullet wind at his ear from Hodge's shot, because now he panicked, too, panicked worse than Boyd, fired his big gun twice in the direction of Coop and Hodge, sent pebbles and moss flecks flying between the brothers, then turned and ran, fired once more wildly into the trees, sprinted down the trail, a hitch in his gait like some character in a cartoon.

No one moved for ten hammered heartbeats, nothing stirred. The shots had stopped the forest: not a bird, not a squirrel. The cop's cruiser hissed and settled, dripped bits of clicking glass.

Coop leapt to Hodge, put a hand on that broad back, stroked him: "I shot you," he said hotly.

Hodge said, "Fuck," only that, but with a kind of irony, like maybe getting shot in the chest was a joke.

"He's hurt," Coop shouted. Hodge burped and slumped further. Coop held him up—heavy—tried to turn him toward the cabin, thinking how you'd pull open the shirt, how you'd look for any wound, how it wouldn't be so bad.

But Hodge wouldn't take a step. He burped again. He said, "It's burning me."

Boyd quickly stomped out on the cabin porch, listened for the cop's progress. Hearing nothing, he strode over. Bailey tripped out next, rushed over, then Tricia, who floated. Madeline's muffled wail came from the house, grew louder as she untangled herself from the coats and blankets and boxes and bags.

Bailey said: "Baby. Oh, baby, I knew it. Y'all're shot?"

Friendly and Coop got Hodge more or less walking, helped him up onto the porch, laid him there with his feet hanging off the steps. Tricia was calmest. She opened Hodge's shirt. Hodge hiccupped again, burped. "Okay," he said.

"Oh Lord," Bailey said. Gently she touched Hodge's chest.

At the very top of the muscles of his stomach, in the resilient skin there and at the place where the ribs stopped, a bruised fold of skin showed—that's all—a bruise of skin like a hole in maybe a nice chair (Coop thought), a hole in something valuable, a hole into which a bored child (Coop himself) had stuffed raspberries (that's what it looked like), a hole that if you put your little finger in you'd feel the old brittle stuffing. No bleeding at all. One very small hole in, raspberry pink, no hole out.

Friendly found Coop's eye and held it coldly.

"Okay," Hodge said, last breath.

9

Roddy, hi. You'll get this letter and I'll already be back. I guess this will be a lot of writing—you asked for a long letter! Sorry to type. This is Dad's new computer, quite a machine for the slide-rule guy. They're asleep. Okay, okay, here we go. I'll get it in writing. A good idea—thanks for your good ideas. I miss you and your good ideas.

It's been difficult here, you could say, but not terrible. In fact, not terrible at all, but a huge relief (as you predicted it would be). And the transition you predicted has maybe happened. I don't know if it's adolescence I'm leaving behind (at my age, Christ, Rod, thanks a lot), but for the first time since I was about nine my parents seem like people to me, very vulnerable and sad.

Okay. Here's how it went, as requested.

I didn't wait, first of all. I got here yesterday afternoon, early, and unpacked in my old room (Hodge's room, too) and just went right down the stairs and found Mom and Dad again in the kitchen and said, "Okay, please come into the parlor. I've

got some things to speak to you about before Cindy gets here."
Something like that. And of course they knew it was going to
be about Hodge. So we all sat ourselves down beside the little
parlor fireplace. My medal from Sapporo is in a very fancy
bronze frame over the mantle there, you'll be glad to know.
They fixed their gazes upon me expectantly and I just started
in, something like, "Listen, I've been lying to you guys for
years."

And my mother nodded her head and my father shook his,
ever so slowly. They weren't going to be happy with anything
but the truth. They knew roughly what was coming, in their
hearts, or deeper than that, and despite my bullshit, they've
always known.

I said the speech, all planned: "Hodge died August 2, 1969,
the day before my sixteenth birthday, just between the first
moon landing and Woodstock, as it happens. Mom and Dad,
I was with him."

The three of us sat there in Grandma Vanderhoop's fancy
parlor chairs quite a long time, with the fire going. A big pot
roast was cooking in the kitchen and the aroma carried all
kinds of other memories, Roddy, and these floated in the air
around me along with the memory of Hodge.

"Thirty years," my father said, looking down. He's old now,
he's wiry and withered. Then he said it again, with the old
anger, the old instant rage, and I started to react with the old
fear and the old rebellion, sat up straight, you know, and Mom
gasped the way she always gasped when her boys squared off.
Dad got up on his feet and stormed right up to me sitting there
in one of Grandma's delicate parlor chairs, practically pushing
his chest into my face, and he said, "Dead, is he?" meaning a
whole list of hurts and questions and doubts and fears but
challenging me, too, and I stood up fast and there we were, face
to face, and he was shouting at me, "Goddamn liars! Goddamn

dead, is he!" These odd phrases, and then he *pushed my chest,*
pushed me ineffectually, meant to shove me back over the
chair, would have those years ago, but pushed me and gave me
an actual chop at the neck when I wouldn't fall, a kind of old-
man's ineffectual karate chop, and I don't know, I stepped into
him and Mom gasped like I was going to break him, but just
out of nowhere I *hugged* him. I hugged him, Roddy, I held him
and squeezed him with full love and he was writhing in my
grasp and punching at me—getting some good shots in, too,
and I hugged him and finally he just went limp and his arms
fell from hitting me onto my shoulders and then he was bawling and I was bawling and he was hugging me back and we
were in this embrace with my mom at our sides and Dad and
I were embracing and crying and Roddy, *it was our first hug.*

Mom joined in then—she's tall, still—joined in with an
arm around us both. She had tissues up her sleeve like the old
lady she is and passed them to us and we were all blowing our
noses and holding each other, and then suddenly laughing as
we have never done, great gales of laughter, finding one
another's eyes, then crying again, Jesus, holding on to one
another.

And in that rare huddle I just said the next thing and the
next—all this stuff I planned in the car, all the stuff I've been
practicing on you. Snuffling, like, "He was going to kill more
people. *You* know he was dangerous. He was vicious and
deceitful and cruel and maybe not entirely sane and he was
going to hurt a lot more people before he got done. It was *revolution,* in his eyes. Any number of deaths were justified, in his
eyes. I'll bet even his own, if we could ask him."

Mom broke the hug, sat back in her seat. You could actually
feel her emotion pushing the air out of the room. My father, he
pushed me then—pushed me again—that's how he broke the
hug. He shoved me in the chest, knocked me back in my chair,

flung his hands up, covered his face, just stood like that in
front of me. And my mother hunkered in her chair, you know.
The hug had surely passed, the laughter.

I didn't care anymore. I said, "He was shot." I said, "Right
here." I pointed to my chest. "I must have hit his heart or
aorta," I told them. And that was the way I let it out: *I* must
have hit. The only time I've ever said it, except to you. I said,
"He died in maybe five minutes' time." And let it all tumble
out, said, "We buried him well. We just didn't want anyone
to know. We thought that was a way to keep him alive. So the
establishment wouldn't know. You remember how it was. And
you were part of the *establishment*. We buried him really well,
just above a river, the Stillaguamish River, Cascade Mountains,
up there in view of Mount Baker, in the valley of Mount Baker."
You know, just talking really fast to Dad's hands in his face. I
said, "Madeline and I, we hiked back in there with a granite
headstone ten years ago, heavy as hell. So it's marked now. It's
a beautiful, protected place. I can take you, if you want. I'll take
you guys!"

Imagine *that* trip, Rod. Still, I'm glad I said it.

The parlor fire burned and the pot in the kitchen bubbled
and there was the deep smell of my mom's cooking and a feeling of stability in this house that I hadn't really caught onto
before: fifty years of marriage. We were just frozen in our
places like that till Dad said something, something I couldn't
hear, into his hands. And then I could hear it: *"Sorry, sorry,"*
and an intense whisper, you know, how it was his own damn
fault, and *"If I were a better man,"* like that. Then something
about love, something I couldn't hear except for love, the first
time ever I'd heard him say anything in that way or with that
word. Never took his hands from his face, layering the blame
on himself, hunching lower and lower till he turned and just
shuffled out of the room, his hands still on his face, shuffled

out of the room and outside. And out there we heard him fire
up his high-tech mulching mower a couple of times. He didn't
mow. In the end he got in his car and locked the door, just sat
there in the driveway two hours. He's old, Rod. I think I have
his forgiveness. I believe I forgive him, too.

Now I had my mother alone. So, onward to the next dis-
agreeable news: "Madeline and I have decided to split up."

Mom said, "Oh, Coop." That's all.

"It's related to all this about Hodge," I said. Then I tried to
say how my marriage could possibly be related to Hodge—hot,
wet mouthfuls of words about how Madeline's and my whole
life together was based on Hodge, on guilt over that, and guilt
over his crimes which were our crimes. But none of that abstraction you and I have been practicing made any sense to
her till I let out that last little puzzle piece, which I'd meant to
hoard. I said, "Madeline was there." I told her, Roddy, I broke
that last vow.

And Mom was like, *"Madeline knew your brother!"* Hoarse
whisper, the whole thing. Overwhelmed. She didn't say anything more for maybe fifteen minutes. We just sat in our chairs
and studied Dad's perfect logs burning. When she finally broke
the silence it was something else altogether, the thing I'd
skimmed past. She said something like, "Wait Cooper, just wait
one moment. Earlier, you made a reference I don't understand.
You said, *you* shot him?"

Not too calmly I said, "Yes, I did say that. In the heat of the
shoot-out, if that's what it was, with that cop at the trial? The
older cop at the trial? You remember him. I had Grandpa's
little gun, one of Grandpa's little guns from the attic on
Boylston Street. You know, your father and his guns. Hodge
was going to just *murder* that cop, the cop who came up to the
DuPont cottage, the cop who was at the trial. In the heat of

that moment I just did it, I just acted, I wasn't thinking. Hodge was going to *kill* that man."

And then we could look at each other. Mom searched my eyes so long I had to look down, the two of us sitting bolt straight on the proper parlor chairs both sides of a dancing, happy fire. Abruptly her hand flew to her face, covered her eyes. And Roddy, my stolid mother wept. She cried sitting up straight and very still, at first quietly, then sobbing, but not moving otherwise, simply holding her hand over her eyes. I had never seen her cry, though I had heard her once, around the time Hodge left home, heard her in her room, closed door. Anyway, after a long time she plucked the next tissue out of her sleeve and blew her nose carefully and wiped her eyes carefully, always dignified, never bowed. If anything, she sat up straighter yet, that strong Mom of my youth.

She said, "What will Madeline do?"

I said, "Madeline is in love with someone."

And she said, "Oh, Coop."

"And I am moving to Vermont. I have a ski-team job at UVM." Too many points of news. I'm going to save you and us for later. You were right about that, you were right.

She said, "I'm not judging you."

"Okay."

"I think I may have done in the past."

"Not so bad," I said. "And I've done, too."

The fire crackling. Dad out in his car. The kitchen noises cheerful. Mom said very softly, "Hodge thought he was doing good deeds."

Long pause to think. And I said, "I'm not sure he thought like that, Mom."

Another silence. "He was an idealist."

Another long pause. "He was violent."

Then quickly: "And the world really did change because of all your idealism. I mean your generation's idealism."

"The world changed a lot."

The fire, the kitchen sounds, Dad out in his car. Hodge dead.

Mom said, "You, Anthony, I'm so sorry. You must have been terribly frightened! All these years! How hard your life has been!"

The first thing I thought to say was subterfuge: "Not so horrible." Then I tried again: "Pretty bad sometimes."

Roddy, our talk the other night about making a kid—I do want to, I do—but thinking about it has made me see what my mom has gone through, what this old woman has gone through—for once I'm thinking of her. Dad, too, I'm thinking of him, sitting out alone in his car.

Mom stood quite suddenly, stepped over suddenly to give me a pat on the shoulder, then flew into the kitchen, and instantly everything was a great banging of pots and pans. That woman chopped and poured and slammed and sliced. She flipped open high cabinets, pulled down obscure cruets and casseroles. Her one son was dead, the next son responsible. She opened the cabinet under the stove, unleashed a tremendous crashing cascade of broiler pans and cookie sheets and wire racks and griddles. She didn't exclaim, didn't fuss, didn't acknowledge the mess in any way. She simply kicked aside the things she didn't want till the right pan met her eye, and this she picked up. Then back to her cooking.

I washed up in my childhood bathroom, changed my clothes for dinner. Dad was out there, still sitting in the car. I looked out the little window down at him and felt affection well up, affection and forgiveness, and not just guilt. Back in the parlor, I took my same seat, waited in front of the fire as edgy as waiting at the gate, Rod, waiting for the buzzer, biggest race of your life.

At long, long last, Mom came in wiping her hands on a tattered kitchen towel. She said, "I think we can close the book."

I said, "What about Dad? Won't he want to call the FBI?" Allowing myself the old sardonic edge.

And Mom went all warm to cut past all that, the hand on my shoulder again, said very softly, like imparting a secret, something like, "You misunderstand your father. He really misses his big boy, his Hodge baby. He always really missed his big boy. Even when your brother was still in this house we missed him." No eye contact, just the warm hand on my shoulder, the warm, confiding voice. "Your father always blamed himself. I blame myself, too, for that matter. You, you blame yourself, too. That's the family curse, I do believe. But Hodge was never . . . normal, Coop. Not after about grade *seven*."

She produced another tissue, offered it to me, that dry hand on my shoulder. When I was quiet she said, "And now I think your Daddy misses you, Anthony. You are his biggest big boy. That will be hard to fathom, I imagine. He heard what you said, today, never fear. He heard you. But he'll come back in and be cheerful, you watch. And then we'll close the book. He wants to close it, just as you do. Just as I do. We don't have to live back there anymore. The only thing left is to tell your sister and brothers. May I tell the others tomorrow when they're here?"

Something like that, Rod. And Leslie Adams Keepnews Henry and Anthony Cooper Henry hugged again, just the two of us, hugged for the first time like that in as many as forty years. After which tender embrace the formidable Mrs. Henry rushed back to her kitchen—plenty work to do.

That's enough for now. Cindy's due any time with her kids,

and Jeremy's coming too, with his. Morton is due tomorrow, with his new boyfriend and miraculously healed, at least for now.

You'll like them all, Roddy. The kids are incredible fun. You'll come for Christmas, maybe. I haven't been down here for Christmas in years.

So there's just this, just the last bit I haven't told you, or anyone. And then it's over, longest letter of your life, just a little bit more about that day, that last day. Let me get it said.

Boyd Friendly—I've told you about Boyd—Boyd Friendly and I struggle and get Hodge dead into his heavy sleeping bag. We bend his arms in—Boyd very curt with me. Instructions and advice, no recriminations. We pull the sleeping bag ties tight over Hodge's head, heave him with great effort into that old VW bus, working like zombies, in shock. Bailey is frozen solid, can barely move. She's the girl I told you about, from Texas. She's devastated by all of this. But the cops are going to turn up in force and soon. All that old cop has to do is get to a phone. Boyd and Madeline and I have to actually put Bailey in the bus like she's dead, too. And Boyd collects shell casings and beer cans and all the other fingerprinted evidence in a whirlwind of criminal experience, Madeline trailing him shivering with *excitement*. Looking back, I believe it's *excitement*, though I used to think just terror.

Who drives? Tricia, of course, brilliant in an emergency (I've told you about Tricia): we zip, bang, zoom, out of the woods. Boyd wants shovels, which we find in the barn by the DuPonts' so-called cottage. And we scram, a mile west to a logging road, then maybe fifteen miles north on more logging roads, a maze that Boyd knows well, crash up and over a gap and into the valley of Mt. Baker above the Stillaguamish River in the glorious Cascade range. Not a soul in sight.

Boyd knows a place, directs Tricia bluntly. When we're there

we open up the bus and carry Hodge, all of us, Bailey too,
Bailey who's coming out of her shock, all of us silent and efficient, a couple hundred yards straining and puffing past colossal guardian boulders—no loggers will disturb this spot. And
there we dig. The earth under those old trees is deep and the
digging goes fast, a clean, cold hole: not a rock, not a root. We
roll Hodge in, sleeping bag and all, and hear the thump. No
one is crying. And I climb in there and arrange him and Boyd
hands me Grandpa's hunting rifle, which I place across my
brother's angry chest to protect him in eternity.

And Boyd Friendly hands me Grandpa's *Little Pal.* This I
take without surprise, breaking Boyd's hard gaze, and put it at
Hodge's right hand. The .45 is not forthcoming. I climb out of
the hole never looking again in Friendly's eye, never again. The
two of us shovel dirt on top of Hodge.

Tricia says something like, "Let us never tell, not ever, not
anyone."

And we all agree: never tell.

And Tricia says, "Let us make a pact over his grave." That is
her sensibility: Ouija boards, Tarot decks, pacts.

Madeline says something about the presence of his spirit,
and for once I'm not making fun.

And we hold hands in a circle over the fresh dirt. Only I in
that circle and very likely Boyd know exactly what happened
to Hodge, though Madeline will find out eventually: Hotel
Jerome, to be exact, Aspen Colorado, twelve years later, over
drinks.

"Solemn oath," Tricia says, something like that.

I'm not yet registering that it's *all over,* that I'm heading to
jail and court and then back to Connecticut and haircuts and
high school, ski team, pot parties, debauchery, rebellion, fame
and failure, years of increasingly crushing guilt.

Boyd pulls Madeline's hand immediately and they slip away

into the trees, hike full-speed down to the river and disappear. Madeline has never said the first thing about what the two of them did after that, not the first word, though I've asked. The other girls and I, we can't leave the fresh dirt so fast. We linger. We do hold hands.

Then, with few words between us—Bailey speaking softly— we make the decision to drive back to Seattle and turn our- selves in straightaway. Bailey, she outlines our strategy, what we should say if they separate us, as of course they will and do: we know nothing at all; we were along for the ride; Boyd and Hodge said something about escaping to Ireland. Tricia's at the wheel, the three of us abreast, one of the shovels stuck with dirt in the rear, a talisman for years to come. On the ride out of the mountains, Bailey sings all the sad songs she knows. I'm like a boy under an avalanche of rock and trees and earth, barely breathing, hugely relieved when a state police cruiser pulls up behind us (then another and another) as we tumble out of the mountains toward the freeway in that VW bus.

The rest of the story is well known. No one has to tell my folks or anyone this part, though I'll tell you, Roddy: twenty cop cars at the very least pull up and surround us in the middle of the highway lanes, forty-some cops point an arsenal at us, push us down, stamp their boots on our necks. Already I'm saying it: Hodge and Boyd are headed for Ireland. Those old-fashioned cops beat the piss out of me, right there on the highway shoulder and later in my cell—a peace officer has been fired upon, and I'm the closest thing to a man they have to make pay. They break my arm, loosen my front teeth, leave me bashed and bleeding, every blow a kind of relief. The bruises to my face gain me sympathy in the Seattle District Federal Court in the weeks to come. My grandmother, con- nected, gets us set up with the best trial lawyers in the United States of America. And Tricia and Bailey and I, we betray

Hodge and Boyd but hold our own, we take the grand jury
stand as state's evidence, portray ourselves with the help of our
lawyers as dupes, innocents, babes, incidentals, none of which
is entirely untrue, all of which is lies. The old cop from
Silverton backs us up, astonishingly, says he thought I was
a *girl* at the shootout: that's how innocent. Madeline, she's
never mentioned once. The feds launch a manhunt for the two
Boeing Bombers, and the manhunt is in the news for months.
But Boyd Friendly, he slips away. And only five people in the
world know where Hodge is.

I never said one word more, not a word till the other night,
Roddy, talking to you. And just a little more today, here where
Hodge and I once lived, a word to his mother and father, and a
little more tomorrow, a word to his brothers and sister, a word,
as my mother says, to close the book.

ACKNOWLEDGMENTS

Warm thanks to a very long list of friends, colleagues, teachers, agents, and editors who have been my readers and advisors along the way in this project. I am also grateful for other sorts of support from the MacDowell Colony, The Ohio State University, The University of Maine at Farmington, and the Ohio Arts Council. My deep thanks go to Betsy Lerner for unflagging help and friendship over the long haul and to Dawn Seferian for calm and clarity. Last and most: all my love to Juliet, and to my parents, Jack and Reba, the best.